Eyewitness Testimony

Éyewitness Testimony

Elizabeth F. Loftus

HARVARD UNIVERSITY PRESS
Cambridge, Massachusetts
London, England 1979

Library of Congress Cataloging in Publication Data

Loftus, Elizabeth F   1944-
  Eyewitness testimony.
                                                  Bibliography: p.
  Includes index.
  1.   Witnesses — United States.   2.   Psychology, Forensic.
  3.   Crime and criminals — Identification.   I.   Title.
    KF9672.L63   345'.73'066   79-13195
            ISBN 0-674-28775-4

For Geoffrey R. Loftus,
my closest friend

Foreword
by John Kaplan

IN BY FAR THE MOST THOUGHTFUL and complete work on
the subject to date, Professor Loftus has directed attention to an
area of our law of evidence that has been inadequately discussed
before, despite its importance—the reliability of eyewitness accounts. Lawyers have innumerable rules involving hearsay, the
character of the defendant or of the witness, opinions given by a
witness, and the like, which are in one way or another meant to
improve the fact-finding process. But more crucial than any one
of these—and possibly more crucial than all put together—is the
evidence of eyewitness testimony; yet there are virtually no rules
which govern what witnesses may say they saw with their own
eyes.

The problem is that such evidence is often extremely unreliable. We have long known that mistaken eyewitness testimony is
the major cause of conviction of the innocent in the United States.
The insidious combination of the unverifiability of this kind of
evidence with the positiveness and good character of those who
put it forth makes it too easily accepted by jurors—and that is the
thing we must fear most in our trials.

Of course the reliability of eyewitness accounts is affected by
many variables—stress, cross-racial aspects of identification, and
the effect of intervening observations and events, an area of inquiry which Professor Loftus' own research has investigated. One
might be surprised that the courts have done so little to protect
litigants—and especially criminal defendants—from the dangers
of unreliable eyewitness testimony. The Supreme Court's rules on

lineups and suggestive identifications have been the only devices directed specifically at unreliable identification, and the full range of problems, as Professor Loftus shows, makes it quite clear that this is not nearly enough.

On the other hand, there is still a great deal that we do not know about eyewitness identification. First of all, considering the high reliance on eyewitness identification in our courts despite its potential for inaccuracy, one would expect that far more convicted defendants would be shown by subsequent confessions of the guilty parties, or by the later discovery of physical evidence, to have been innocent. These events, of course, do occur, but considering the large number of subsequent confessions to previously unsolved crimes and the volume of new evidence that constantly turns up, the number of cases where someone already convicted is later shown to be innocent is far less than one would expect.

Perhaps part of the reason for this is the enormous differences among individuals in their ability to make identifications. Personally, I rarely can identify someone whom I have seen only a few times, and I have great difficulty recognizing most of my students until I have grown to know them over a period of many meetings — on the order of dozens. As a result, the following event made quite an impression on me:

During the student protest days at Stanford, about ten students disrupted a faculty meeting and, to their great consternation, were photographed in the act by a university photographer. Since Stanford is a large university, it was no easy matter to identify all of the students for disciplinary action. Although some of the students were well known by the administration, one proved especially difficult to identify. She was found, however, after a police officer saw the picture. He said that he did not know her name but had seen her once before, at night, several weeks earlier in a large crowd demonstrating its dissatisfaction with Stanford by throwing rocks through the library windows. He did not approach her, and there were far too many people present to arrest, but he had jotted down the license plate number of the Porsche that she had driven away in. It turned out to belong to a Stanford student, who, when located, was quite clearly the person pictured in the photograph.

To this day I cannot understand how the police officer identified the woman after seeing her on one fleeting occasion, at a moment of considerable stress, with bad visibility as well — but he had indisputably done it.

Granted that some people can make reliable identifications and others cannot, is it possible that juries, aided by cross-examination, can tell which is which? We do not know — but until more research is done on this issue, it remains a possibility.

It is also possible that juries give less weight to unreliable eyewitness accounts than the statistics on the amount of eyewitness testimony introduced in court would lead us to believe. There are two quite different kinds of eyewitness identification. One involves deciding whether a particular person seen for the first time at the scene of the crime is the same person as the one in a police photograph, a lineup, or a courtroom. It is this kind of identification which is quite dubious. The other kind of identification — a girl properly recognizing her boyfriend who beat her up or someone recognizing his own brother-in-law — raises very different questions and presumably is a great deal more reliable. It is likely that this is the kind of identification much more often believed by juries — at least let us hope so.

Be that as it may, Professor Loftus is undeniably right in suggesting that we are much too cavalier about eyewitness testimony. The real problem is that it is very hard for our legal system to do anything about this weakness. Allowing psychologists to testify about the unreliability of identification has certain advantages and is growing in popularity; but before long we will see experts testifying on the other side as well. And we have already seen the serious — some might say disastrous — consequences of permitting psychiatrists to take the witness stand and tell juries how to decide cases. Allowing a courtroom battle of experts among psychologists (and it would take somebody far less cynical than I to assert with a straight face that one could not find psychologists on all sides of any particular narrowly drawn issue) might well compound the problem, and delay and confuse our trials as well.

It may be that we are better off trusting the common sense of judges and juries informed by this book and the research which will follow it. The message need not have reached all jurors, since those who know may be able to persuade the others. It is not only the jurors, however, who will have to take account of this knowledge. If they are to do their jobs at all right, the judges, in deciding whether to affirm convictions, will have to pay a great deal more attention than in the past to the variables which determine the reliability of eyewitness evidence heard by the jury. This, indeed, would be in keeping with a more general trend in the law of admitting some types of evidence, particularly hearsay and opinion, even though we have been traditionally less confident of their reliability. But, as the judges admit more material that might influence juries' decisions, they are becoming increasingly aware of the need to supervise more closely the sufficiency of the evidence, not only in formal terms but as a practical psychological matter as well. In this effort, Professor Loftus' role as a public educator will be invaluable.

Preface

A MAJOR REASON for my writing this book has been a long-standing concern with cases in which an innocent person has been falsely identified, convicted, and even jailed. Too often these events receive some publicity but then are quickly forgotten. This happened in the case of Edmond D. Jackson, who was convicted in 1970 of the murder of a New York bartender. The murder took place while fifty customers scrambled for cover. The subsequent investigation focused on four witnesses who looked at numerous mug shots and said one resembled the gunman. Later the defendant was convicted solely because he had been identified by these witnesses, who had seen the gunman in the bar for only a few seconds. While in prison Jackson "prayed and prayed" for his release — prayers which were not to be answered for nearly eight years. In August of 1978 the United States Court of Appeals set aside Jackson's conviction. The court found that the eyewitness testimony presented by the prosecution was so tainted by the suggestive procedures of the police investigators that its admission into evidence against Jackson constituted a denial of due process.

In this book I have tried to draw together into one coherent framework the empirical work on eyewitness testimony, and to examine the role that this testimony has played in the American legal system. For nearly a century experimental psychologists have been conducting research on human perception and memory. A portion of this work has involved the use of materials that bear a reasonable resemblance to real-life experiences — for example, staged events or films of crimes or traffic accidents. There is now a substantial body of research that bears directly on the perception, memory, and recall of complex events of the kind involved in eyewitness testimony. I have tried to integrate this research into a theoretical framework that views eyewitness testimony in terms of a three-stage process. During the first stage — acquisition — an event is perceived and information about it is initially stored in memory. In the second stage — retention — information is resident in memory. In the final stage — retrieval — memory is searched and pertinent information is retrieved and communicated.

Different variables affect the different stages. The specific variables affecting the acquisition, retention, and retrieval stages are dealt with in chapters 3, 4, and 5. Some of the work conducted in my own laboratory is described in chapter 4 — the retention chapter — since my principal concern has been with the effects of events that occur while the to-be-remembered information is resident in the memory system. For example, the way a question is phrased and the assumptions it makes have a subtle yet profound effect on the stored information. In one experiment we conducted, witnesses were shown a movie of an automobile accident and afterward were questioned about it. One of the questions, the critical one, was phrased in two different ways to two different groups of witnesses. One group was asked, "How fast were the cars going when they smashed into each other?" The other group was asked, "How fast were the cars going when they hit each other?" A week later, all witnesses returned and were asked, "Did you see any broken glass in the accident?" In actuality, there had been no broken glass, but witnesses who were originally queried with the verb "smashed" were substantially more likely to erroneously report (that is, to remember) the presence of broken glass than were subjects originally queried with the verb "hit."

This result raises obvious issues about the whole process of questioning witnesses, whether by the police prior to trial or by counsel during trial. In either case the questions asked may deposit information in memory that radically alters subsequent testimony. The theoretical account of this and similar effects involves the postulation of two types of information in the memory: information acquired during the acquisition stage and information acquired during the retention stage. These two types of information may become inextricably integrated, and the person may therefore be unable to distinguish them at the retrieval stage.

Subsequent chapters tie other important issues in the area of eyewitness testimony into the three-stage theoretical framework. These issues are the degree to which information stored in memory is permanent or immutable (chapter 6), the factors that affect one's ability to recognize previously seen human beings (chapter 7), and individual differences in the accuracy with which complex information is remembered (chapter 8).

It is a commonly held belief that information, once acquired by the memory system, is unchangeable, and that errors in memory result either from an inability to find stored information (failure at the retrieval stage) or from errors made during the original perception of the event (failure at the acquisition stage). An alternative position is that stored information is highly malleable and subject to change and distortion by events (such as misleading questions, overheard conversations) occurring during the retention stage. In chapter 6 evidence is presented that supports the conclusion that once the memory for some event is distorted by intervening events, the information acquired during perception of the original event may never be recovered.

Chapters 2, 9, 10, and 11 are primarily concerned with the impact of eyewitness testimony, particularly on the legal system. Chapter 2 provides some information on the enormous credibility that eyewitness testimony is likely to have in jury trials. Chapter 9 provides an account of common but mistaken beliefs about eyewitness testimony and assesses the degree to which such beliefs can lead to erroneous decisions. Chapter 10 is somewhat akin to a legal brief, delineating the legal status of eyewitness testimony and the role of expert testimony on the matter. Finally, chapter 11 provides a detailed account of a single case in which eyewitness testimony played a key role; expert testimony by a psychologist on this subject was presented to the jury and seems to have affected the outcome of the trial.

This is a book that faces in two directions. It faces inward to the field of experimental psychology with the purpose of providing a theoretical framework in which a diverse collection of empirical findings are integrated. It faces outward toward the rest of the world in an attempt to say how this body of research should be fitted into society as a whole, and into the legal system in particular.

I owe a great debt to the National Institute of Mental Health, the National Science Foundation, and the United States Department of Transportation, all of which have supported my research at various times over the last ten years. The manuscript was written while I had the privileges of fellowship at the Center for Advanced Study in the Behavioral Sciences, 1978-79; financial support from the Andrew W. Mellon Foundation and the National Science Foundation to the Center is gratefully acknowledged. I also wish to thank the people at Harvard University Press, especially Eric Wanner and Susan Wallace, for very useful comments and suggestions. Finally, I am indebted to a century of researchers whose work was essential to the development of this book.

In descriptions of crimes, police investigations, and trials, many names have been changed to protect the privacy of those involved.

March 1979   E.F. L.
Stanford, California

Contents

Eyewitness Testimony

1

Mistaken Identification

ON THE AFTERNOON of April 15, 1920, Mrs. Annie Nichols was taking a short break from her household chores when she happened to look out her window and see two men leaning against a nearby fence. Two more men appeared, a factory cashier and his bodyguard, each carrying a black bag containing the combined amount of over $15,000. Suddenly, one of the men who had been leaning against the fence sprang forward, pulled a gun from his pocket, and fired directly at the bodyguard. The factory cashier was gunned down as he attempted to flee, still clutching his black bag. Mrs. Nichols, frozen in horror, next saw a car pull up near the bodies. The two men piled into it and it sped away. The payroll bags were nowhere in sight.

Neither Mrs. Nichols nor others who had seen the killings could give the police precise descriptions of the gunmen. One witness thought one of the men looked "awful" dark, while another said he had very light hair and looked to be either a Swede or Finn. A third witness thought the driver of the car had a mustache, but shortly thereafter decided the man had been smooth shaven. While no agreement could be reached about the descriptions of the gunmen, it was clear that the factory employees had been shot by an automatic pistol that fired .32 calibre, steel-jacketed bullets.

A few weeks later, Nicola Sacco, a shoemaker, and Bartolomeo Vanzetti, a fish peddler, were arrested. They were both armed, Sacco with a .32 calibre Colt automatic; neither had a criminal

1

record. The police, convinced that they had the culprits, attempted to obtain identifications using procedures that are unacceptable by today's standards. Witnesses were invited to view the two in jail and to indicate whether these were the gunmen who did the shootings.

Their trial opened on May 31, 1921. The prosecution introduced the testimony of five witnesses who identified Sacco. However, one of these had testified at a preliminary hearing that her opportunity to see the robbers was too limited for her to say that Sacco was one of them. Another told a policeman that she had not seen the faces of the robbers. Another claimed, at the time of Sacco's initial arrest, that he had not seen enough to be able to identify anybody. A fourth had told three people that he would not be able to identify any of the robbers.

Four witnesses placed Vanzetti at or near the scene of the murders. One of these had told a friend, shortly after the shootings, that he had ducked as soon as he saw a gun and thus would not know the robbrs if he saw them again. As the friend related the conversation: "He said there was some fellows went by in an automobile and he heard the shots, and . . . one of them pointed a gun at him and he . . . ducked in the Shanty. I asked him if he knew them. He said, no, he did not . . . He said all he could see was the gun and he ducked" (Frankfurter 1927/1962, p. 27-28). Yet at the trial, this witness made a positive identification.

How can a witness go from being so unsure to being absolutely certain? Legal scholars who analyzed the identification techniques claimed that numerous improper methods produced this result. Other reports indicated that not a single person could originally identify Vanzetti, but that the repeated showing of his photographs to various witnesses finally produced identifications from a number of them. This type of influence can also be seen in a case brought against Vanzetti shortly before he stood trial with Sacco for the Braintree, Massachusetts, murders. Several eyewitnesses claimed to have seen Vanzetti at an attempted holdup of a Bridgewater, Massachusetts, payroll in 1919. One witness told a detective on the day of the crime that he had not gotten a good look at the robber's face. Two weeks later he repeated this statement to another detective. After Vanzetti's arrest, the witness was taken to view him, and later, at Vanzetti's preliminary hearing, the witness's description was suddenly quite complete: the gunman had a dark complexion, high cheekbones, red cheeks, hair cut close in back, and a trimmed mustache. At Vanzetti's trial, a few other features were added to the list, and the witness was now certain that he had gotten a very good look at the assailant. Vanzetti was found guilty and sentenced to a term of twelve to fifteen years. With that conviction in hand, the police pressed on toward what was to become one of the most disputed criminal cases in history—the conviction of Sacco and Vanzetti.

While the prosecution had its eyewitnesses, the defense had what they regarded as airtight alibis. Sacco claimed that on the day of the murders he had left his hometown, on a train headed for Boston, where he went to the Italian consulate to apply for a passport. A consular clerk remembered him well: Sacco had tried to use a large family group photo for his passport picture, and this unusual incident made the clerk laugh, leaving a special impression. Vanzetti claimed to be peddling fish in Plymouth on the day of the murders. A merchant from whom he had bought a length of cloth remembered him.

The transcript of the trial of Sacco and Vanzetti ran to over 2,200 pages, beginning with the clerk's opening statement and ending with the jury's verdict (Feuerlicht 1977). In the end, the jury must have believed the eyewitnesses over the alibi witnesses, for they convicted Sacco and Vanzetti on July 14. The two were put to death in the electric chair at Charlestown Prison at midnight on August 23, 1927. As Vanzetti was being strapped into the electric chair, he said something like, "I wish to tell you that I am an innocent man. I never committed any crime but sometimes some sin. I wish to forgive some people for what they are now doing to me." His many years in prison were finally over. At that moment hundreds of people stood in anxious vigil watching the light in the prison tower; they had been told it would fail at the moment of death (Porter 1977).

The case of Sacco and Vanzetti inspired a rash of books based on their trial and their long wait for death. The debate has, of course, focused on the pivotal question of guilt or innocence, but this question has in turn led to a welter of other uncertainties, many of which concern eyewitness testimony. Why, for instance, did so many witnesses, once so uncertain, make positive identifications of Sacco and Vanzetti at the trial? Were these witnesses improperly influenced by the police, and if so, how was this influence achieved? Why did the jurors believe Sacco's and Vanzetti's eyewitness accusers, even in the face of plausible alibis? Was the jury correct to give so much credence to these eyewitness accounts?

In the case of Sacco and Vanzetti, we cannot say whether the identifications were erroneous or not, but there are many less famous cases where error is known to have occurred. These are not easy to come by, since someone else must later confess or some bit of evidence must later be produced that will exonerate a once-identified person. This sort of outcome occurred in the case of the Sawyer brothers (Pearlman 1977).

The Sawyer brothers, eighteen-year-old Lonnie and his twenty-year-old brother Sandy, came from the small town of Mint Hill, North Carolina. To their horror, they were arrested for a kidnapping that took place on May 15, 1975. Robert Hinson, assistant manager of Collins' Department Store in Monroe, North Carolina, was forced into a car by two men, one of whom pointed a gun at him and demanded that he lie down in the back of the car. He got only a glimpse of his abductors before they pulled stocking masks over their faces, preventing any further view. The men planned to drive Hinson to the store where he would open the safe for them. However, Hinson convinced them that he did not know the combination, and they then took thirty-five dollars from his wallet and let him go.

Hinson had little to say about his abductors. He reported that one of them looked Hispanic, that they drove an off-white 1965 Dodge Dart, that the car was similar to one owned by a woman who worked at the store. He claimed that one kidnapper looked similar to a man who had recently applied for a job at the store, and from the bits of information he could provide, a composite sketch of one of the suspects was created.

Three days after the incident, the police stopped a 1965 white Plymouth Valiant and arrested the driver and passenger, Sandy and Lonnie Sawyer. The Valiant looked similar to a 1965 Dodge. However, neither man looked like the composite sketch, neither had applied for a job at the store, and both vehemently denied knowing anything about the kidnapping.

At their trial, the prosecution introduced the testimony of the victim, Robert Hinson, who positively identified the Sawyers as the men who kidnapped him at gunpoint. Like Sacco and Vanzetti, the Sawyers had alibis. Four witnesses testified that Sandy was at home at the time of the kidnapping, and four witnesses testified that Lonnie was at a printing plant, where he was visiting his girlfriend. After two hours the jury was deadlocked, nine for conviction. The judge instructed the jurors to try hard to reach a unanimous decision, and within a few minutes all twelve jurors voted to convict. The younger brother was sentenced to twenty-eight to thirty-two years, and the older one received thirty-two to forty years (in part because of a prior conviction). As the boys were led out of the courtroom, Lonnie yelled to his father and mother, "Momma, Daddy, appeal this. We didn't do it."

Ordinarily there would not be much hope. But because of the perseverance of their family, friends, a tenacious private detective, and a television producer who had become interested in the case, the Sawyers did have a chance. These people all believed in the results of a lie detection examination indicating that the brothers had nothing to do with the crime. And then in 1976 a prisoner at the youth center where the Sawyers were taken swore that Robert Thomas, an inmate, had admitted to being one of Hinson's kidnappers. With this rumor in hand, the private detective talked further with Hinson and discovered important information that he had initially given to the police but that the police had kept from the defense. This included Hinson's first description of the abductors, the composite sketch produced by the police, and Hinson's thought that one of the men resembled someone who had recently applied for a job at the store.

The detective searched the job applications on file at the store and found one, dated a week before the crime, that had been filled out by Robert Thomas, the inmate who had supposedly admitted to being one of the kidnappers. The detective would later find out that Thomas had a friend whose mother owned a 1965 Dodge Dart. The pieces were coming together, but the job was not over.

Those trying to free the brothers were still puzzled by one fact. During the trial a large number of witnesses said that the Sawyers could not have been the kidnappers, and only one — the victim — disagreed; yet the jury believed the one rather than the many others. Why? Several jurors were interviewed and subsequently confessed that they had eventually caved in to the majority, voting guilty simply because they were tired.

From that point it should have been easy: there was a new suspect, new evidence, and the jurors' admission that they had not voted their consciences. But it was not easy. The Sawyers were almost granted a new trial, but a judge ruled, despite the existence of new evidence, that too much time had passed. The defense attorneys petitioned the governor for a pardon. Robert Thomas confessed in writing and on camera, then recanted, then recanted his recantation. It was not until January 7, 1977, that the case was finally over. On that day the governor of North Carolina pardoned the Sawyers, but only after the brothers had lost nearly two years of their lives, their impoverished family had collected and spent thousands of dollars, and many people had suffered through a nightmare.

Like the case of Sacco and Vanzetti, the Sawyer case raises many important questions about eyewitness testimony — questions even more pointed here because it is apparent that reliance on eyewitness testimony caused a terrible error. Why did an eyewitness falsely identify someone whom he had actually never seen before? How is it that a witness can get a poor glimpse, have little confidence in his future ability to make an accurate identification, and yet ultimately make a positive identification? Why will jurors believe a single victim-eyewitness over five, ten, sometimes dozens of alibi-eyewitnesses who claim that the defendant was nowhere near the scene of the crime? Are errors of this sort rare and isolated events? Or is it possible that the reliability of eyewitness testimony is systematically overestimated by the courts?

Eyewitness testimony arises in instances that deal not only with someone's ability to identify a person but with his or her ability to accurately recall other kinds of details that were part of an important incident. Here, too, errors are abundant. For example, an article in *Flying Magazine* (July 1977) reported a major fatal aircraft accident. The crash of a small plane killed all eight people aboard and one person who was on the ground. Sixty eyewitnesses were interviewed, although only a few appeared at a hearing called to investigate the accident. Two of these people had actually seen the airplane just before impact, and one of them was certain that "it was heading right toward the ground — straight down." This witness apparently did not know that several photographs taken of the crash site made it absolutely clear that the airplane hit flat and at a low enough angle to skid for almost a thousand feet.

Whether we are concerned with the identification of a person or the accurate recounting of the details of an event, there can be problems posed by evidence of eyewitness testimony. The problem can be stated rather simply: on the one hand, eyewitness testimony is very believable and can wield considerable influence over the decisions reached by a jury; on the other hand, eyewitness testimony is not always reliable. It can be flawed simply because of the normal and natural memory processes that occur whenever human beings acquire, retain, and attempt to retrieve information.

2

Impact of Eyewitness Testimony

IN THE LAST DECADE two notorious cases of mistaken identification in England have caused grave concern within the British legal community. The first involved a Mr. Dougherty, who served nearly nine months' imprisonment of a fifteen months' sentence for theft. He was later awarded an *ex gratia* payment of 2,000 pounds. The second case involved a Mr. Virag, who had served nearly five years of a ten-year sentence for a number of offenses, including wounding a police officer with intent to resist arrest. He was later awarded an *ex gratia* payment of 17,500 pounds.

A committee to review these cases in particular and identification procedures in general was established in May 1974 under the chairmanship of Lord Devlin, the distinguished former law lord who is reputed to be a master of criminal law and procedure. The committee reported its results in April 1976 in what has come to be informally called the Devlin Report (Devlin 1976). The Devlin committee examined all lineups (or identification parades, as they are called in the British Isles) that were held in England and Wales during the year 1973. Their analysis produced the following interesting results: There were 2,116 lineups in all and the suspect was picked out in 45 percent of these. After being identified at a lineup, 850 people were prosecuted; 82 percent of these were convicted. More interesting is the fact that 347 people were prosecuted even though the *only* evidence against them was the identification by one (169 cases) or more (178 cases) eyewitnesses. And of those 347 cases, 74 percent resulted in conviction. This figure of 74 percent indicates that when no other evidence is available, the testimony of one or more eyewitnesses can be overwhelmingly influential. A jury seems to find it proof enough when a single person implicates another with a remark such as "I am certain that's the man!"

Jurors have been known to accept eyewitness testimony pointing to guilt even when it is *far* outweighed by evidence of innocence. This happened in the case of Harry Cashin (Wall 1965), whose trial arose out of an incident in a New York City speakeasy in mid-February of 1931. Two men entered the speakeasy to rob it, two policemen followed, and a gun battle ensued in which a robber and a policeman were killed. After identifying the dead robber, the police sought his friends and acquaintances and ended up questioning a former employee of the speakeasy, nineteen-year-old Harry Cashin. When Cashin arrived at the police station for questioning, all the witnesses to the robbery were there, but none identified him. A couple of months later a prostitute who supposedly had been in the speakeasy identified Cashin; he was arrested for murder and placed on trial. If convicted, he could have been put to death.

At Cashin's trial the only evidence of guilt was the identificacation of the prostitute. On the side of innocence there were many points. No other witness could identify Cashin. He did not even resemble the description of the robber originally given by the witnesses. The prostitute who identified him had previously sworn she could not identify him. There was evidence that the fleeing robber had been wounded, whereas just a few hours after the incident Cashin was free of injury. Cashin's alibi was supported by both his fiancée and her aunt. And so on. But having heard both sides of the case, the jury nevertheless found Harry Cashin guilty of murder in the first degree. The conviction was later reversed.

Ideally, we would like to ascertain the impact of an eyewitness account by conducting a trial that contains such an account and comparing the outcome to that identical trial when conducted without an eyewitness account. In the real world this is impossible. However, in the laboratory it is not.

In an experiment conducted several years ago (Loftus 1974), subjects were asked to play the role of jurors trying a criminal case and to come to a decision about the guilt or innocence of the defendant. The subject-jurors were given the following general description of the crime: On Friday, November 12, 1970, Mr. X, the owner of a small grocery store, was confronted by a man who demanded money from the cash register. Mr. X immediately handed $110 to the robber, who took the money and started walking away. Suddenly, and for no apparent reason, the robber turned and fired two shots at Mr. X and his five-year-old granddaughter, who was standing behind the counter. Both victims died instantly. Two-and-a-half hours later the police arrested a suspect, who was charged with robbery and murder. A trial date was set for February 3, 1971.

The subject-jurors were then presented with the following arguments from the prosecution: the robber was seen running into an apartment house — the same apartment house in which the defendant lived; $123 was found in the defendant's room; traces of ammonia used to clean the floor of the store were found on the defendant's shoes; and paraffin tests, used to determine whether a person has gunpowder particles on his hands from firing a gun, indicated that there was a slight possibility that the defendant had fired a gun during the same day.

From the defense the jurors learned that the defendant took the stand in his own behalf and claimed that he did not commit the crime, that the money found in his room represented his savings for a two-month period, that the ammonia tracings could have been obtained at a different place since he worked as a delivery man, and that he had never fired a gun in his life.

What percentage of the jurors, given this evidence, believe the defendant is guilty? Of the fifty jurors, only 18 percent judged the defendant to be guilty. However, for fifty new jurors we added an additional piece of prosecution evidence: a store clerk's testimony that he saw the defendant shoot the two victims. Of the fifty jurors who received the second "eyewitness" version of the case, 72 percent judged the defendant to be guilty.

In a third version of the case with fifty other jurors the defense attorney discredited the eyewitness by showing that the witness had not been wearing his glasses on the day of the robbery, and since he had vision poorer than 20/400, he could not possibly have seen the face of the robber from where he stood. Of the jurors who heard about the discredited witness, 68 percent still voted for conviction, in spite of the defense attorney's remarks. This result suggests that jurors give eyewitness testimony much more weight than other sorts of evidence when reaching a verdict.

Another line of research indicates just how heavy this weight is. Tversky and Kahneman (1977) presented their subjects with the following problem: A cab was involved in a hit-and-run accident at night. Two cab companies, the Green Cab Company and the Blue Cab Company, operate in the city; 85% of the cabs in the city are green and 15% are blue. A witness identified the cab as a blue cab. The court tested the witness's ability to identify cabs under the appropriate visibility conditions. When presented with a sample of cabs (half of which were blue and half of which were green), the witness made correct identifications on 80 percent of the cases and erred on 20 percent of the cases. Question: What is the probability that the cab involved in the accident was blue rather than green?

The several hundred subjects who were given various versions of the problem answered that the probability was about 80 percent. In this particular version, even though there were many more green cabs, people still thought it was much more likely that the cab was blue. Apparently, they trusted almost totally the witness's report and largely disregarded objective information about the percentages of blue and green cabs. When these percentages were changed, people still based their answers on the witness's credibility rather than on the relative frequency of blue and green cabs. (Of course, in the extreme case, where all the cabs were green, this would not happen.) For example, if the witness was tested and found to be correct in 60 percent of the cases, people would answer 60 percent; if the witness was correct in 30 percent of the cases, people would answer 30 percent, and so on.

I used a version of this problem to find out how credible subjects believe the *ordinary* witness to be. No information about the witness's credibility was given, except to note that his vision was "normal." Under these conditions, subjects' answers to the problem should tell something about how much faith they would put in the eyewitness testimony of a normal human being. Here is the problem, just as it was presented to the subjects: A cab was involved in a hit-and-run accident at night. Two cab companies, the Green and the Blue, operate in the city; 85 percent of the cabs in the city are green and 15 percent are blue. A witness identified the cab as a blue cab. The court tested his vision and found that it was normal. Question: What is the probability that the cab involved in the accident was blue rather than green?

Most people placed the probability that the cab was blue at

over 70 percent, even though blue cabs are much rarer than green ones. In fact, one subject wrote, "The probability is 98 percent that the car was blue. Because of the relative rarity (15 percent) of blue cabs, the witness was probably correct." Many of our subjects gave a response similar to this one—they felt that a person who claimed to have seen something that was relatively rare was probably right. However, a number of our subjects felt that it is difficult for people to distinguish blue from green at night. For this reason, these few individuals indicated that the chances that the cab was blue were about 50 percent. In other words, the witness might be right but might also be wrong.

The problem was changed slightly to indicate that the accident occurred during the day, and was then given to another group of subjects. In this case just about everyone said the chances that the cab was blue were over 80 percent. The demonstration is telling. People pay attention to what a witness says, and from a witness's report they decide what reality is.

Another way to find out something about the importance of eyewitnesses is to ask the prosecutors, who, along with the police, ordinarily have the most contact with these people. The prosecutor is the person who initially makes the decision to prosecute a defendant and who presents the eyewitnesses at the defendant's trial.

Lavrakas and Bickman (1975) asked fifty-four prosecuting attorneys in a large metropolitan community to judge the effect that various witnesses' attributes have on the outcome of four major stages of prosecution: felony review, preliminary hearing, plea bargaining, and trial. Prosecutors were asked to indicate the importance, for example, of the witness's memory of the defendant's face, the witness's age, and the witness's race. A five-point scale was used, in which a rating of one meant that the attribute was totally unrelated to the outcome of a particular stage of prosecution and five meant that the attribute was closely related to the outcome.

The investigators found that an attribute which was deemed important at one stage of the proceedings tended to be important at other stages. For example, having a witness who could positively identify the defendant was believed to be crucial to the outcomes of each stage of prosecution. Because of this consistency, the investigators presented the averages that each attribute achieved across the four different stages of prosecution. Some of the attributes, along with the importance rating that they received, are shown below:

Attribute	Mean rating
Whether the victim is available for testimony	4.53
Whether there is a witness with a good memory of the defendant's face	4.44
Whether the victim remembers the incident clearly	4.37
The age of the witness	3.62
Whether the witness is an addict	3.55
The intelligence of the witness	3.46
Whether the witness has a prior arrest record	3.40
Whether the witness speaks English	2.70
The socioeconomic status of the witness	1.90
Whether the witness is of the same race as the defendant	1.88
The race of the witness	1.59

It is clear that availability of the victim and of additional witnesses for testimony is of great importance to a successful prosecution. An eyewitness identification and the victim's memory of the incident (which is also an eyewitness account) are far more important than any other characteristics a witness possesses, such as age, race, or level of income. Lavrakas and Bickman interpreted the prosecutors' responses to mean that having a witness who could recall events accurately was absolutely crucial to the just resolution of criminal cases.

There are other, seemingly irrelevant, factors that can also affect the way in which a jury receives an eyewitness's account. For example, the sheer likableness of the witness makes a difference. An experiment that shows this effect was conducted by Garcia and Griffitt (1978). The subjects acted as jurors in a trial that resulted from an automobile accident involving a pedestrian. The key question at the trial was whether the defendant had run through a red light at the time he struck the victim. The jurors read the testimony of two eyewitnesses who had been present at the scene of the incident. The prosecution's witness testified that the defendant had run through the red light, while the defense witness testified to the contrary. In addition to the testimony, the jurors received written descriptions of the witnesses, which consisted of either a positive or a negative report by a psychologist who was supposedly observing the trial. The investigators were well aware that formal presentations of evidence of this type would be inadmissible in a real trial. However, the positive or negative information presented in this format provided the subjects with a basis on which to form impressions of the witnesses. In a real trial, jurors would be likely to form these sorts of impressions from observations of the witnesses' behaviors.

After the subjects finished reading their material, they were asked to rate the guilt of the defendant on a seven-point scale where one represented not guilty and seven represented guilty. The subjects were also asked to indicate how credible they found each witness. The results of this study, presented in table 2.1, can be summarized easily. When the witness, whether prosecution or defense, is characterized in likable terms, he is perceived as more credible than when he is described in unlikable terms. The guilt ratings also were affected by witness likableness. Subjects were more certain of the defendant's guilt when the prosecution witness was characterized positively rather than negatively and when the defense witness was characterized negatively rather than positively.

In addition to what a witness is like, *how* a witness presents testimony can alter the reception that it gets. Speech factors have been found to be critical in the overall chemistry of the trial

Table 2.1. Mean ratings of defendant's guilt and witnesses' credibility as a function of psychologist's descriptions of witnesses. (From Garcia and Griffitt 1978.)

Description of witness[a]		Mean rating of guilt	Credibility rating of witness[b]	
P	D		P	D
Positive	Positive	3.25	22.10	25.20
Positive	Negative	4.10	26.00	17.80
Negative	Positive	2.50	16.10	27.00
Negative	Negative	3.45	16.80	19.80

a. P = prosecution; D = defense.

b. Credibility ratings are expressed such that the higher the rating, the more credible the witness was perceived. Guilt is rated on a scale of one to seven, where seven represents guilty.

courtroom. The following are versions of hypothetical excerpts from a trial transcript:

Q. What was the nature of your acquaintance with her?
A. We were, uh, very close friends. Uh, she was even sort of like a mother to me.
Q. What time did she leave the party?
A. If I'm not mistaken, it seems like it was, perhaps midnight.

Q. What was the nature of your acquaintance with her?
A. We were close friends. She was like a mother to me.
Q. What time did she leave the party?
A. It was just after midnight.

The law of evidence would hold that these are equivalent presentations of facts, but O'Barr and his colleagues (O'Barr and Conley 1976; Erickson et al. 1978) have shown that subtle differences such as these can influence a jury. What exactly are the differences? To answer that question, the investigators turned to the work of Lakoff (1975), a linguist, who pointed out the following characteristics which, she maintains, distinguished female speech from male speech:

(1) a high frequency of hedges, such as "I think," "It seems like," "If I'm not mistaken," "Perhaps," "Kinda";
(2) rising intonation in declarative statements; for example, if asked about the speed at which a car was traveling, the speaker would answer, "Twenty, twenty-five?" uttered with rising intonation as if the speaker were seeking approval for the answer;
(3) repetition indicating insecurity;
(4) intensifiers, such as "very close friends" instead of "close friends" or just "friends";
(5) a high degree of direct quotation indicating deference to authority;
(6) empty adjectives, such as "divine," "charming," "cute."

With these ideas in mind, O'Barr and Conley analyzed a collection of tapes from trials that occurred in Durham, North Carolina. They noted that the style of speaking that Lakoff attributed to women occasionally appeared in the speech of men.

Furthermore, not all women talk in this manner. Thus, they felt that a "power language" continuum could be developed ranging from powerless speech (characterized by the attributes listed above) to powerful (lacking the above characteristics). Individuals of either sex might vary along this continuum.

O'Barr and Conley constructed their experiment from one ten-minute segment of an actual trial which was the result of a collision between an automobile and an ambulance. The patient in the ambulance, already critically ill and en route to the hospital, died shortly after the accident. The patient's family was suing the ambulance company and the driver of the automobile to recover damages for the patient's death. During the trial a neighbor and friend who had accompanied the patient in the ambulance was being examined by a defense lawyer. In one of O'Barr and Conley's versions of the testimony, the witness used relatively powerful speech during the interrogation, and relatively powerless speech in the other. In the powerful version any hedges were removed, repetitions and intensifiers were minimized, and the testimony in general lacked most of the characteristics that are indicative of powerless speech. A powerful and a powerless version were recorded by both a male and a female "neighbor."

One of the four versions of the tape was played to each group of subjects; all subjects were told that they were listening to excerpts from a real trial and were asked to respond in writing to a number of questions. An analysis of these responses indicated that the subjects viewed the witnesses with the powerful speech very differently from the witnesses whose speech was powerless. The "powerless" witnesses were rated significantly less intelligent, competent, likable, and, most importantly, believable. These effects applied to both male and female witnesses speaking in a powerful versus powerless mode. Some of the data from this experiment are given in table 2.2.

After indicating how believable, likable, and so on the witness was, each subject in this experiment was asked to decide the amount of money to be awarded, ranging from none to $50,000. As can be seen from table 2.2, more money was awarded when the witness spoke in a powerful manner. When the witness was a female speaking in a powerful style, the average jury award was well over $29,000. When a man testified in a powerless way, the award was only $19,000. Thus, it would appear that the way a witness gives testimony can affect the monetary award to a plaintiff.

Table 2.2. Mean ratings given to female and male witnesses who spoke in a powerful versus powerless mode. Higher values indicate a rating in the direction of the particular characteristic. Ratings of zero to eleven were possible. (Data provided by William M. O'Barr.)

Characteristic	Female witness		Male witness	
	Powerful speech	Powerless speech	Powerful speech	Powerless speech
Competent	8.61	6.85	8.44	6.18
Intelligent	8.57	5.77	7.80	6.18
Likable	8.48	6.54	8.52	7.23
Believable	9.70	7.88	10.24	8.86
Amount of damages	$29,608	$22,730	$25,319	$18,909

There are many other extra-evidential factors besides witness likableness and the way a witness speaks that contribute to jurors' verdicts (see Gerbasi et al. 1977). Jurors choose to believe the testimony of one witness and disbelieve the testimony of another for a number of reasons. In the cases of Sacco and Vanzetti and the Sawyer brothers, presumably the jurors felt that the defense witnesses had a motive to distort the truth, whereas the prosecution witnesses did not, and this almost certainly contributed to the greater believability of the prosecution witnesses' accounts. Likableness or credibility probably played a somewhat different role in the jurors' evaluation of the defendants themselves than they played in their evaluation of witnesses who were not seen by the jurors to be particularly motivated to recall the past in one way or another. In other cases when witnesses disagree and neither has a motive to recall the facts in a particular way, the jury will undoubtedly tend to believe the more credible and likable witness. But then this is true of most situations in which one person obtains information from another.

Wall (1965) cites a number of instances in which jurors themselves have been asked after the trial what they thought of the eyewitness testimony. From these cases Wall concluded that juries are often unduly receptive to evidence of identification. One of his examples is, again, the case of Sacco and Vanzetti. The prosecution introduced some eyewitness testimony that one would have thought would be too weak to bring within ten feet of a courtroom. A witness, Mary Splaine, claimed to have seen the Braintree murderers riding in a car which passed no closer to her than sixty feet and which she had in view only for the period of time it took the car to travel fifty or sixty feet. Despite these difficult conditions, she positively identified Sacco, and her testimony was most detailed, as this excerpt shows (p. 20):

Q. Can you describe him to these gentlemen here?
A. Yes sir. He was a man that I should say was slightly taller than I am. He weighed possibly from 140 to 145 pounds. He was muscular—he was an active looking man. I noticed particularly the left hand was a good-sized hand, a hand that denoted strength or a shoulder that . . .
Q. So that the hand you said you saw where?
A. The left hand, that was placed . . . on the back of the front seat. He had a gray, what I thought was a shirt—had a grayish, like navy color, and the face was what we would call clear-cut, clean-cut face. Through here [indicating] was a little narrow, just a little narrow. The forehead was high. The hair was brushed back and it was between, I should think, two inches and two-and-one-half inches in length and had dark eyebrows, but the complexion was a white, a peculiar white that looked greenish.

In commenting upon the testimony of Mary Splaine, a psychologist said: "Such perception and memory under such conditions can be easily proved to be psychologically impossible. Every psychologist knows that—so does Houdini" (Frankfurter 1927/1962, p. 14). The prosecution must have thought the testimony would be useful, otherwise why introduce it? Did the jury rely on it? Six of the jurors were polled in 1950, and at least two of them indicated they were greatly impressed by it.

In a study conducted by Wells and his colleagues (1978), jurors were asked to indicate their impressions of an eyewitness who tesified during a mock trial. The study was conducted in two phases, the crime phase and the trial phase. During the crime phase, subjects (three in each session) sat for a few minutes, whereupon a "thief" entered, posing as a co-participant. She soon "discovered" a calculator that had apparently been left by a previous subject. After examining the calculator, she stated that she wanted it, put it in her purse, and left the experimental room. The entire incident lasted just a few minutes. About thirty seconds later the experimenter came into the room, gave each witness a questionnaire requesting a description of the thief, and then asked the witnesses to try to identify the thief from a set of six pictures. The witnesses responded individually by checking one of the six pictures (or indicating "none") and also giving a confidence rating.

In phase two, the trial phase, a new group of subjects—the jurors—were told about the staged theft and the witnesses' identifications. Then the jurors were asked to watch a cross-examination of one of the witnesses who had made an identification, and decide whether or not the particular witness was or was not mistaken in his or her identification. Some of the jurors watched the testimony of a correct eyewitness while others watched the testimony of an incorrect eyewitness. Finally, the jurors were asked for their reactions to the eyewitness. The results were striking. Overall, the jurors tended to believe the eyewitness testimony about 80 percent of the time. However, the jurors were just as likely to believe a witness who had made an incorrect identification as one who had made a correct identification.

The confidence of the witness played a role here. Jurors tended to believe witnesses who were highly confident more than those who had less confidence. This experiment leads to the conclusion that eyewitness testimony is likely to be believed by jurors, especially when it is offered with a high level of confidence, even though the accuracy of an eyewitness and the confidence of that witness may not be related to one another at all. All the evidence points rather strikingly to the conclusion that there is almost nothing more convincing than a live human being who takes the stand, points a finger at the defendant, and says "That's the one!"

3

Perceiving Events

ACCORDING TO Hugo Munsterberg (1908), one of
the earliest experimental demonstrations of eyewitness
fallibility took place about 1902 in Berlin.

A few years ago a painful scene occurred in Berlin, in the University
Seminary of Professor von Liszt, the famous criminologist. The Professor had spoken about a book. One of the older students suddenly
shouts, "I wanted to throw light on the matter from the standpoint of
Christian morality!" Another student throws in, "I cannot stand that!"
The first starts up, exclaiming, "You have insulted me!" The second
clenches his fist and cries, "If you say another word _____" The first
draws a revolver. The second rushes madly upon him. The Professor
steps between them and, as he grasps the man's arm, the revolver goes
off. General uproar. In that moment Professor Liszt secures order and
asks a part of the students to write an exact account of all that has
happened. The whole had been a comedy, carefully planned and re-
hearsed by the three actors for the purpose of studying the exactitude
of observation and recollection. Those who did not write the report at
once were, part of them, asked to write it the next day or a week later;
and others had to depose their observations under cross-examination.
The whole objective performance was cut up into fourteen little parts
which referred partly to actions, partly to words. As mistakes there
were counted the omissions, the wrong additions and alterations. The
smallest number of mistakes gave twenty-six per cent of erroneous
statements; the largest was eighty per cent. The reports with reference
to the second half of the performance, which was more strongly emotional, gave an average of fifteen per cent more mistakes than those of
the first half. Words were put into the mouths of men who had been
silent spectators during the whole short episode; actions were attrib-

uted to the chief participants of which not the slightest trace existed;
and essential parts of the tragi-comedy were completely eliminated
from the memory of a number of witnesses.

According to Munsterberg, this dramatic but somewhat helter-
skelter experiment opened up a long series of similar tests in a
variety of places, with a steady effort to improve the conditions of
experimentation. Today, these experiments are still being performed, each one designed to uncover a bit more knowledge
about the workings of the eyewitness's mind. Some of this work
will be examined with an eye toward illustrating just what is
known about the nature of perception and memory that might be
of interest to the legal field.

When we experience an important event, we do not simply record that event in memory as a videotape recorder would. The
situation is much more complex. Nearly all of the theoretical
analyses of the process divide it into three stages (see, for example, Crowder 1976; Loftus and Loftus 1976). First, there is the
acquisition stage—the perception of the original event—in which
information is encoded, laid down, or entered into a person's
memory system. Second, there is the *retention* stage, the period
of time that passes between the event and the eventual recollection of a particular piece of information. Third, there is the *retrieval* stage during which a person recalls stored information.
This three-stage analysis is so central to the concept of the human
memory that it is virtually universally accepted among psychologists.

When a complex event is experienced, some of the features of
that experience are extracted first to be stored and later to be
utilized in arriving at action decisions. Early on, in the acquisition stage, the observer must decide to which aspects of the visual
stimulus he should attend. Our visual environment typically contains a vast amount of information, and the proportion of information that is actually perceived is very small. The process of
deciding what to attend to can be broken down into an even finer
series of decisions, each corresponding to where a person will
make his next eye fixation.

Once the information associated with an event has been encoded or stored in memory, some of it may remain there unchanged while some may not. Many things can happen to a witness during this crucial retention stage. The witness may engage

in conversations about the event, or overhear conversations, or read a newspaper story—all of these can bring about powerful and unexpected changes in the witness's memory.

Finally, at any time after an event a witness may be asked questions about it. At this point the witness must recreate from long-term memory that portion of the event needed to answer a specific question. This recreation may be based both on information acquired during the original experience and on information acquired subsequently. In other words, both the acquisition and the retention stages are crucial to what happens during retrieval. The answer that a person gives is based on this recreation.

Any thorough analysis of the memory process must account for events during each of the three stages. One of the most critical problems in research on human memory is to account for a person's inability to retrieve information accurately. Events at any one or several of the stages can be the cause of this retrieval failure. The information may simply not have been perceived in the first place—a failure at the acquisition stage. The information might be accurately perceived, but is then forgotten or interfered with during the retention stage. And finally, information may have been accurately perceived in the first place but may become inaccessible during questioning—a failure at the retrieval stage. It is usually a very difficult task to determine which stage is the source of failure. This chapter will focus on causes of failure at the acquisition stage.

Before a witness can recall a complex incident, the incident must be accurately perceived at the outset; it must be stored in memory. Before it can be stored, it must be within a witness's perceptual range, which means that it must be loud enough and close enough so that the ordinary senses pick it up. If visual details are to be perceived, the situation must be reasonably well illuminated. Before some information can be recalled, a witness must have paid attention to it. But even though an event is bright enough, loud enough, and close enough, and even though attention is being paid, we can still find significant errors in a witness's recollection of the event, and it is common for two witnesses to the same event to recall it very differently. Why? There are two groups of variables during the acquisition stage that affect a witness's ability to perceive accurately: event factors and witness factors.

Event Factors

Inherent in the incident itself are a number of factors that can reduce a witness's ability to report accurately. An obvious one is the amount of time that a witness has to look at whatever is going to be remembered later on; the less time a witness has to look at something, the less accurate the perception. As early as the turn of the century Whipple (1909) noted that an eyewitness should be better able to recall an event when the event transpired and was observed over a longer period of time. Yet, even when our intuitions tell us how a factor ought to operate, psychologists still feel it is necessary to conduct experiments, since intuitions and actuality do not always match.

Exposure Time

Laughery and his colleagues (1971) asked subjects to look at four slides showing different candid positions of a particular human face, one at a time. Some subjects viewed these slides for ten seconds (two and a half seconds each) while others viewed them for thirty-two seconds (eight seconds each). Two different target faces were used in the experiment—subjects either saw a Caucasian male with fair-colored hair and complexion, wearing glasses, or they saw a Caucasian male with darker-colored hair and complexion, without glasses. Approximately eight minutes later, the subjects viewed a test series of 150 projected slides of human faces. The subjects' task was to indicate on an answer sheet whether each slide in the test series was or was not the target.

As expected, these investigators found that subjects were much more accurate at remembering a face they had seen for thirty-two seconds than a face they had seen for ten seconds. Fifty-eight percent of subjects who had viewed the faces for thirty-two seconds correctly said yes when the target face appeared in the test series, whereas only 47 percent of those who had viewed the faces for ten seconds correctly said yes.

The investigators asked their subjects which features they used in the recognition process and tabulated the number of times various features were mentioned by the different subjects. While the data were not presented separately for the two exposure times, the responses of 128 subjects are shown here:

General structure	73
Eyes	66
Nose	53
Skin	42
Mouth	33
Lips, chin	31
Hair	28
Ears	19

The features mentioned by subjects in two subsequent studies were reasonably consistent with those shown above. The eyes were mentioned quite often while the ears were rarely mentioned. The investigators did not make much of these results, only to say that the question of which features subjects use in the identification process is an important issue and deserves more extensive and elaborate investigation. Obviously the more time a person has to look at a face, the more features can be perceived and used for the later recognition of that face.

Frequency

Frequency, another event factor, refers to the number of opportunities that an individual has to perceive particular details that are to be remembered later. Perhaps because this factor is so much a part of common sense, it has not been examined within the context of experiments on eyewitness reports. However, the effect that frequency of exposure has on memory is well established. Even before the turn of the century Ebbinghaus (1885/ 1964), who is famous for his studies of recall of nonsense syllables using himself as his most valuable subject, established that one's ability to relearn previously seen material was improved by repeated prior study of the material. His usual procedure was as follows: He first studied a list of, say, sixteen nonsense syllables a given number of times, ranging from zero to sixty-four. After a day or so elapsed, he would study the lists again until he recalled all of the syllables. He found that the time required to correctly recall all the syllables was reduced as a function of the number of repetitions on the previous day.

Ebbinghaus's results have been obtained in many other laboratories, using a wide range of materials and learning and testing conditions. Burtt (1948), writing on the subject of memory for the details of a crime, pointed out that something that is experienced many times is going to be remembered better than something that is encountered only once. "A person who saw the same suspect go into a certain door repeatedly will presumably remember it better than a person who saw that event only once" (p. 302).

Detail Salience

When a complex incident is witnessed, not all of the details within that incident are equally salient, or memorable, to the viewer or hearer. Some things just catch our attention more readily than others. A salient detail is one that has a high probability of being spontaneously mentioned by individuals who witness a particular event.

The importance of the salience of a detail can be seen in an experiment reported by Marshall and colleagues (1971). These investigators showed a movie to a total of 151 witnesses, all of whom were males between twenty-one and sixty-four years of age. They were recruited through several community service clubs and through the Fire Department of Ann Arbor, Michigan. The movie was in color, with sound, and lasted about two minutes. The following description of it was taken from the original article:

> Two college-age boys are seen throwing a football. The camera pans
> from them, showing a large building and parking lot and stops at the
> doorway of a supermarket from which several people emerged. A
> young man and woman carrying packages and engaged in conversa-
> tion come from the doorway and walk behind a row of cars. The man
> says he forgot to get something and leaves. The woman continues
> walking and is struck by a car backing out of the parking line. She
> loses hold of her package and falls to the pavement. The car stops; the
> driver gets out, approaches the woman and says, "Don't you ever
> watch where you're going?" The woman gets up and swears at him.
> Her companion returns running and shouts something. A scuffle en-
> sues between the companion and the driver. The companion is pushed
> to the pavement, spilling the contents of his package. The boys who
> played football earlier in the picture appear, ask what happened, and
> restrain the men. One of the boys trots off in the direction of the super-
> market entrance saying he will call the police. (p. 1662)

After the witnesses had finished viewing the film, they were given the following instructions: "You were all witnesses to the events shown in the film. Each of you will be interviewed by a man who is an expert legal interviewer. He will want to find out everything that you, as a witness, saw and heard in this film. He hasn't seen the film, so he doesn't know what the real facts are. Therefore, it will be very important for you to be careful and precise in answering his questions." The witnesses were assigned to separate rooms where individual interviews were conducted. Only about two or three minutes elapsed between the film and the beginning of the interview. Each witness was urged to be as complete as possible and as accurate as possible, that is, "to tell the truth, the whole truth, and nothing but the truth" as if he were in a courtroom.

Before the experiment began the investigators tested the movie to determine the salience of the perceivable items by simply measuring the frequency with which they were mentioned. The film was shown to high school students and to staff members who worked with one of the researchers. These individuals simply listed what they had seen. Of the nearly nine hundred possible items that were present, some were never mentioned while some were mentioned by almost everyone. The latter items can be considered to be highly salient items.

The investigators wanted to determine whether the salience of items affected the accuracy and completeness of a witness's report about those details. To determine the accuracy score for, say, highly salient items, the investigators examined only the responses referring to highly salient items. The accuracy score was calculated by dividing the number of items mentioned correctly by the total number of sample items mentioned. The completeness score was calculated by dividing the number of sample items in a category mentioned by the total number of sample items that could have been mentioned. In this same way both accuracy and completeness scores could also be obtained for less salient items.

The results shown in table 3.1 were obtained when subjects were quizzed using a multiple-choice format only (for example, "Where did the incidents happen: in a vacant lot, in a street, on a sidewalk, in a parking lot, or someplace else?"). Subjects were much more complete and accurate when reporting items of higher rather than lower salience. Items that were highest of all in salience received accuracy and completeness scores of 98. Those that were lowest in salience received scores below 70.

In this experiment the salience of an item was determined by the ratings of individuals. It is not always possible to know on what bases these ratings were made. Is a highly salient item one that was visible for a long period of time, in the center of the field

Table 3.1. Average accuracy and completeness index scores for items according to their level of salience.[a] (Adapted from Marshall et al. 1971.)

Salience category	Accuracy	Completeness
0.00	61	64
.01- .12	78	81
.13- .25	81	82
.26- .50	83	92
.51-1.00	98	98

a. 0.51-1.00 means that the item was highly salient, that is, noticed by over 50 percent of a group of people who viewed the movie. Data are presented for conditions in which witnesses were tested with a multiple-choice format.

of view, very large in size, bright or well lighted, in motion or highly active, or rather important in function? Any of these could contribute to an item's being declared salient rather than non-salient. It is likely that we would see effects for each of these different "ways of being salient" in terms of an item's memorability. Many of them were captured in Gardner's (1933) remark: "The extraordinary, colorful, novel, unusual, and interesting scenes attract our attention and hold our interest, both attention and interest being important aids to memory. The opposite of this principle is inversely true—routine, commonplace and insignificant circumstances are rarely remembered as specific incidents" (p. 324).

Type of Fact

In addition to the salience of some particular detail that a witness might be asked to remember, another event factor, the *type* of detail or type of fact being queried, must be considered. Is the witness being asked to remember the height or weight of a criminal, the amount of time an incident lasted, the speed of a car before an accident, the details of a conversation, or the color of the traffic signal? These different types of facts are not equally easy to perceive and recall.

Cattell (1895) provided one of the earliest studies to examine recall of various types of information. During March 1893 he posed a series of questions to the fifty-six students in the junior class who were present on the particular day he chose for conducting his study. His first question was, "What was the weather a week ago today?" The answers that the students gave were pretty much equally distributed over all kinds of weather which was possible at the beginning of March. Of the fifty-six people who answered, sixteen said it had been clear, twelve said it had been raining, seven said snow, nine said stormy, six said cloudy, and six said partly stormy and partly clear. Actually, on the day in question it had snowed in the morning and cleared in the late afternoon. Reflecting upon his findings, Cattell remarked, "It seems that an average man with a moderate time for reflection cannot state much better what the weather was a week ago than what it will be a week hence" (p. 761).

Next, Cattell asked his students a few questions designed to tap the ordinary accuracy of observation: "Do chestnut trees or oak trees lose their leaves the earlier in the autumn?" "Do horses in the field stand with head or tail to the wind?" "In what direction do the seeds of an apple point?" Although these questions were answered correctly more often than incorrectly, the difference was slight. The students were correct about 60 percent of the time. Thirty students thought that chestnut trees lose their leaves the earlier in autumn, while twenty-one were of the opposite opinion. Thirty-four students thought that horses in the field stand with tails to the wind, and nineteen thought they stand facing it. Twenty-four thought the seeds of an apple point "upward" or "toward stem" while eighteen thought they pointed "toward center," thirteen said "downward," and three said "outward." Cattell left it to the readers of his article to munch an apple and decide for themselves which direction the seeds in fact point. The important question he hoped to raise was this: What information can we possibly obtain by looking at the collection of answers that people give to a question?

Later in the questioning Cattell sought to determine the average accuracy in estimating weight, distance, and time. He asked his students to estimate the weight of the textbook the class had been using (William James' *Briefer Course in Psychology*), the distance between two buildings on the college grounds, and the time usually taken by students to walk from the entrance door of the building to the door of the lecture room.

The book actually weighed 24 ounces, whereas the average student's estimate was 17 ounces, a bit low. The distance between the two buildings was actually 310 feet; the estimate, 356 feet. The time taken to walk from the door to the lecture room was actually 35 seconds, whereas the average estimate was 66 seconds. Thus, Cattell provided one of the first demonstrations of the invariable human tendency to overestimate the amount of time that some activity either took or generally takes.

The students were also asked questions designed to tap their recollection of statements that were made by the lecturer one week before and their recollection of details of the building in which the class had been meeting. Recollection in these areas was so poor that Cattell was prompted to remark that his findings were worthwhile if only to "emphasize the worthlessness of many hundred casual observations as compared with one measurement" (p. 764).

Cattell felt that his work and all work in the area of accuracy of observation would find useful application in courts of justice. He thought the probable accuracy of a witness could be measured and the witness's testimony could be weighted accordingly. "A numerical correction could be introduced for lapse of time, average lack of truthfulness, average effect of personal interest, etc. The testimony could be collected independently and given to experts who could affirm, for example, that the chances are 19 to 1 that the homicide was committed by the defendant, and 4 to 1 that it was premeditated" (p. 765-766). Here Cattell went a bit too far. Based upon the collection of studies on the accuracy of observation, experts are in no position to declare a defendant guilty or not. However, they are in a reasonably good position to describe in detail some of the factors that influence a witness's observation and some of the conditions that make accurate observation difficult.

After Cattell's initial work, many investigators produced evidence of marked inaccuracies in the reporting of details such as time, speed, and distance. The judgment of speed is especially difficult, and practically every automobile accident results in huge variations from one witness to another as to how fast a vehicle was actually traveling (Gardner 1933). In one test administered to air force personnel who knew in advance that they would be questioned about the speed of a moving automobile, estimates ranged from ten to fifty miles per hour. The car they watched was actually going only twelve miles per hour (Marshall 1966/1969, p. 12).

As Cattell found out, most people have enormous difficulty estimating the duration of an event. But in this case the errors are practically always in the same direction: people overestimate the amount of time an event took. In order to study the effects of eyewitness testimony in a realistic setting, Buckhout and his colleagues staged an assault on a California state university campus (Buckhout 1977; Buckhout et al. 1975). A distraught student "attacked" a professor in front of 141 witnesses. The entire event was recorded on videotape so that the actual incident could be compared with eyewitness accounts. The attack lasted only thirty-four seconds, and after it was over, sworn statements were taken from each of the witnesses. One question about the duration of the incident produced an average estimate of eighty-one seconds. Thus, the witnesses overestimated by a factor of almost two and a half to one.

Two additional studies show the same tendency to overestimate time. In the first (Marshall 1966) the subjects watched a forty-two-second film in which a young man rocks a baby carriage and then flees when a woman approaches him. A week after the subjects had seen the picture and after they had made written or oral reports on their recollection, they were asked how long the picture had taken. On the average the subjects thought it had lasted about a minute and a half. In the second study (Johnson and Scott 1976) unsuspecting subjects who were waiting to participate in an experiment overheard either a neutral or violent conversation going on in the next room. A person, referred to as the "target," then departed from the room, spending approximately four seconds in the presence of the waiting subjects. Both males and females overestimated the amount of time they thought they had viewed the target. Females reported that they had viewed him for an average of twenty-five seconds while males claimed it had been seven seconds, on the average. Thus, we have ample evidence that people overestimate the amount of time that a complex event takes. Furthermore, there is evidence that when a person is feeling stress or anxiety, the tendency to overestimate the passage of time is increased even further (Sarason and Stoops 1978).

Despite this lack of ability, witnesses are often asked to give time estimates in courts of law. The amount of time that something took can be critical to the outcome of a case. For example, several years ago I worked with the Seattle Public Defender's office on a case involving a young woman who had killed her boyfriend. The prosecutor called it first-degree murder, but her lawyer claimed she had acted in self-defense. What was clear was that during an argument the defendant ran to the bedroom, grabbed a gun, and shot her boyfriend six times. At the trial a dispute arose about the time that had elapsed between the grabbing of the gun and the first shot. The defendant and her sister said two seconds, while a prosecution witness said five minutes. The exact amount of elapsed time made all the difference to the defense, which insisted the killing had occurred suddenly, in fear, and without a moment's hesitation. In the end the jury must have believed that the prosecution's witness had overestimated the time, for it acquitted the defendant.

In sum, there is solid evidence that errors occur in people's estimates of the duration of an incident, and the errors are in the direction of overestimation. Of course there are errors involved in the estimation of height and weight, shapes and colors, facial characteristics, and so on, but the errors do not tend to be in one particular direction. If people have difficulty perceiving this sort of information in the first place, then we can be sure that their later recall will reflect this difficulty.

Violence of an Event

Clifford and Scott (1978), wondering whether people differ in their ability to perceive violent versus nonviolent events, constructed two black-and-white videotapes which showed two policemen searching for a criminal and eventually finding him with the reluctant help of a third person. In one tape—the nonviolent version—the third person's reluctance resulted in a verbal exchange among the three people and a number of weak restraining movements by one of the policemen. In the violent version, one of the policemen physically assaulted the third person. The critical sequences were spliced into the middle of the videotape so that the beginning and end of the two tapes were identical.

Forty-eight subjects, half men and half women, looked at one of the two versions of the tape. After some intervening activities, the subjects answered a forty-four-item questionnaire. For both men and women the ability to recall events was significantly worse for those who had seen the violent event than for those who saw the nonviolent version (fig. 3.1). Clifford and Scott argued that the effect might be due to the greater stress produced by the violent event. Whatever the exact reason for the reduced performance in the case of a violent incident, the practical significance is clear: testimony about an emotionally loaded incident should be treated with greater caution than testimony about a less emotional incident.

Witness Factors

In addition to factors inherent in the event itself that affect a witness's ability to perceive, there are also factors inherent in the witness. For example, the amount of stress or fear that a witness is experiencing will influence perception, as will the prior knowledge or expectations that a witness brings to bear upon the event. What a witness does during the event will matter. For example, some witnesses try very hard to remember all of the details that they can, while others are preoccupied with thoughts such as, "How can I get myself out of this situation?"

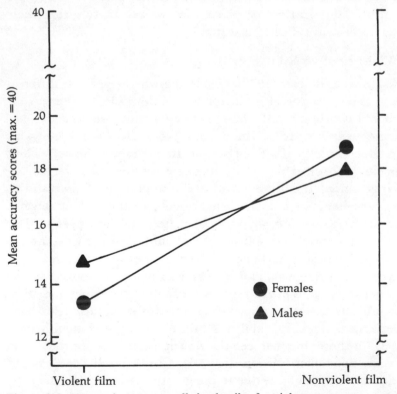

Figure 3.1. Men and women recall the details of a violent event more poorly than a nonviolent event. (Data from Clifford and Scott 1978.)

Stress

The role that stress plays at the time a witness is perceiving a complex event is captured in the Yerkes-Dodson law, named in honor of the two men who first noted it in 1908. The law states basically that strong motivational states such as stress or other emotional arousal facilitate learning and performance up to a point, after which there is a decrement. The location of the point at which performance begins to decline is determined by the difficulty of the task. Hilgard and his colleagues state the law this way: "A mild level of emotional arousal tends to produce alertness and interest in the task at hand. When emotions become intense, however, whether they are pleasant or unpleasant, they usually result in some decrement in performance" (1975, p. 357). At very low levels of arousal (for example, when one is just waking up) the nervous system may not be functioning fully and sensory messages may not get through. Performance is optimal at moderate levels of arousal. At high levels of arousal performance begins to decline. The optimum level of arousal and the shape of the curve differ with different tasks. A simple, well-learned habit would be much less susceptible to disruption by emotional arousal than a more complex response that depends upon the integration of several thought processes. In a moment of intense fear a person would probably still be able to spell his name, but his ability to play a good game of chess would be seriously impaired.

Yerkes and Dodson proposed their law on the basis of experiments with mice, in which electric shock was used as the stressor and light discrimination was the simple task to be performed. However, the law—and particularly the implication that performance suffers under extreme stress—has been shown to hold with human beings performing a variety of tasks. Baddeley (1972), in a most interesting discussion, writes that one way to obtain evidence of the effects of stress is to watch the performance of soldiers in combat. In the heat of a battle the probability that a soldier will use his rifle effectively is much lower than in training. For example, during the battle of Gettysburg in the American Civil War, over two hundred of the muzzle-loading rifles used were found to have been loaded five or more times without being fired. One had even been loaded twenty-one times without being fired a single time.

However, the battlefield is not exactly the ideal place for gathering data. Thus, several investigators attempted to simulate the battlefield, that is, to simulate a dangerous situation, in order to observe performance decrements. In one such experiment stress was induced in army recruits who were on a simulated tactical exercise. They were totally isolated except for a telephone link. Some were made anxious by telling them that they were being shelled with live ammunition by mistake or that they had mistakenly been put in an area subject to intense accidental atomic radiation. After an army recruit had been sufficiently stressed, he was required to contact headquarters by radio. The radio, however, was broken, and in order to repair it he had to follow certain complicated instructions. The simulated danger situations definitely produced a good deal of anxiety and also tended to impair performance (Berkun et al. 1962).

This last experiment was conducted in the early 1960s—a time when there were very different ethical standards for what a psychologist could do in the name of scientific experimentation with human beings and other animals—and it might very well be in violation of today's standards. Nonetheless, it does provide some useful information on the effects of stress on cognitive abilities. Simulated danger research is stricken with problems, not only practical ones but moral ones. Many investigators feel that experimental subjects should not be exposed to such high levels of stress, even for the sake of scientific inquiry. For this reason a number of investigators have chosen to conduct their studies on people who voluntarily subject themselves to real danger in such activities as parachute jumping, rock climbing, and deep-sea diving. In one study army parachutists were asked to perform a task well before, immediately before, and immediately after jumping. Performance on the task immediately before the jump was impaired for the novice parachutists but not for the experienced parachutists. This makes sense if we assume that the experienced parachutist is less anxious because he is more competent and more confident in his ability. Another interpretation is that the experienced parachutist learns to inhibit anxiety because it tends to be disruptive of performance. This explanation appealed to Baddeley, who said, "It seems then that subjects who are repeatedly exposed to a dangerous situation can in some as yet unspecified way learn to inhibit their anxiety and displace it away from the point of maximum danger" (1972, p. 544). This is likely to be useful in terms of survival, since it means that at the crucial moment performance will not be impaired.

Most individuals are not repeatedly exposed to dangerous situations and thus for most there will be a deficit in performance. It is reasonable at this point to ask why the impairment occurs. One promising explanation is that increases in stress produce a narrowing of attention. Under high stress people concentrate more and more on but a few features of their environment, paying less and less attention to others (Easterbrook 1959). Thus, a crime victim might spend a great deal of time concentrating on the gun that the assailant is waving about, and much less time processing other aspects of the situation. In fact, there is some evidence that this is exactly what people do. The term *weapon focus* has been used to refer to the situation in which a crime victim is faced with an assailant who is brandishing a weapon. The weapon appears to capture a good deal of the victim's attention, resulting in, among other things, a reduced ability to recall other details from the environment, to recall details about the assailant, and to recognize the assailant at a later time.

The phenomenon of weapon focus was at work in the experiment, already described, in which an unsuspecting subject sat outside the experimental laboratory waiting to participate in an experiment (Johnson and Scott 1976). A receptionist sat with the subject for a few minutes then excused herself to run an errand, leaving the subject alone. In the "no-weapon" incident the subject overheard an innocuous conversation about an equipment failure, after which an individual (the target) entered the reception room, holding a pen with grease on his hands, uttered a single line, and left. In the "weapon" incident a different waiting subject overheard a hostile interaction — one that ended with bottles breaking, chairs crashing, and the target bolting into the reception room with a bloodied letter opener. The target uttered a single line and left. In both cases the target was in the presence of the subject for about four seconds. Either immediately or one week later the subjects were interrogated about the incident they had witnessed. Nearly every subject in the weapon phase described some sort of weapon, whereas very few of the subjects in the no-weapon phase described the comparable item. Furthermore, the presence of the weapon was associated with a reduced ability to identify the target accurately from a set of fifty photographs. All subjects looked at the photographs and received the following instructions: "A photograph of the suspect in question may or may not be included in this album of photographs. Moreover, his photograph may or may not be a current one. Please view them carefully and tell me if you see a photograph of the person you saw in the other room." With no weapon present, 49 percent of the subjects correctly identified the target; when a weapon was present only 33 percent did so.

A word of caution is in order. The experiment was far from a perfect test of the effects of the presence of a weapon, because the two situations varied in a number of different ways, not simply in the presence or absence of a weapon. In one, the target's hands were bloodied while in the other they were full of grease; in one a hostile conversation preceded the target's entrance into the reception room whereas in the other the conversation was innocuous; the statements uttered by the target in the presence of the subject were also different. Thus, we can only say that the study is suggestive in terms of providing evidence for the phenomenon of weapon focus, but it is far from conclusive.

Expectations

Sometime in the late 1950s a hunting party of five men went out one afternoon to shoot some deer. While driving through a soggy field, their car became stuck in the snow and eventually its transmission broke down altogether. Of the five men, two volunteered to fetch help at a nearby farmhouse. Of the remaining three, one remained in the car while the other two stood just in front of it. Meanwhile, one of the two men on his way to the farmhouse decided that there was no reason for both to go after help; instead he thought he would spend his time trying to scare up a deer. The men who remained by the car did not know that their friend was circling around down a hill in front of them. One of the men who stayed by the car saw something moving and said to his friend, "That's a deer, isn't it?" The friend replied that he thought so too, and the first man then took a shot at the deer. The deer pitched forward and cried out—a sound which seemed like the cry of a wounded deer. When the deer started to run again, the friend yelled, "Don't let him get away; please get him for me." The first man fired another shot. Since the deer still moved, a third shot was fired and this brought the deer to the ground. The men ran toward it. Only then did they see that it was not a deer at all, but their friend. And the friend was dead (Sommer 1959).

Expectations clearly played a role in this dreadful episode. The hunters who eagerly scanned the landscape for a deer perceived the moving object as a deer. They expected to hear the cry of a deer and they heard their friend's cry that way. "In my thoughts and my eyes, it was a deer," remarked one of the men at the court case arising from the incident. Yet a policeman testified that when he later observed a man under the same conditions, he perceived the object as a man. The policeman had gone to the scene on the day after the incident and surveyed it carefully. He stated that he had no difficulty seeing with his naked eye up until nearly five o'clock. Yet the policeman knew he was supposed to be looking at a man; thus, he perceived the object he saw as a man. His perceptions, too, were influenced by his expectations.

A psychologist, Robert Sommer, who was asked to testify at the trial, gave a description of how people see the world, and then focused his testimony on the effects of past experience on perception. Sommer based his testimony on the research of others and on his own research concerning the role of expectations. That expectations play an important role in eyewitness reliability was nothing new. It had been known for some time. For example, Whipple (1918) commented that "observation is peculiarly influenced by expectation, so that errors amounting to distinct illusions or hallucinations may arise from this source . . . We tend to see and hear what we expect to see and hear" (p. 228).

We can identify four different sorts of expectations that will affect perception: cultural expectations or stereotypes, expectations from past experience, personal prejudices, and momentary or temporary expectations. When any of these are present, they can distort perception; the perceptual material that enters stored memory will accordingly be distorted in a manner consistent with the expectation.

Cultural expectations. A cultural expectation is simply a belief held by a large number of people within a given culture. Sometimes it is a trait attributed indiscriminately to all members of a group or to all situations of a given type. Thus, many people believe that persons of Asian background are particularly tidy, or that fat people are jolly, or that pool halls are sleazy. Cultural expectations, occasionally referred to as stereotypes, are usually simple and widely accepted, but are often highly inaccurate. That cultural expectations can dramatically affect perception was effectively shown in an experiment by Allport and Postman (1947).

These two investigators showed their subject a semidramatic

picture that contained a large number of related details (see fig. 3.2). The scene was a New York subway train filled with people, most of whom were sitting, two of whom were standing up and talking to each other: a black man wearing a tie and a white man holding a razor blade. Typically, the subject viewed the picture briefly, then proceeded to tell a second subject (who had not seen the slide) all he could recall about the picture. The second subject then told a third subject and so on, through about six or seven subjects. Over forty groups of subjects were used, including college undergraduates, army trainees, members of community forums, patients in an army hospital, and police officials in a training course. Children and adults participated, as did blacks and whites.

In over half of the experiments with this picture, the final report given by the last subject indicated that the black man, instead of the white man, held the razor in his hand. Several times he was reported as "brandishing it wildly" or as "threatening the white man with it." Here is a typical report by the last subject in the chain: "This is a subway train in New York. There is a Jewish woman and a Negro who has a razor in his hand. The woman has a baby or a dog" (p. 57). The result is due to expectancy. As the investigators themselves said: "Whether this ominous distortion reflects hatred and fear of Negroes we cannot definitely say . . .

Figure 3.2. Cultural expectations can dramatically affect perception, as revealed by subjects' reports on the contents of this picture. (After Allport and Postman 1947.)

Yet the distortion may occur even in subjects who have no anti-Negro bias. It is an unthinking cultural stereotype that the Negro is hot tempered and addicted to the use of razors and weapons" (p. 63). At least it may have been a cultural stereotype in 1947 when this study was published.

In discussing the importance of expectations, Allport and Postman aptly remark: "Things are perceived and remembered the way they usually are. Thus a drugstore, in one stimulus picture, is situated in the middle of a block; but, in the telling, it moves up to the corner of the two streets and becomes the familiar 'corner drugstore.' A Red Cross ambulance is said to carry medical supplies rather than explosives, because it 'ought' to be carrying medical supplies. The kilometers on the signposts are changed into miles, since Americans are accustomed to having distances indicated in miles" (p. 62). This study provides us with one of the nicest examples of the impact of cultural expectations on perception.

Expectations from past experience. Two men are seen leaving the scene of an apartment that they have just burglarized. A witness gets a closer view of one of the men and recognizes him as an acquaintance. Although she did not get as good a look at the other man, she identifies him as being a very close friend of the first man. The second person has an ironclad alibi: he was in another state at the time of the burglary.

These facts are hypothetical, but they are similar to actual events that have taken place in real criminal situations. The hypothetical mistaken identification of the second person indicates the important role that past experience plays in perception. The witness got a good look at the first man, knew him to be a good friend of someone in particular, and inferred that the second person must be that friend.

The role of expectations can be seen in a fascinating experiment by Bruner and Postman (1949). These investigators briefly showed subjects a display of playing cards (twelve aces from all four suits) and asked them to report everything they saw or thought they saw. After a brief glance, most subjects reported that they saw three aces of spades. Actually, there were five, but two of them were colored red instead of black. People did not see the red aces of spades because they are not used to seeing spades that are red; when they see one that is red, they apparently dismiss it immediately. Occasionally a subject would look at a red ace of spades and call it "purple" or "rusty black" — a compromise between what they actually saw and what they expected to see. They remembered the color in such a way as to make it more in keeping with their normal expectations about what colors go with what suits. Other subjects got upset. In response to a red spade card, one thoroughly disrupted subject said: "I can't make the suit out, whatever it is. It didn't even look like a card that time. I don't know what color it is now or whether it's a spade or heart. I'm not even sure now what a spade looks like! My God!" (p. 218). This classic experiment shows the important role that a person's prior experience plays in what we perceive and recall. In concluding, Bruner and Postman remarked that when expectations are violated by the environment, "the perceiver's behavior can be described as resistance to the recognition of the unexpected or incongruous" (p. 222).

Personal prejudices. Just as it is true that large groups of people can hold certain stereotypic beliefs that will affect perception, so it is true that an individual can have a personal prejudice that will affect perception. Like cultural stereotypes, these personal beliefs are usually simple, are usually applied to a given person, group, or situation, and are often untrue. Thus, if someone believes that all women are lousy drivers, this can affect his ability to accurately perceive a situation in which a woman is at the wheel.

Nowhere has this effect been shown as beautifully as in the study by Hastorf and Cantril (1954). The two psychologists studied people's perceptions of a football game between Dartmouth and Princeton — one of the roughest and dirtiest games ever played by either team. That game, played one brisk Saturday afternoon in November of 1951, was important for both colleges because it was their last game of the season and one in which a Princeton player, Dick Kazmaier, was receiving All-American mention and had just appeared as the cover man on *Time* magazine. Kazmaier was playing his last game for Princeton, which had won all its games so far.

Only minutes into the game the referees were blowing whistle after whistle and penalties abounded. The Dartmouth players were out to get Kazmaier — they tackled him, piled on him, and mauled him. Barely into the second quarter he left the game with a broken nose. During the third quarter a Dartmouth player was carried off the field with a broken leg. Tempers flared. Fistfights broke out. Many injuries were suffered by both sides.

Later, a curious thing happened: the versions of the game that appeared in the Princeton newspapers were very different from those in the Dartmouth papers! Had the writers of these stories been seeing the same thing? For example, Princeton's student newspaper wrote: "This observer has never seen quite such a disgusting exhibit of so-called 'sport'. Both teams were guilty but the blame must be laid primarily on Dartmouth's doorstep. Princeton, obviously the better team, had no reason to rough up Dartmouth. Looking at the situation rationally, we don't see why the Indians should make a deliberate attempt to cripple Dick Kazmaier or any other Princeton player. The Dartmouth psychology, however, is not rational itself" (The *Princetonian*, November 27, 1951). And from the *Princeton Alumni Weekly*: "But certain memories of what occurred will not be easily erased. Into the record books will go in indelible fashion the fact that the last game of Dick Kazmaier's career was cut short by more than half when he was forced out with a broken nose and a mild concussion sustained from a tackle that came well after he had thrown a pass. This second-period development was followed by a third quarter outbreak of roughness that was climaxed when a Dartmouth player deliberately kicked Brad Glass in the ribs while the latter was on his back. Throughout the often unpleasant afternoon, there was undeniable evidence that the losers' tactics were the result of an actual style of play, and reports on other games they have played this season substantiate this" (November 30, 1951).

But . . . through the editorial eyes of Dartmouth's student newspaper: "However, the Dartmouth-Princeton game set the stage for the other type of dirty football. A type which may be termed as an unjustifiable accusation. Dick Kazmaier was injured early in the game . . . After this incident [the coach] instilled the old see-what-they-did-go-get-them attitude into his players. His talk got results. Gene Howard and Jim Miller [from Dartmouth] were both injured. Both had dropped back to pass, had passed, and were standing unprotected in the backfield. Result: one bad leg and one leg broken. The game was rough and did get a bit out of hand in the third quarter. Yet most of the roughing penalties were called against Princeton" (*Dartmouth*, November 27).

Clearly there was disagreement about what people had seen during the game. The two psychologists, Hastorf and Cantrill, decided to make a simple study: they showed a film of the game to students on each campus and asked them, while watching the film, to note any infraction of the rules they saw and whether these infractions were "mild" or "flagrant." The subjects were told to be completely objective. The results indicate that there was a huge difference in the way the game was viewed by the students at each university. On the average, Princeton students saw the Dartmouth team make 9.8 infractions, over twice as many infractions as they saw their own team make (4.2). Further, they saw the Dartmouth team make over twice as many infractions as Dartmouth students saw their team make (4.3). Princeton students thought the violations made by the Princeton team tended to be mild ones, whereas the violations made by the Dartmouth team tended to be flagrant ones. As for the Dartmouth students, when they looked at the film, they saw about the same number of infractions—4.3 by Dartmouth and 4.4 by Princeton. However, they too tended to see violations made by the opposing team as being more flagrant than violations made by their own team.

Clearly, this experiment shows a strong tendency for the students to see their fellow students as victims of illegal aggression rather than as perpetrators. "It seems clear that the 'game' actually was many different games and that each version of the events that transpired was just as 'real' to a particular person as other versions were to other people" (p. 132).

Temporary biases. Biases play a role in the perception of all sorts of incidents—crimes, traffic accidents, hunting accidents. Hunting accidents particularly offer many opportunities for seeing how powerful temporary biases can be. Most people are not aware of just how many hunting tragedies occur because of misleading expectations. During the hunting season of 1974-75, for example, hunting accidents took the lives of at least seven hundred people (*New York Times*, November 12, 1976). The nation's newspapers occasionally report these incidents, but this does not stop them: "At least six hunters, two of them 15 years old, were shot to death during the first 48 hours of the deer hunting season" (UPI). "A 16-year old Wilmington boy, wearing a squirrel-skin cap, was shot to death Saturday morning on a hunting trip with his cousin. Cumberland County Coroner Alph Clark said Archie Lee Butler III was killed when struck in the head by a bullet fired by his cousin, Willie Butler, 16" (*Raleigh Times*). "An 18-year old Kalispell deer hunter has been shot to death only 10 days after his father died in a hunting accident" (AP). Many of these deaths are especially tragic because the victims are shot by a relative or close friend. If people were a bit more aware of the significant role their temporary biases or expectations play, perhaps these accidents could be avoided.

A good experimental example of the effects of temporary biases can be found in a study performed by Siipola (1935). Two groups of subjects were given a set of words (or quasi-words); however, one group was told that the words would pertain to animals or birds (group A), while the other group was told that the words would pertain to travel or transportation (group T). The words were presented to the subjects in a tachistoscope — an optical device (sometimes called a t-scope) with which words or pictures can be shown to a subject very briefly, as small as a fraction of a second if the experimenter wishes. A series of ten items was used, and each was presented for approximately 0.1 seconds. Some actual words were presented, such as "horse," "baggage," and "monkey"; some quasi-words were shown, such "sael," "wharl," and "dack." The subjects were asked to simply record the words which they perceived.

Siipola collected results from 160 subjects, 80 in each group. In the case of real words, the most frequent response was the correct perception of the word. (There was one exception; persons in group T often looked at the word "monkey" and said "money.") But for ambiguous words the results were striking. The subjects clearly tended to perceive the ambiguous words according to their expectations. Thus, "sael" was perceived by group A as the word "seal," whereas it was perceived to be "sail" by group T. Similarly, "wharl" was seen as either "whale" or "wharf," depending upon the subject's prior expectation. "Dack" was "duck" if viewed by a group A subject, or "dock" or "deck" if viewed by a group T subject. The tendency to perceive real words was so strong that correct reports of the actual stimulus were exceedingly rare. For example, of those subjects in group T, 89 percent gave "deck" or "dock" as the response, while only 3 percent correctly perceived "dack"; of group A, 80 percent gave "duck," while only 7.5 percent gave "dack."

The work of Siipola indicates that people will convert ambiguous words into words that are appropriate to their momentary expectations about the words that they will see. But can our momentary biases affect the way we perceive a picture? The answer to this question is yes. The picture shown at the top of fig-

ure 3.3 has been called the "rat-man" figure since it can be perceived as either a rat or a man. If a subject expects to see faces of
people, the figure will be seen as a man. On the other hand, if the
subject expects to see an animal, the figure will be seen as a rat.
These expectations can be created quite simply. If before looking
at the rat-man figure the subject is shown the faces at the bottom
of figure 3.3, an expectation is created that the figure will be a
face. If before looking at the rat-man figure the subject is shown
the animals at the bottom of figure 3.3, an expectation will be
created that the figure will be an animal. Bugelski and Alampay

Figure 3.3. Rat-man figure and series of drawings that produce temporary
biases. (After Bugelski and Alampay 1961.)

(1961) found that 85 to 95 percent of their subjects perceived the rat-man figure as a man if they saw other human heads first, and as a rat if they saw the animals first.

The same result has been obtained with other drawings. Is the drawing at the top of figure 3.4 a woman's figure or a man's face? Most people who view it after looking at the first row of drawings shown below perceive a man's face, while those who view it after looking at the second row of drawings perceive a woman's figure (Fisher 1968).

Before leaving the subject of temporary biases, let us examine one last experiment, conducted by Peterson (1976) with highly naturalistic materials. The subjects, 256 students, witnessed a videotaped disruption and fight. The tape lasted approximately seven minutes and showed events occurring at a forum that had supposedly met at the University of California in Los Angeles. The purpose of the forum was to consider the proposed impeachment of Richard Nixon. The events that the subjects watched on tape were as follows:

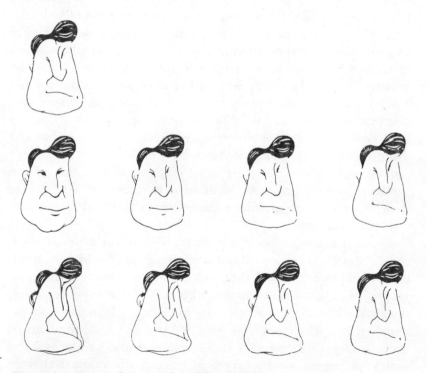

Figure 3.4. Face or figure? (After Fisher 1968.)

A pro-Nixon speaker was introduced by a moderator. The speaker began to defend Nixon. His speech was soon interrupted by comments from members of the audience. The speaker continued for several minutes and members of the audience continued to comment sporadically. While the speaker was still talking, two students got up from the audience and went on stage. One student walked behind the speaker to a blackboard. There he substituted "Closed" for "Open" Forum and wrote "impeachment" on the blackboard. The second student went immediately to the speaker. He took the microphone from the speaker and began speaking for impeachment. The anti-Nixon speaker talked for over a minute. Then the speaker attempted to reach for the microphone. With this, the speaker and both students got into a pushing match. From off stage, the moderator told them to stop. The moderator returned to the stage and told the students to sit down. The students left the stage, but the speaker refused to continue.

Before viewing the disruption, all subjects saw one of two preliminary videotapes that provided substantially different explanations for the motives of the two actors principally involved in the disruption and fight. In one version—the "guilt" tape—the students were portrayed as threatening, angry radicals who intended to prevent a speaker from completing a controversial talk. In the other version—the "no-guilt" tape—the two actors became polite students who were concerned about free speech and who wanted to be sure that both sides of the controversial subject would be heard. The guilt tape was designed to bias the witnesses toward believing that the disrupting students intended to prevent one side from speaking, and to attack or harm that speaker. The no-guilt tape sought to bias the witnesses toward believing that the disrupting students meant no harm but only intended to present their side of the argument. After viewing one or the other of the preliminary tapes and then the disruption videotape, all subjects then answered some questions about events that took place during the disruption.

The two biasing tapes did produce significant differences in the witnesses' conclusions about what happened. While witnesses of both tapes concluded that the disrupting students had improper intentions, the witnesses who viewed the tape depicting the students as angry radicals—the guilt tape—held this opinion strongly. But what about memory for the details of the disruption? As might be expected, those witnesses who had viewed the guilt tape remembered a larger proportion of details that were consistent with their conclusion that the demonstrators had behaved improperly. For example, here are some facts that are consistent with this conclusion. (Assume *A* and *B* refer to two of the disrupting students in the videotape.)

(1) *B* noisily rattled papers at the beginning.
(2) *A* said several times, "Tell us about the Watergate tapes."
(3) At the blackboard, *B* erased the word "open" and wrote "closed forum."

These kinds of details, consistent with improper behavior, were more likely to be remembered by subjects who had viewed the guilt tape than by those who had viewed the other tape.

On the other hand, witnesses of the guilt tape were less likely than the other witnesses to remember facts that were consistent with the conclusion that the actors behaved properly, facts such as these:

(1) *A* took the microphone without touching the speaker.
(2) *A* said "Excuse me" to the speaker.
(3) When the moderator told them to sit down, *A* and *B* left the stage.

A witness's memory for details consistent with his initial conclusion tended to be much stronger if a reasonable period of time passed between the disruption and the witness's recollection of it. When time passes, the witness's memory is weaker, and any faulty conclusions are less likely to conflict with other memories. This observation suggests that biases have at least some effect on the memory that exists after the initial perception has taken place. In fact, over the years there has been something of a theoretical controversy among psychologists about the role of expectations in perception. Some psychologists believe that expectations cause a real change in what a person perceives. If a person expects to see a woman's figure rather than a man's face or a bunch of guilty hoodlums rather than a peaceful lot, the attributes corresponding to those expectations are clearer and more vivid in perception. They stand out more. We pay them more attention. Yet, other psychologists believe that our expectations do not affect perception itself but rather they affect how we interpret what we have seen, or how we respond to what we have seen. Whichever of these theories is correct (and there is some possibility that both may be true in part), one thing is clear and accepted by all: expectations have an enormous impact on what a person claims to have seen.

Perceptual Activity

While an event is being experienced by a witness, there are many types of activities that he can engage in. For example, an eyewitness to a robbery could spend a good deal of time examining the individual features of the face, or he could spend most of his time staring in the direction of the face but might actually be trying to figure out how to escape from an unpleasant situation. The activity that a witness engages in is important in determining how well various aspects of an incident will be remembered.

A simple demonstration of this point can be found in the work of Bower and Karlin (1974), who presented pictures of human faces to subjects while the subjects performed one of several tasks on the faces. Some subjects were asked to judge the sex of the face, which was thought to be a superficial judgment. Other subjects were asked to judge the likableness or honesty of the face, which was thought to be a deeper judgment. On a later recognition memory test, performance was high for pictures that had been judged for likableness or honesty, and low for pictures judged for sex. This effect held up both for subjects who knew they would be tested on the faces and for those who did not know. Bower and Karlin offer a practical prescription in their conclusion: "If you want to remember a person's face, try to make a number of difficult personal judgments about his face when you are first meeting him" (pp. 756-757).

The original result reported by Bower and Karlin has been repeated many times in different laboratories around the world. In a study by Mueller and colleagues (1977), one group of subjects judged pictures of faces according to a personality trait, like generosity or friendliness, while another group judged on the basis of some physical feature of the face, such as height of forehead. The former subjects outperformed the latter on an unannounced recognition test. In a study by Patterson and Baddeley (1977), some subjects judged faces according to various personality traits, such as whether the person was nice or nasty, while others judged on the basis of facial features, such as whether the nose was small or large. Again, perceiving faces in terms of personality characteristics produced better recognition scores than perceiving them on the basis of facial features.

Why is recognition better after a personality judgment than after a judgment about either the sex of the person or some physical feature of his face? Perhaps it is because the latter judgment can be made by noting a single cue or concentrating on a single feature — the presence of a necktie or beard, short hair or bushy eyebrows, a high forehead. By contrast, judging honesty or likableness may require a greater scan of the entire face. Perhaps the subject tries to think of a person he knows who is honest or likable and then judges the similarity of the stimulus face to the known person just retrieved from memory. Whatever the process by which these complex judgments improve one's ability to recognize previously seen faces, it is clear that they work. They provide compelling evidence for the importance of a witness's perceptual activity for the accuracy of a later recollection.

A Little Bit of Knowledge . . .

Expectations and perceptual activity — both factors influencing a witness's perception of an incident — can actually be shown to be interrelated. Having a bit of knowledge about an incident *before* it even occurs can influence how we view it, what we look at, what we pay attention to, how much attention we give to various details. Put another way, what a witness knows in advance can affect what the witness does at the time of a critical incident.

To examine this relationship, Leippe and colleagues (1978) asked a simple question: If a witness knows in advance that a particular object is expensive, will this influence the subsequent accuracy of identification of a person who is seen stealing that object? Students were gathered in an experimental room, whereupon the experimenter entered and made this inquiry: "I have a subject on the phone from an earlier session who says she left a bag here. Has anyone seen it?" One of the subjects who was actually a confederate in the experiment pointed to a brown paper bag sitting on a nearby table and asked, "Is that it?" At this point, the experimenter replied, "Yes, that's it; that's her calculator," indicating that the object was expensive. For other groups of subjects the word "cigarettes" was substituted for "calculator," indicating that the object was inexpensive. The experimenter left the room, at which point the confederate grabbed the paper bag and began to leave the room. On the way out he dropped the bag, picked it up, then rushed out. (This was to ensure that all subjects would attend to the theft.) The experimenter returned about one minute later and asked about the paper bag. Upon being informed that a thief had taken it, the experimenter noted it was probably too late to catch the thief, but he could probably be tracked down later. After a few minutes the subjects were individually escorted to another room where they were told that the theft had been staged. They were then shown a six-person photospread and asked to identify the thief.

It is important to report that the subjects perceived the object as being more expensive when it was a calculator than when it was cigarettes. The average estimated value of the stolen object was $46.44 in the first case, and $1.49 in the second case. And the seriousness of the crime affected identification accuracy. When the object was believed to be expensive and the crime serious, 56 percent of the subjects made an accurate identification. When the crime was not serious, only 19 percent made an accurate identification. Thus, these investigators have found that the perceived seriousness of a crime—in this case advance knowledge of the value of a stolen item—can be a significant determinant of accuracy in eyewitness identification. It is important that the knowledge be acquired in advance for, as was shown in other versions of the experiment, when it is acquired after the thief has vanished, it has no effect whatsoever. The researchers believe that advance knowledge works because it motivates the witness to actively attend to the criminal. Possibly more facial characteristics are examined than people usually attend to and this is why identification accuracy increases. In other words, the advance knowledge may cause people to process information differently, to change their perceptual activity.

When a witness sees a serious event such as a crime or traffic accident and then must recall it later, three major stages can be identified: the acquisition stage, the retention stage, and the retrieval stage. In the acquisition stage, there are numerous factors that will affect the accuracy of the initial perception. Some of these factors, such as the amount of time the witness had to look at whatever is going to be remembered, are inherent in the situation itself. Other factors, such as the amount of stress a witness is experiencing, are inherent in the witness. Both event factors and witness factors can dramatically affect a witness's ability to perceive accurately.

Once information enters memory, it may reside there for a while before the witness attempts to retrieve it. At this point a new set of factors come into play. The next chapter is devoted to a discussion of events that take place during the retention stage and how they affect the witness's ultimate recollection.

4

Retaining Information in Memory

ON APRIL 6, 1975, a man whom I will refer to as Aaron
Lewis was arrested after leaving a grocery store carrying
bottles of wine and beer for which he had not paid. The arrest
came about because a clerk in the store called the police and
stated that the man leaving was the same man who robbed him at
knifepoint on February 15, 1975. The police picked up Lewis a
few blocks from the store, took him to police headquarters, and
booked him for the armed robbery that had occurred seven weeks
before.

Although Lewis admitted to having shoplifted the beer and
wine (he was caught red-handed), he denied having committed
the armed robbery, a much more serious offense. He protested
his arrest, arguing that the clerk had made a mistaken identification. The clerk, on the other hand, said that even though it had
been seven weeks, he was sure that it was Lewis who had robbed
him. Thus, the only piece of evidence against Lewis at his trial for
armed robbery was the word of a single eyewitness. Incidents such
as these cause us to wonder what happens to a person's memory
over a period of time such as seven weeks. What about periods
that are shorter, or those that are even longer?

When a witness perceives a complex event, a number of factors, such as the exposure time, or the salience of the event, or the
witness's prior expectations, will affect the accuracy of what is
perceived and stored in memory. But to compound the problem,
once the material has already been encoded, further changes can
take place. The time between a complex experience and a wit-

52

ness's recollection of that experience is a crucial period. Both the length of this retention interval and the events that take place during it affect a witness's testimony.

It is by now a well-established fact that people are less accurate and complete in their eyewitness accounts after a long retention interval than after a short one. The classic research, conducted by Ebbinghaus in 1885, is probably the most often cited study dealing with the loss of retention with the elapse of time. Ebbinghaus used only a single subject in his experiments—himself. Typically, he learned a list of nonsense syllables, put them away for a certain interval of time, and then relearned them. He recorded the saving in time or the saving in number of readings necessary for relearning, assuming that the better his memory, the less time it would take to relearn the material. His results (which he plotted on the now-famous "forgetting curve") showed that we forget very rapidly immediately after an event, but that forgetting becomes more and more gradual as time passes.

Ebbinghaus's findings have been confirmed again and again in subsequent research, using different types of people and different types of learning materials. Shepard (1967) tested thirty-four clerical workers for recognition of pictures after intervals of two hours, three days, one week, or about four months. Shepard found that the retention of the picture material dropped from 100 percent correct recognition after a two-hour delay to only 57 percent correct after four months. While 57 percent may seem high, it actually represents mere guessing on the part of the subjects: the test consisted of showing individual pictures to subjects and asking them to say yes if they recognized the picture as one they had seen before and no if they did not; a person who had never seen the pictures could guess correctly half of the time (obtaining a score of 50 percent) simply by chance.

An even more realistic event was shown to the subjects who participated in Marshall's study (1966), which was mentioned briefly in the previous chapter. Subjects looked at a forty-two-second film which Marshall describes as follows (pp. 53-54):

> The picture which we showed had background music through most of the sequence. It opened with a boy lowering a mosquito net on a baby carriage. The boy was in his late teens or early twenties, of average build, wore a dark jacket, lighter baggy slacks, and a white shirt open at the neck. There were white buttons on the jacket and around his neck there were two strings or chains with a flute or whistle on one and

a looking glass on the other. He had sideburns, curly hair. The baby was crying. At the beginning, the boy was smiling at the baby carriage. He appeared uncertain or nervous. He faced the baby carriage and touched the handle and started rocking it, then he removed his hands from the handle. The baby cried louder. The boy rocked the baby carriage back and forth, shifting his weight from foot to foot. The rocking became more violent and he pulled the carriage backward off the grass on which it had been to the driveway. A woman called out or shouted, "Mrs. Gerard, Mrs. Gerard, quick! Someone's running away with your baby." The boy turned toward the fence of the yard and then toward the house. A woman came running from the house toward the boy and the carriage. The woman was young. She wore a white smock and a darker skirt. She shouted, "You bad boy! You bad boy!", and waved her left arm as she ran. The boy hesitated, looked startled, ran through the gate and crouched in a corner by a white picket fence near a bush growing through the fence.

It is obvious that the movie contained quite a few details and the subjects in this experiment — 167 law students, 102 police trainees, and 22 low-income people — answered questions about them either immediately after the movie was shown or after a one-week interval. The subjects were consistently more accurate when they answered items immediately than when they answered them after a one-week interval. Referring to this decline as a "slippage of memory," Marshall indicated that he would have liked to see what would have happened to his subjects' memories after an interval of a month, or even a year. The answer seems clear. The accumulation of research tells us that after a year, memory will be less accurate than after a month; after a month it will be less accurate than after a week. This is, of course, another way of stating the result that Ebbinghaus discovered nearly one hundred years ago.

Postevent Information

Time alone does not cause the slippage of memory. It is caused in part by what goes on during the passage of time. Often after witnessing an important event, one is exposed to new information about it. For example, a person sees an automobile accident and then learns from the newspaper that the driver of the car had been drinking before the accident. Or one witnesses an argument between two people, and then overhears a friend tell a third person all the gory details of the argument. Evidence has recently been accumulating to indicate that postevent experiences such as exposure to newly released information can dramatically affect our memory of the original event. Bird (1927) provides an early example. During the course of a routine classroom lecture, the instructor was discussing the results of a series of experiments. A well-meaning but not very thoughtful reporter on the local newspaper printed an account of the lecture that was riddled with errors. Many students read the newspaper account, and nearly all of these thought it was an accurate report. The instructor gave an exam at the end of the week and after the usual set of exam questions he asked each student to indicate whether or not the student had read the press account. Those who had read the article made many more errors on the exam; they remembered the erroneous information that was in the newspaper, assuming that they had learned it from the instructor's original lecture.

The same sort of thing happens when witnesses to an event later read or hear something about it and are subsequently asked to recall the event. Postevent information can not only enhance existing memories but also change a witness's memory and even cause nonexistent details to become incorporated into a previously acquired memory.

Enhancing Memory

It is quite common for witnesses to a serious event to discuss the event after it is over. For example, the robbers leave the grocery store and one checker says to another, "Did you get a look at the guy with the green hat?" For a moment, let us suppose that one of the robbers actually was wearing a green hat. What are the consequences of the first checker's remark for the second checker's memory? As it turns out, this remark can increase the likelihood that the second checker will also claim to have seen the green hat.

This was demonstrated in the following experiment (Loftus 1975). Subject-witnesses were shown a film of a multiple-car accident in which one car, after failing to stop at a stop sign, makes a right-hand turn into the main stream of traffic. In an attempt to avoid a collision, the cars in the oncoming traffic stop suddenly and a five-car bumper-to-bumper collision results. The film lasted less than one minute and the accident itself occupied a four-second period. At the end of the film, the subjects were given a diagram of the accident, in which the letter A represented the car that turned right and ran the stop sign, while B through F represented the cars involved in the collision. All subjects were asked a series of ten questions. The first question in the series asked about the speed of the car that caused the accident in one of two ways:

(1) How fast was car *A* going when it ran the stop sign?
(2) How fast was car *A* going when it turned right?

Seventy-five subjects were asked the first question, and seventy-five different subjects were asked the second question. The last question in the series, question 10, was identical for all subjects; it asked whether the subject had actually seen a stop sign for car *A*. If the earlier question had mentioned a stop sign, 53 percent of the subjects reported later on that they had seen a stop sign. However, if the earlier question had not mentioned a stop sign, only 35 percent of the subjects claimed to have seen the stop sign when asked later on. Thus, by simply mentioning an existing object, it is possible to increase the likelihood that it will be recalled later on.

Compromise Memories

What happens when a witness sees some event and later learns a piece of new information which conflicts with some aspect of what was previously seen? It appears that when possible many witnesses will compromise between what they have seen and what they have been told later on.

In one experiment (Loftus 1975) forty subject-witnesses were shown a three-minute videotape taken from the film *Diary of a Student Revolution*. The incident involved the disruption of a class by eight demonstrators. The confrontation, which was relatively noisy, caused an interruption in a professor's lecture and finally ended when the demonstrators left the classroom. At the end of the videotape the subjects received one of two questionnaires containing one key question and nineteen filler questions. Half of the subjects were asked, "Was the leader of the four demonstrators who entered the classroom a male?" whereas the other half were asked, "Was the leader of the twelve demonstrators who entered the classroom a male?" The subjects responded to all of their questions by circling yes or no. One week later, all subjects returned to answer a new set of questions. The critical question at this time was, "How many demonstrators did you see entering the classroom?" Those subjects who had previously been asked the "twelve" question reported having seen an average of 8.9 people when questioned one week later, whereas the subjects interrogated with the "four" question recalled an average of 6.4 people. When the individual responses were examined, it was noted that most subjects tended to compromise between what they had actually seen, namely eight, and what they had been told later on — four in one case, twelve in the other.

In a second study showing the compromise response (Loftus 1977), a series of thirty color slides depicting an auto-pedestrian accident was shown for three seconds each to one hundred subjects. In this series a red Datsun is seen traveling along a side street toward an intersection. The car turns right and knocks down a pedestrian who is crossing at the crosswalk. A green car drives past the accident but does not stop (fig. 4.1). A police car arrives, the officer attempts to help the victim, while a passenger who had been in the Datsun runs for help.

Immediately after viewing the slides, the subjects answered a series of twelve questions. For half of the subjects, question ten falsely informed them that the car that drove past the accident

Figure 4.1. Black and white reproduction of one of thirty color slides depicting an automobile-pedestrian accident. Subjects' memories of the critical item — the green car seen at the center of this picture — tended to be a compromise between the green they saw and the blue they were told they saw. (From Loftus 1977.)

was blue rather than green. The other half of the subjects (the controls) received no color information. After a twenty-minute filler activity, a color recognition test was administered. All subjects were shown a color wheel containing thirty color strips and were given a list of ten objects. For each object their task was to pick the color that best represented their recollection of the object.

The results showed that the subjects who had been given the blue information tended to pick a blue or bluish-green as the color that they remembered for the car that passed the accident. Those not given any color information tended to choose a color near the true green. Thus, the introduction of the false color information significantly affected the ability of subjects to correctly identify a color that they had seen before.

Introducing Nonexistent Objects

When estimating numbers of people, or when recalling colors, witnesses can readily compromise between what they actually saw and what they were told. The compromise could be conscious and deliberate, or it could be unconscious. However, with other kinds of objects such compromise is not easy. For example, suppose a witness saw a car speed through a stop sign and later learned that the traffic sign was actually a yield sign. It would probably be the unusual witness who could come up with some compromise sign; most would stick to the stop sign that they actually saw, or decide upon the yield sign that they learned about later on. In fact, this is what people tend to do.

In an experiment by Loftus and colleagues (1978) nearly two hundred subjects viewed a series of thirty color slides depicting successive stages in an auto-pedestrian accident. The auto was a red Datsun shown traveling along a side street toward an intersection with a stop sign for half of the subjects and a yield sign for the remaining subjects (fig. 4.2). The Datsun became involved in an accident with a pedestrian, as described in the last section. Immediately after viewing the slides, the subjects were asked some questions, one of which was critical. For about half of the subjects the critical question asked was, "Did another car pass the red Datsun while it was stopped at the stop sign?" The remaining subjects were asked the same question with the words "stop sign" replaced by "yield sign." For some of the subjects, the sign mentioned in the question was the sign that had actually been seen; in

Figure 4.2. Critical slides used in an experiment which showed that eyewitnesses can "remember" seeing nonexistent objects. (From Loftus et al. 1978.)

other words, the question gave them consistent information. For the remaining subjects, the question contained misleading information.

After completing the questionnaire, the subjects participated in a twenty-minute filler activity, which required them to read an unrelated short story and answer some questions about it. Finally, a recognition test was administered. Pairs of slides were presented to the subjects and they had to indicate which member of each pair they had seen before. The critical pair was a slide depicting the Datsun stopped at a stop sign and a nearly identical slide depicting the Datsun at a yield sign.

The results indicated that when the intervening question contained consistent information, 75 percent of the subjects accurately responded. When the question contained misleading information, only 41 percent of the subjects accurately responded. If the subjects had been simply guessing, they would have been correct about half the time, or 50 percent, so the misleading question reduced their accuracy below that which would have been expected from a person who was merely guessing.

I have conducted numerous demonstrations showing how nonexistent objects can be introduced into people's recollections. For example, college students were presented with a film of an accident, followed by a misleading question (Loftus 1975). Some subjects were asked, "How fast was the white sports car going when it passed the barn while traveling along the country road?" A control question asked other students, "How fast was the white sports car going while traveling along the country road?" One week later, all of the students were asked whether they had seen a barn. In fact, no barn existed, but over 17 percent of the students whose question mentioned the nonexistent barn claimed to have seen it later on. In contrast, less than 3 percent of control subjects recalled a barn. Thus, casually mentioning a nonexistent object during the course of questioning can increase the likelihood that a person will later report having seen that nonexistent object.

The basic phenomenon noted here, namely, that nonexistent objects can become incorporated into people's memories, has been observed by other investigators. Two psychologists, Lesgold and Petrush (1977), conducted a study in which ninety-nine subjects saw a series of slides depicting a bank robbery. Every slide was accompanied by a narration of approximately sixty words which tied the slides together so that the subjects definitely felt as if they were experiencing a unified event. In each slide there was one detail (such as an alarm button) that was either present or not present (fig. 4.3). Following the slides, a series of questions was asked, some of which mentioned the existence of the key objects and others of which did not. Finally, all subjects were given

Figure 4.3. Slide from bank robbery series. A companion slide, seen by half of the subjects, did not contain the key item—an alarm button. (From Lesgold and Petrush 1977.)

the names of the key items, and some filler items, and were asked to indicate whether each item had actually been seen. The two psychologists found that simply mentioning a nonexistent object after the bank robbery slides had long since been viewed was sufficient to increase the likelihood that subjects would think they had seen the object.

In addition to the laboratory studies, demonstrations outside the laboratory have uncovered the same phenomenon at work. For example, some years ago during a course on cognitive psychology I gave my students the following assignment: I told them to go out and create in someone's mind a "memory" for something that did not exist. My hope was that they would discover how relatively easy this can be, and, further, that they would see that a memory so acquired can be as real to a person as a memory that is the result of one's own ordinary perceptual sensations. One group of students conducted their study in train stations, bus depots, and shopping centers, proceeding as follows: Two female students entered a train station, one of them leaving her large bag on a bench while both walked away to check the train schedules. While they were gone, a male student lurked over to the bag, reached in, and pretended to pull out an object and stuff it under his coat. He then walked away quickly. When the women returned, the older one noticed that her bag had been tampered with, and began to cry, "Oh my God, my tape recorder is missing!" She went on to lament that her boss had loaned it to her for a special reason, that it was very expensive, and so on. The two women began to talk to the real eyewitnesses who were in the vicinity. Most were extremely cooperative in offering sympathy and whatever details could be recalled. The older woman asked these witnesses for their telephone numbers "in case I need it for insurance purposes." Most people gladly gave their number.

One week later an "insurance agent" called the eyewitnesses as part of a routine investigation of the theft. All were asked for whatever details they could remember, and finally, they were asked, "Did you see the tape recorder?" Although there was in fact no tape recorder, over half of the eyewitnesses "remembered" seeing it, and nearly all of these could describe it in reasonably good detail. Their descriptions were quite different from one another: some said it was gray and others said black; some said it was in a case, others said it was not; some said it had an antenna, others claimed it did not. Their descriptions indicated a rather vivid "memory" for a tape recorder that was never seen.

In real life, as well as in experiments, people can come to believe things that never really happened. One of the nicest examples of this can be found in the reminiscences of the psychologist Jean Piaget (1962):

> There is also the question of memories which depend on other people. For instance, one of my first memories would date, if it were true, from my second year. I can still see, most clearly, the following scene, in which I believed until I was about fifteen. I was sitting in my pram, which my nurse was pushing in the Champs Elysees, when a man tried to kidnap me. I was held in by the strap fastened round me while my nurse bravely tried to stand between me and the thief. She received various scratches, and I can still see vaguely those on her face. Then a crowd gathered, a policeman with a short cloak and a white baton came up, and the man took to his heels. I can still see the whole scene, and can even place it near the tube station. When I was about fifteen, my parents received a letter from my former nurse saying that she had been converted to the Salvation Army. She wanted to confess her past faults, and in particular to return the watch she had been given as a reward on this occasion. She had made up the whole story, faking the scratches. I, therefore, must have heard, as a child, the account of this

story, which my parents believed, and projected into the past in the form of a visual memory. (pp. 187-188)

Central Versus Peripheral Details

Dritsas and Hamilton (1977) noted that the misleading bits of information in much of the previous research dealt with items that were not central to the actions being observed by witnesses. They became interested in comparing the ease with which one could modify memory for a salient detail—one that is perceived easily and has a high chance of being recalled accurately. The investigators hypothesized that peripheral items would be easier to modify than central, salient items, and they set out to test their hypothesis.

Seventy-two subjects looked at a videotape of three industrial accidents. In one, a male job trainee is hit by a metal chip in the cornea of the right eye. In a second, a maintenance man is struck in the back by a spinning metal rod and thrown to the ground, injuring his head and neck. In the third, a woman's right hand is caught in a punch press. Thus, the subjects viewed relatively stressful events which—if they had happened in real life—would probably lead to a fairly rigorous questioning of witnesses by investigators. It took eleven minutes to view all three tapes.

After watching the videotape, each subject completed a questionnaire which included thirty questions on both central and peripheral details. (The details had been rated as either central or peripheral on the basis of the responses of an independent group of twenty-five students.) Six of the thirty questions—three central and three peripheral—were misleading in that they contained false information intended to alter the subjects' later recollection of the event.

The results indicated that salient or central items were recalled with significantly greater accuracy and were much more difficult to alter with misleading information than were peripheral items. Eighty-one percent of the central questions were accurately answered, while only 47 percent of the peripheral questions were correctly recalled. Misleading information about central items altered subsequent recall 47 percent of the time, whereas misleading information about peripheral items altered subsequent recall 69 percent of the time. Thus we can conclude from this study that it is harder to mislead a witness about important, salient, or central aspects of an event than about peripheral ones.

Timing of Postevent Information

Consider the following dilemma: A witness to an accident has actually seen a vehicle run through a red light. The witness will be leaving town for a week and will then return to testify about the accident. An unscrupulous lawyer for the driver of the vehicle has been granted a few minutes with the witness and wishes to use that time to suggest to the witness that the light was actually green. Which time would be best for him to query the witness — right after the accident or one week later, just prior to the time the witness must testify? (For the moment, set aside the ethics of this demonstration and consider only the effects of the lawyer's behavior on the witness's final testimony.)

When people are asked to predict when the misleading information will have the greatest impact, those who vote for the earlier input often say something like, "You have to put the new information into the person's memory close in time to the actual event so that they will be stored in memory near each other." Those who vote for the later input often remark, "If you put the new information in too early it will conflict with what the witness already has in memory; if you wait until later, the memory will be weaker and will not conflict as much." Who is right? An experiment my colleagues and I conducted suggests an answer (Loftus et al. 1978).

The question asked in this study is: Does information introduced subsequent to an event have a different impact depending upon whether it is introduced immediately after the event or just prior to the time the event is to be recalled? Over six hundred participants saw the series of thirty color slides described previously, which included one slide showing a red Datsun stopped at either a stop sign or a yield sign. A questionnaire was administered, followed by a final forced-choice test; this test occurred after a retention interval of either twenty minutes, one day, two days, or one week. Half of the subjects answered the questionnaire immediately after viewing the accident slides (the "immediate" questionnaire), and the other half answered it just before the final forced-choice test ("delayed" questionnaire). In addition, another group was both questioned and tested immediately after seeing the accident. In each group of subjects, some received information on their questionnaires that was consistent with what they had seen (that is, they actually saw a stop sign and were told

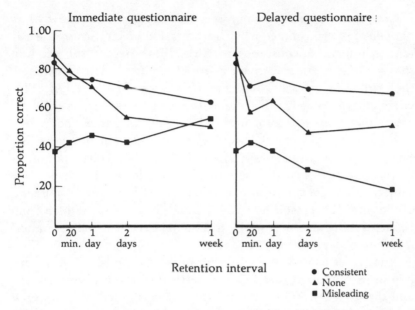

Figure 4.4. Proportion of subjects who correctly selected the slide they had seen before. The subjects were tested after an interval that ranged from immediate to one week. They were given either consistent information, misleading information, or no information about the critical sign. Their information came either immediately after the accident slides or else it came just prior to the final test. (From Loftus et al. 1978.)

it was a stop sign); others received information on their question naires that was misleading (they actually saw a stop sign but were told it was a yield sign), and still others received no information about the signs. Our major interest was performance on the final test, during which the subjects were shown the two critical slides, one containing a stop sign and the other containing a yield sign. What proportion of them correctly chose the sign they had actually seen before?

The results are shown in figure 4.4. The curves marked by triangles show what happens to performance when no relevant information is introduced during the retention interval. Performance on the test is quite high immediately after the slide sequence — almost 90 percent accuracy. It drops gradually as the interval increases, and by the time two days pass, subjects are performing at about 50 percent correct, a figure which of course means that the subjects are simply guessing. These data constitute additional support for the claim that people are less accurate after a long interval than after a short one.

Now, look at the curves marked with circles. These show what happens to performance when information given during the retention interval is consistent with the film. Here a subject was shown a stop sign, was given a questionnaire which mentioned the existence of this stop sign, and then was finally tested. The circle curves are generally higher than the triangle curves, indicating that consistent information boosts performance above that of a group of subjects who were given no relevant information. For example, after a two-day interval, the subjects given no information are performing at about a chance level. However, the subjects given consistent information are correct over 70 percent of the time. This result lends additional support to the idea that by mentioning an object which did in fact exist, one may enhance a witness's memory for that object.

Finally, let us examine what happens when misleading information is presented to a subject between the initial experience and the final test. The data in the curves marked with squares correspond to this situation. When misleading information is given immediately, the subjects answer correctly just over 50 percent of the time after a retention interval of one week. When misleading information is given just before the test, subjects are correct a mere 20 percent of the time after a retention interval of one week. Thus, misleading information more severely retards performance when it is delayed. Why is this? If misleading information is given immediately after the slides, one week later both the information from the slides and the new misleading information have faded. When tested, the subject can only guess, and he is correct about half of the time. However, when the misleading information is delayed for a week, the information from the slides has faded but the misleading information which has just been introduced is quite strong. Thus, the subjects tended to "recall" the misleading information and thus to perform incorrectly on their final test.

This experiment shows that, in general, longer retention intervals lead to worse performance; consistent information improves performance and misleading information hinders it; and misleading information that is given immediately after an event has less of an impact on the memory than misleading information that is delayed until just prior to the test. Apparently, giving the event information a chance to fade in memory makes it easier to introduce misleading information.

However, if one desires to get the witness to completely reorganize the full content of the critical event, rather than simply to change memory for a detail (as was the aim of the experiment just described), different timing may be called for. In research by James Dooling and his colleagues, subjects were presented with written passages; one, for example, was about a ruthless dictator (Sulin and Dooling 1974):

> Gerald Martin strove to undermine the existing government to satisfy his political ambitions. Many of the people of his country supported his efforts. Current political problems made it relatively easy for Martin to take over. Certain groups remained loyal to the old government and caused Martin trouble. He confronted these groups directly and so silenced them. He became a ruthless, uncontrollable dictator. The ultimate effect of his rule was the downfall of his country.

Subjects in one group believed that the dictator was the fictitious Gerald Martin. Subjects in another group were told after reading the passage that the main character was really Adolph Hitler; these subjects could then understand the passage with respect to their prior knowledge about Hitler. In the final test given to all subjects, seven sentences from the passage were randomly mixed together with seven false sentences. Of special interest was the subjects' performance on critical false sentences such as, "He hated the Jews particularly and so persecuted them." This sentence did not occur in the original passage and thus would not apply to the fictitious Gerald Martin but would be true of Hitler. When the test was delayed for one week, subjects in the group which had been told that the passage was about Hitler were much more likely than the other group to answer that they had read this critical sentence.

But what about the timing of the Hitler information? Would final test performance depend upon whether the Hitler information was presented just after the reading of the passage or just before the final test? It does matter. Manipulation of the main character immediately after the reading of the passage led to more errors on the final test (Dooling and Christiaansen 1977). The explanation offered for this finding is quite speculative: the investigators argue that those subjects who were given the Hitler information immediately had to perform a difficult cognitive manipulation to comprehend the material. They integrated passage information with new information, and the new information showed up in their memories when tested one week later. On the other hand, subjects who were given the Hitler information one week later, just before the test, did not have much specific memory for the passage, and thus they did not have as much passage information to integrate with the new information. Why under these conditions the subjects do not rely *more* heavily on their general knowledge store is still something of a mystery.

One Year Later

Most psychologists have studied memory using retention intervals of a day, a week, or occasionally a month or so. Shepard (1967) looked at memory for pictures after a four-month interval, and that was quite rare; it requires a good deal of effort to round up a group of subjects four months after their initial learning. But Davis and Sinha (1950) were sufficiently enterprising to get some of their subjects back after a full year had elapsed since an initial learning experience, in order to investigate the influence of postevent information.

The subjects in this experiment, university students, were presented with a 750-word story about a feud between two families and their reconciliation in the betrothal of the son of one with the daughter of the other. The last part of the story described a wedding feast. The entire story was written in a rather pompous style, as this excerpt shows:

> The wedding feast, which was held at the Weyden farm,| was honoured even by the sheriff, whose efforts had often been necessary to curb the violence of their quarrels | and to arrange a truce between the families.| Sitting in a high-backed chair | at the head of the broad and laden table,| a dark Holbein cap | almost hiding his white hair | and the velvet of his nobility being somewhat incongruous | in the humble interior of the farmhouse,| he gazed anxiously at Hans Loon,| the uncle of the bridegroom and the brother of the murdered man.| His solemn expression was unsuited | to the rustic boisterousness of the village folk.| But he had reasons to be alarmed,| for several unhappy incidents| made him doubt the permanence of the sudden friendship between the two families|. . . But nothing seemed to daunt the vivacious gossiping of the women,| and as dish after dish was brought | for the guests' pleasure,| and the coloured earthenware pitchers were filled | again and again | with sweet, white wine,| the danger that rancour would flare up again | seemed to grow less.|

Three or four days after reading the story, one group of subjects was shown seven postcards and asked to identify the one that depicted a scene described in the story. One card was picked by all of the subjects: it was a reproduction of Pieter Bruegel the Elder's painting *Peasant Wedding*, which, although it is famous, was not familiar to these subjects (fig. 4.5). Some of the details in the picture were consistent with the story, but there were discrepancies between picture and story as well.

A major interest in this experiment was how the picture influenced memory for the story. Subjects were asked to recall the story on one occasion only, at intervals varying from immediately to more than three weeks. For purposes of analyzing the students' recollections, the investigators divided up the original story arbitrarily into about 120 items as shown in vertical lines in the excerpt. Similarly, the items in each subject's written recollection were enumerated. Of those subjects whose initial recall occurred within about a month, those who had seen the picture listed more items than did those who had not seen the picture. In addition, those who had seen the picture tended to incorporate more totally false items into their story. For example, they claimed to have read about two long tables—an item from the picture but not from the story. Further comparisons revealed a difference in the

Figure 4.5. Pieter Bruegel the Elder's *Peasant Wedding* (c. 1565). Details from this painting were incorporated into subjects' memories of a story they had read one year earlier. (By permission of the Bettmann Archive.)

way the two groups tended to recall the story. The recall of the subjects who saw the picture was fuller and more graphic (see table 4.1).

One year after reading the story, nine subjects who saw the picture and seven who did not were found and asked to come back and recall the story again. The two groups tended to recall different kinds of items. Those who had seen the picture tended to structure their fragmentary recollection around the wedding feast. Those who had not tended to recall the concept of a feud in a peasant society. Most of the former subjects said they could remember the picture better than the story, but in general they could not decide whether a detail which had been recalled came from the picture or the story. Mistakes were numerous, with picture details appearing as intrusions in the story. Thus, their recollection of the story included a memory for "laborers with colored hats" and for "servants carrying plates on a tray," items which were never part of the story at all. It appears that one year later there was a total merging of the ideas from the two separate sources.

Subjective Recollections Can Change

We have seen how postevent information can cause objects to be added to people's memories under some conditions (for example, a barn is introduced) and can also cause objects to be altered in memory (for example, a stop sign becomes a yield sign). It also turns out that postevent information can have a fairly significant impact on people's subjective recollections; people's feelings about how noisy an event was, or how violent it was, can also be changed.

Table 4.1. Performance on memory test by subjects who saw a misleading picture during the retention interval, compared to the performance of subjects who did not. (Data from Davis and Sinha 1950.)

Subjects	Retention interval	Mean number of items recalled	Median number of importations
Saw picture	Less than 8 days	50	4
	21-28 days	43	7
Did not see picture	Less than 8 days	45	3
	21-28 days	24	4

In a study I conducted in collaboration with Altman and Geballe (Loftus et al. 1975), over fifty subjects were shown a three-minute videotape taken from the film *Diary of a Student Revolution*. The sequence depicted the disruption of a class by eight demonstrators; the confrontation was relatively noisy but basically nonviolent, and ended with the demonstrators leaving the classroom.

At the end of the videotape the subjects received one of two questionnaires. The neutral/passive questionnaire contained twenty-five questions, all phrased in a relatively mild way. For example, two of the questions were: Did you notice the demonstrators gesturing at any of the students? Did the professor say anything to the demonstrators? The other questionnaire was more emotional, with questions worded in a more aggressive way. It contained twenty-five analogous questions, for example: Did you notice the militants threatening any of the students? Did the professor shout something at the activists? No instructions were given as to possible future questions that would be asked.

One week later all subjects returned and answered a new series of questions about the disruption. As part of this session, the subjects were asked to indicate their recollection by checking the appropriate place on a five-point scale:

(1) The incident could be described as: quiet __ __ __ __ __ noisy
(2) Would you describe the incident as: peaceful __ __ __ __ __ violent
(3) Do you recall that the demonstrations were: pacifistic __ __ __ __ __ belligerent
(4) In general, the students' reaction to the demonstration was: sympathetic __ __ __ __ __ antagonistic

The subjects responded to these questions by placing an X or a check mark on the line that best reflected their recollection of the incident.

The results are shown in table 4.2. For each of the four critical questions, a single number was obtained for the subjects answering the emotional/aggressive questionnaire and for those answering the neutral-passive one in this way: If a subject checked the first spot on the scale, he received a score of one; if he checked the second spot, he received a score of two, and so on. We then took the average score of the emotional/aggressive subjects and the

Table 4.2. Average responses to four critical questions asked in an emotional/ aggressive or in a neutral/passive manner. (Data from Loftus et al. 1975.)

Average response	Emotional/aggressive	Neutral/passive
Quiet/noisy	3.71	3.04
Peaceful/violent	2.50	2.04
Pacifistic/belligerent	3.33	2.64
Sympathetic/antagonistic	4.50	3.64

average score of the neutral/passive subjects. As the table shows, the subjects who were interrogated with questions worded in an emotional, aggressive manner reported that the incident was noisier and more violent, that the perpetrators of the incident were more belligerent, and that the students in the classroom were more antagonistic than did those subjects whose questionnaires were neutral and passive. Thus, this simple postevent interrogation in which just a few words were changed produced marked changes in people's subjective recollections about the incident.

Nonverbal Influences

The fact that a picture can influence someone's memory for a previously heard story is one indication that postevent information need not be in the form of words or language spoken to a witness after an event is over. Words, in fact, make up only a small part of the information that people convey to one another. The tone of voice, the movements of heads and eyes, the gaze, the posture, and other—sometimes very subtle—behaviors can be used to convey ideas to others.

Several psychologists at Harvard University have been studying the power of nonverbal communication (Hall et al. 1978). Some very interesting studies on nonverbal messages came about as a result of research done by one member of the group on the effect of teachers' expectations on the performance of their pupils. In that research, elementary school children took a standard intelligence test which the teachers were told would distinguish those children who were intellectually gifted. The teachers were then told that certain children who had taken the test (about one-fifth of the class) were expected to be intellectual bloomers. Unknown to the teachers, these children had been chosen at random. After eight months had passed, all of the children in the class were given a second intelligence test, and the random fifth that the teachers believed to be special did in fact outperform the rest of the children. What had apparently happened is that the teachers behaved differently toward these "special" children and unintentionally influenced them to behave as if they were intellectually advantaged. The teachers could have communicated high expectations for the "special" children through some nonverbal channel, perhaps tone of voice used when speaking to the student, facial expressions, or whatever. These positive expectations are known to create a favorable atmosphere for children to develop in.

Another important study (Hall et al. 1978) has indicated that if a scientific experimenter expects research subjects to behave in a certain way, the behavior can be unintentionally influenced through nonverbal communication. Students who were studying psychology were told either that the rats in their experiment were specially bred for high intelligence or that they had been bred to be stupid. The students then studied them as the rats attempted to learn how to navigate a maze. Actually the rats were all from the same source—one was not really smarter than another. Yet the "intelligent" rats learned to run mazes far more quickly and accurately than their "stupid" counterparts. How could this happen? The researchers argue that "the students who had been told their rats were bright said that they handled their animals gently, that they liked them, and that they were enthusiastic about the experiment. The students whose rats supposedly were dull said they handled them less but talked to them more than did students with 'bright' rats" (p. 70). It is thus apparent that nonverbal communication played a part in fulfilling the expectations that the students held about their particular animals. Performance changed in the direction of the student-experimenter's expectations.

People vary in their ability to send and perceive nonverbal messages, but most people have some ability to be swayed by the nonverbal communication that comes their way. In the legal world this can be potentially very important. A police officer may tell a witness that a suspect has been caught and the witness should look at some photographs or come to view a lineup and make an identification. Even if the policeman does not explicitly mention a suspect, it is likely that the witness will believe he is being asked to identify a good suspect who will be one of the members of the lineup or set of photos. It is here that nonverbal as well as verbal suggestions can easily be communicated. If the officer should unintentionally stare a bit longer at the suspect, or change his tone of voice when he says, "Tell us whether you think it is number one, two, THREE, four, five, or six," the witness's opinion might be swayed.

Another area for potential danger has to do with the possible communication from one witness to another. In a lineup situation this has been recognized and has led Wall (1965) to note that "the most important rule here is that each witness must view the line-up separately, unaccompanied by another witness" (p. 49). This eliminates the problem of witnesses either verbally or nonverbally, intentionally or unintentionally, communicating with one another. Of course, no law enforcement procedures can prevent witnesses at the scene of a crime or accident from interacting with each other before the police arrive. Memories may be distorted long before anyone arrives to investigate. This problem became apparent to me several years ago when I arrived at the scene of a serious armed robbery moments after the robbers had fled from the grocery store. Somewhere between four and six intruders had held up the store, made the employees lie on the floor, taken the money, and run. When I arrived the manager was up off the ground, the police had been called, and the witnesses were all agitated and communicating with one another. "Did you get a look at the weird one with the blue cap?" "Boy, that short one was really frightening!" Words were used, but so was nonverbal information through the voice, gaze, and body movements. In this way one witness indicated a great deal of confidence in what she had seen, a confidence that was likely to enhance the probability that her views would be accepted by some of the others who were less confident of what they had seen. In short, there is a problem when witnesses to a crime are friends or fellow employees and have time to compare mental notes with each other before an "official" investigation begins. Nonverbal influences are as worrisome as verbal ones.

Investigations by Police and Attorneys

Recently in a town in Idaho a man raped a young woman, Jane, while forcing her friend Susan to lie with them on the bed.

The two roommates had been asleep in their apartment when Susan heard Jane screaming. Since Jane often had nightmares and occasionally talked in her sleep, Susan began to get up from her bed to go into Jane's room and awaken her. Then she heard a male voice. Before she could even get up, her own bedroom door opened and revealed the intruder holding Jane. The stranger was standing directly behind Jane with his left arm across her upper chest, holding her close to him. He held a long knife — possibly a kitchen steak knife — in his right hand. Jane was forced to lie down on the bed with Susan and both women were told to cover their faces. But Susan looked up periodically. What happened at this point, from Susan's point of view, could be inferred from what she told the police during an interview several hours later (Lewiston, Idaho, December 14, 1977):

Q: What was he doing when you looked up?
A: I don't, he was trying to bother Jane and I just took the pillow away from my face and started to say something to him and he saw me and told me to get my face back down.
Q: What do you mean bother?
A: He was starting to — you know.
Q: Have intercourse with her?
A: Yea, he was just kind of fondling her I guess, I don't know, I didn't see anything he was doing that, you know, she was telling him to stop and please don't do that.
Q: All right, let's go back, you heard the scream?
A: Yes.
Q: And you heard a man's voice?
A: Yes.
Q: The next thing you knew your door opened?
A: Right, it was partway open to begin with.
Q: And then it was just pushed open?
A: Yes.
Q: And then he brought her into your room, into your bedroom, with his hand around her throat, or did he have her in a head lock or . . . ?
A: Yea.

This is a portion of an actual interview conducted after an actual rape had occurred. It may appear as if the purpose of the interview is to get information from the witness, and indeed this is the major purpose. However, such interviews can have side effects which may be unintentional. They can *impart* information to the witness at the same time that they are apparently obtaining information from the witness. This is particularly dangerous when the police have a suspect in mind, or a theory about the case, for their ideas can be transmitted to the witness and can affect the witness's memory. But it is also a danger when there is no theory and the investigating officer or attorney is simply trying to get information from the witness.

Vidmar (1978) studied the effects of various investigative procedures on the ultimate memory and testimony of an eyewitness. Subjects came into the laboratory and were shown a ten-minute incident involving a discussion in a pub that resulted in a fight in which the defendant, Zemp, struck the victim, Adams, on the head with a bottle. The events in the incident were presented via slide projector and tape recorder and were designed to be ambiguous in places, although in one version the incident was clearly biased against the defendant, Zemp. Only after the incident was over were the subjects informed that they were to be called as witnesses in a civil trial to take place in one week. Adams was suing Zemp for damages incurred in the incident.

Between the incident and the trial, a lawyer came to interview each of the student-witnesses. The lawyers were students recruited to play this role. They were given a summary of the suit, statements given by both Zemp and Adams, and some basic information about relevant law, and they were told they would have to prepare and argue a case in front of a judge in a trial to be held in one week. To prepare for that trial each lawyer was given one witness to interview—this was to be the only source of evidence. Some lawyers were told they represented the victim Adams, while others represented the defendant Zemp. Each lawyer was given a "retainer" fee of $2.00 and told that if the judge hearing the case was to decide in favor of his client, he would win an additional $2.00 as his contingency fee; if he lost he would receive nothing.

One week from the incident, after each witness had been interviewed by either the plaintiff's or the defendant's attorney, the witness appeared for the trial. Each was met by a judge, an older student who was very formal in both dress and decorum. The judge did not know what type of lawyer had interviewed the witness. The judge informed the witness that his testimony was being recorded so that the judge could have it for further reference in deciding the case. The witness was then asked to state his or her name and to swear to tell the truth, the whole truth, and nothing but the truth. The witness was asked to recall what had happened while the judge listened passively except for a few prompting cues such as "Is that all?" or "Go on." When the witness completed testimony the judge asked the witness some questions designed to probe the witness's memory for the incident. The judge then made a decision. Was the witness's testimony biased toward the plaintiff or toward the defendant? The results were clear-cut: Even though the case itself favored the plaintiff, witnesses who had been interviewed by attorneys for the defendant gave testimony that was definitely biased in favor of the defendant; their testimony was clearly contrary to the facts of the case. Why did this happen? Vidmar argues that a lawyer for the defendant, Zemp, is confronted with a witness who has seen a version of the incident contrary to the defendant's position. In an attempt to build a case, he must exert substantial effort to find favorable facts in order to increase his chances of winning. Ultimately, this extra effort affected the witness, possibly by changing his memory of the actual incident.

Why Postevent Information Works

How and why do people come to believe that they have seen nonexistent stop signs, tape recorders, alarm buttons, barns? The answer to this question is exceedingly important to understanding how the human mind works. The preliminary ideas I will offer here are best understood in the context of a specific experiment (Loftus and Palmer 1974) in which subjects viewed a film of a traffic accident and then answered questions about the accident. Some subjects were asked, "About how fast were the cars going when they smashed into each other?" whereas others were asked, "About how fast were the cars going when they hit each other?" The former question elicited a much higher estimate of speed. One week later the subjects returned and, without viewing the film again, they answered a series of questions about the accident. The critical question was, "Did you see any broken glass?" There was no broken glass in the accident, but because broken glass usually results from accidents occurring at high speed, it seemed likely that the subjects who had been asked the question with the word "smashed" might more often say yes to this critical question. And that is what we found:

"Smashed"	"Hit"
16 yes	7 yes
34 no	43 no

In discussing our results, we proposed that two kinds of information go into one's memory for some complex occurrence. The first is information gleaned during the perception of the original event; the second is "external" information supplied after the fact. Over time, information from these two sources may be integrated in such a way that we are unable to tell from which source some specific detail is recalled. All we have is one "memory." In the smashed-hit experiment, the subject first forms some representation of the accident he has witnessed. Some bits and pieces of information get into memory. The experimenter, then, while asking, "About how fast were the cars going when they smashed into each other?" supplies a piece of external information, namely, that the cars have indeed smashed into one another. When these two pieces of information are integrated, a subject has a "memory" of an accident that is more severe than the accident in fact has been. This situation is depicted in figure 4.6. Because broken glass is typically associated with a severe accident, the subject is more likely to think that broken glass has occurred.

A more general statement can actually be made. Anytime after a witness experiences a complex event, he may be exposed to new information about that event. The new information may come in the form of questions—a powerful way to introduce it—or in the form of a conversation, a newspaper story, and so on. The implication of these results for courtroom examinations, police interrogations, and accident investigations is fairly obvious: interrogators should do whatever possible to avoid the introduction of "external" information into the witness's memory.

Intervening Thoughts of a Witness

At the Twenty-ninth Annual Advocacy Institute at the University of Michigan, over one thousand lawyers received materials regarding the hypothetical case of *Duncan v. The Americraft Industries, Inc.* (Stein 1978). Although this case was hypotheti-

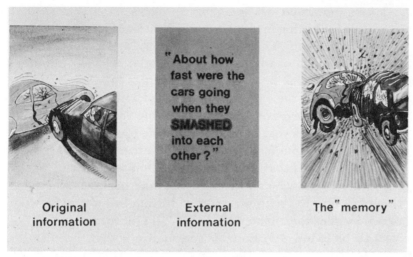

Original information — External information — The "memory"

Figure 4.6. Two types of information in memory. (From Loftus and Loftus 1976.)

cal, it was derived from a couple of actual cases that had occurred in Michigan. The Duncan case arose after David Allen, who worked as a salesman for Americraft, was driving southbound on Ridge Road at about thirty-five miles per hour and struck a four-year-old girl, Mary Lou Duncan. The little girl suffered a broken arm and skull fracture; but perhaps worst of all, she later began having *grand mal* seizures.

Mary Lou's mother, Louise Duncan, who was driving alone in her own car, had been a witness to the accident. Officers attempted to interview her at the scene, but she was hysterical and kept repeating, "My God, there was nothing he could do." Later, at the hospital, she was a bit calmer. She said that she saw her daughter run across the street and then hesitate, as if she wasn't sure she could make it. The car seemed to Mrs. Duncan as if it was going "a mite fast." Yet, she conceded that because the car was coming at her and she was concerned about her daughter, it was difficult for her to tell the exact speed. She restated that there was nothing the driver could do.

Over a year later, a deposition was taken from Mrs. Duncan. She seemed to remember things differently:

Q: Where were the other children when the accident happened?
A: They made it to the other side. I don't know why they weren't holding her hand, but they weren't.
Q: Did you sense that Mary Lou was going to be struck?

A: I sure did. That car was coming like a bat out of hell. I remember hitting my brakes and screaming out, "God, Mary Lou, watch out!" Then she got run down and I don't remember very much of what happened for the next few minutes.

The lawyers at the institute were asked how a person could remember that the driver of a car was going "a mite fast" at one point in time and a year later recall that he was going "like a bat out of hell." To examine this question for ourselves, let us first set aside the possibility that the witness is deliberately lying on one of these two occasions. Next, we might ask whether the witness was exposed to any postevent information during the interval between her two recollections. If no evidence for this sort of external influence can be found, a reasonable alternative is that the witness's own internal thoughts, wishes, and desires intruded during the interval. The witness's thoughts bend in a direction that would be advantageous for her purposes. The strong influences that one's wishes and desires have can be quite unconscious. The witness in this case was suing the driver defendant and the company that employed him. Thus, it was in her best interests to "remember" that the driver was speeding. It would then be far more likely that the jury would find him negligent. The way a person thinks about things clearly affects how they are remembered.

Labeling

The classic study showing that the way a person labels a given object or situation can dramatically affect the way that situation is remembered was conducted in the early 1930s (Carmichael et al. 1932). The subjects in their research were shown nonsense shapes such as those depicted in figure 4.7. Some subjects saw only the shapes listed in the column called "original stimuli." Other subjects were given a label that corresponded to each shape. Thus, the first nonsense shape shown in figure 4.7 might be called "curtains in a window" or it might be called "diamond in a rectangle."

Later on, subjects were asked to reproduce the figures they had seen. Two things happened. First, the subjects who had been given verbal labels reproduced more of the figures. Second, the drawings by subjects who were given verbal labels looked very different from the drawings by subjects who were given no labels. The labels caused the drawings to be distorted in a very specific

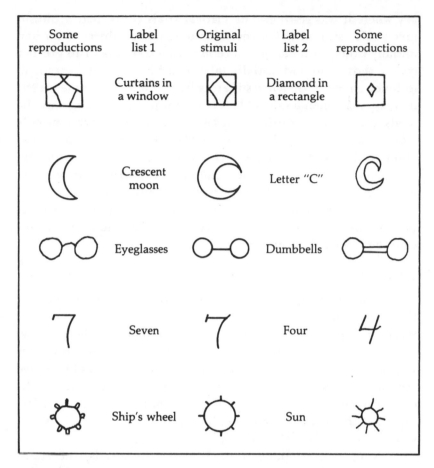

Some reproductions	Label list 1	Original stimuli	Label list 2	Some reproductions
	Curtains in a window		Diamond in a rectangle	
	Crescent moon		Letter "C"	
	Eyeglasses		Dumbbells	
	Seven		Four	
	Ship's wheel		Sun	

Figure 4.7. Stimuli and verbal labels given to subjects, and the reproductions that the subjects produced. (Adapted from Carmichael et al. 1932.)

direction. Thus, a subject who had been given the label "curtains in a window" drew a figure that looked very much like curtains.

Of course in this study the experimenters themselves provided the labels to the subjects. Thus, in a sense the labels acted as a piece of postevent information. But labels thought of spontaneously by the subject also affect later memory. This result was shown in a study of memory for colors (Thomas and DeCapito 1966). The subjects in this study were seated in the experimental room and were told that they would be exposed to a color which they should label. Later they were tested in the following way: Each time they recognized the color that had been initially shown, they should respond by lifting a finger off of a telegraph key where it was resting. The critical trials concerned a bluish-green color stimulus. On the later test, those subjects who had initially called the color green tended to respond later to greener colors; those who had initially labeled it blue tended to respond to bluer colors. Other investigators have found this same effect, namely, that when a subject labels a color in a particular way, he tends to remember it differently than does a subject who initially labels it another way (Bornstein 1974). These investigators have also found, as Carmichael and colleagues did, that when the experimenter provides the label, the same distortions in memory occur (Thomas et al. 1968; Bornstein 1976). Thus, it appears that a subject's linguistic responses to an object can cause distortions similar to those that have been observed when others provide the information externally.

Guessing

It is common practice for witnesses to a robbery to attend a five- or six-person lineup and to be asked to indicate whether they recognize the person who committed the robbery or whether anyone in the lineup resembles that person. When a witness responds with a statement such as, "I'm not really sure, but number five sort of looks like him," the witness is giving a response that is obviously closer to a guess than to a confident report. Unfortunately, this guess has all too often graduated over time to the standing of a confident observation.

Guessing can be dangerous. When a witness is uncertain, guessing can fill gaps in memory. Later, when searching his memory, a witness may incorrectly "recall" something that had earlier been merely a guess but is now a part of memory. Furthermore, while an initial guess may be offered with low confidence, later, when the witness mistakes the guess for a real memory, the confidence level can rise. This seems to occur because a witness is now "seeing" an item that he himself has constructed in memory.

In the first experiment in a set of studies designed to explore these phenomena (Hastie et al. 1978), undergraduates were shown a slide show depicting a street scene which involved four actors in a simulated mugging: a thief, a victim, and two bystanders. The show included twenty-five slides and was displayed at a two-second rate so that the entire series lasted about one minute. After a short filler activity, subjects were presented with a booklet containing a number of questions about the slide show.

They were asked about particular objects, as well as things like: What was happening in the street scene? What were the motives of each of the characters? What do you think happened in the scene after the slide show was finished? One group of subjects was told that if they could not remember a particular detail, they should answer the question anyway, guessing if they had to. Another short filler activity was presented, and finally the subjects' memories were tested. They were asked questions about details from the slide show, such as: "Was the male bystander wearing glasses? Yes or no?" "What color was the victim's coat? Black, green, or brown?" For each question they were encouraged to say "I don't know" if they had no memory. Guessing was discouraged.

Subjects who had guessed on the earlier test were significantly less accurate on this final test than were subjects who had not guessed on the earlier test. The subjects who had guessed earlier were less likely to use the "I don't know" response category and more likely to produce an error by giving an answer that was simply wrong.

The second experiment in this series gave essentially the same result. Subjects viewed a short film depicting an automobile-pedestrian accident. After a short filler activity, they answered some questions about the accident. A critical question was posed to a portion of these subjects. It asked, "What color was the stationwagon that passed the accident?" when in fact there was no stationwagon in the film. The subjects were urged to guess when uncertain. After another filler activity, the subjects took a test. The critical question on this test was, "Did you see the stationwagon that passed the accident?" Subjects answered the questions and then gave their confidence in their answer by responding on a five-point scale, "one" indicating that the subject was guessing and "five" indicating high confidence. Two days later the subjects returned and took the identical test again.

The results of this experiment were clear. The subjects who had initially been asked to guess about the color of the stationwagon were more likely to think they had seen such a vehicle when asked later on. Furthermore, their confidence continued to rise between their first test and their second one. Control subjects who had not guessed about the stationwagon were less likely to think they had seen one, and their confidence was lower on the second test than the first.

There are several explanations for why these guessing effects may occur. One is that guessing causes a change in the witness's underlying memory representation. A witness to a fast-moving event forms a skeletal representation of that event. Gaps in that representation are filled by whatever means are available. If the witness guesses the color of a supposed stationwagon, this information may be used to fill out the schematic representation. A stationwagon of some given color is essentially added to the representation. Later on, when queried about the stationwagon, the witness may retrieve from memory the stationwagon that he himself has constructed. It appears to be more vivid each time it is recalled, and this accounts for the witness's greater confidence. In addition, there are undoubtedly great pressures upon witnesses to be complete and accurate. Furthermore, there are social pressures to be sure of one's views. It may be that once a witness has given his response, he has a need to indicate that he is confident of his response, not wishy-washy. It is likely that both memory and social factors operate in this sort of eyewitness situation.

Freezing Effects

When a person is asked to recall some previously learned material, statements that appear in an early recollection tend to reappear later on. Thus, if a witness to an accident reports early on that the driver of the damaged vehicle ran a red light, this detail would be likely to appear in later recollections, whether it was true or not. This high degree of persistence in the contents of one's recollection has been called the freezing effect, and is closely related to the guessing problem. In essence, early comments are frozen into place in one's memory and pop up frequently when the witness recalls his experiences at later times. The problem here lies in the fact that, although the early comments may often be true reflections of reality, sometimes they may not. It is not uncommon for false comments to persist as well.

Nowhere have freezing effects been shown as effectively as in the study by Kay (1955), whose work was substantially influenced by the work of Bartlett during the 1920s and 1930s. Bartlett (1932) presented subjects with a story or drawing and later asked people to repeat or reproduce this information several times. Among other things, Bartlett reported great inaccuracy in people's reproductions; but of real interest here is the great persistence he found in the content of a reproduction once the first version had been given. Kay has also noted that the content of people's recollections, though often far from accurate, is stubbornly maintained. Kay put the question in an interesting way: "Why should the initial reproduction be so stable when that version itself is an inaccurate reproduction of the original? or alternatively, Why can accuracy of reproduction be achieved between one inaccurate version and another and not between the original and its first reproduction?"

Kay's experimental procedure was straightforward. Prose passages were read to subjects, who were asked to reproduce them five minutes later. The passages were read again, and the subjects reproduced them again. One week later the subjects attempted another reproduction, followed by the originals being read to them again, and this routine was followed the next week. The experiment was conducted on these lines until six reproductions in all had been made. Four months after this they attempted one last reproduction. The following example gives some idea of the passages that Kay used:

> Wanted stenographic position—I take shorthand notes quicker than a new band of Oklahoma outlaws can spring up. I lay a smoke screen with a typewriter, and I do not stay long with one firm because I work so fast I burn the office down.

> References: several large firms in Oklahoma City had complete new furniture of steel installed after I had worked there a few days, and the police raiding squad stationed me with a typewriter, and copying the encyclopedia, in front of the door of a speakeasy to smoke out the bootleggers instead of throwing tear gas bombs into the building. Warning—I advise the person who contemplates hiring me to have his office heavily insured, because if I work for him he will have a sure case of conflagration on hand.

When Kay examined the various reproductions, he found that any one version bore a much greater resemblance to its immediate predecessor than either one of them bore to the original material. If only correct information persisted, this would be a fine result. The problem is that errors persist as well. In fact, as many as 95 percent of the errors that existed in one version might persist in the next version, despite the fact that the original material had been presented again between the two versions. One subject used the expression "the entire stock" in all seven of his reproductions when the original passage he heard had said "the whole stock." Another kept using "a vague urge" when the original had said "a vague impulse." Another kept saying "a half forgotten geography lesson" when the correct phrase was "subconscious memory of a geography lesson." These verbal changes might perhaps be considered minor. But others are major. One subject persistently remembered something about "the grandmother in Australia" when he had actually heard about "the geography lesson on Australia" and "the recollection of his grandmother"—an interesting amalgamation. Errors persisted in people's memories of the passage about the stenographic position, quoted above. For example, one subject insisted on interpreting "several large firms" as "the last three firms" and in two versions she also "set fire within three days" to the offices, while another subject kept repeating "three weeks" for "a few days." One subject maintained throughout that it was the "Oklahoma City Police Vice Squad," while another made it "F.B.I. officials"; a third described it as "the police riot squad," while a fourth related how "the State Police hired me to sit on the sidewalk."

In the typical eyewitness situation, or even the typical memory experiment, a subject is presented with information once; his memory or recollection is tested at a later time, perhaps on several occasions. Kay's experiment is unusual—and his results more striking—because the person's memory for the original material is refreshed by presenting the original again, and yet inaccurate recollections persist.

The important role that the intervening thoughts, remarks, and recollections of a witness can have upon a final account—say, in court—were well known long before Kay did his work. Whipple (1909) wrote, "When a given reporter is called upon to make his report several times, the effect of this repetition is complex, for (1) it tends in part to establish in mind the items reported, whether they be true or false, and (2) it tends also to induce some departure in later reports, because these are based more upon the memory of the verbal statements of the earlier reports than upon the original experience itself" (pp. 166-167). Whipple felt the judicial system should act on this knowledge and argued that "most writers . . . believe that legal procedure should, insofar as possible, be arranged to reduce the number of times that witnesses are called upon to testify."

During the time between an event and a witness's recollection of that event—a period often called the "retention interval"—the bits and pieces of information that were acquired through perception do not passively reside in memory waiting to be pulled out like fish from water. Rather, they are subject to numerous influences. External information provided from the outside can intrude into the witness's memory, as can his own thoughts, and both can cause dramatic changes in his recollection.

People's memories are fragile things. It is important to realize how easily information can be introduced into memory, to understand why this happens, and to avoid it when it is undesirable.

5

Retrieving Information from Memory

THE FOLLOWING DESCRIPTION of an eyewitness scenario is hypothetical, but it is based on actual cases that occurred in Santa Clara County, California (Woocher 1977):

A young woman named Mary Smith is walking home after midnight, having just finished her work on the night shift at the phone company. On her way she passes a tavern where she hears someone step away from the entrance and begin to follow her. Suddenly in a dark section of the street, a man rushes on her, knocks her down, waves a gun in front of her face, and demands her purse and jewelry. She sees that he is a tall black man, and, frightened, she obediently complies. The man runs off, and Mary — in a total state of panic — rushes home and calls the police. Just ten minutes later, the police arrive and Mary tells them all she can remember, trying her best to describe her attacker — he was a tall, fairly dark-complexioned black man in his early twenties, of medium build, with a large, flat nose and medium Afro. Pressed to "remember something else," Mary remarks: "Well, he might have had a beard or something, like a goatee . . . Yeah, I think he had a goatee." Further interrogation continues at the police station, and again after five weeks when the police have a suspect. It is the conditions that prevail during these interrogations, when the witness is being asked to retrieve information from memory, that are of central interest in this chapter. As a number of experiments have shown, these conditions are critically important in determining the accuracy and completeness of an eyewitness report.

Retrieval Environment

Over thirty-five years ago E. M. Abernathy (1940) showed that college students performed much worse on their examinations when classroom learning was tested in a different room from the usual classroom. The students also scored more poorly when the proctor for the exam was different from the usual instructor. And when both the room and the proctor were changed, the students performed worst of all. This is a curious result, but it is not an isolated finding. There is reason to believe that it would also hold up in an eyewitness situation where the "learning" that is taking place is the taking in of information about a crime or accident or other important event, and the "testing" is the retrieving of that information during interrogation.

Long ago, Gustave Feingold (1914) looked into the problem: "An individual is seen lurking in a building, let us say. Subsequently it is discovered that a robbery or a murder or what not, took place in that building. Some days or weeks later an arrest is made, and the persons who had seen this lurking individual are summoned to the police court for the purpose of identifying a suspect. Assuming that the individual under arrest is the one who had been seen lurking in the building, what is the probability that he will be recognized in the new surroundings?" (p. 39).

The answer to Feingold's question is best stated, "It depends." It depends for one thing on whether the new surroundings provide a condition favorable to successful recognition. Feingold's experimental research used picture postcards representing every conceivable object, scene, and situation that a person may well observe in life and then be called upon to recognize. The cards were grouped in pairs on the basis of their similarity. Thus, a picture of a red rose and another of a gray church building were totally dissimilar. Pictures of two different churches might be judged to be quite similar. The subjects in this experiment were trained psychologists who had never seen the cards before. They were shown a single card for about five seconds. Then came an interval of twenty seconds during which the observer was required to retain in memory as much of the material he had just seen as he could. Finally, a new card was shown and the subject was asked to say whether the second card was identical with the first or not. If not identical, the observer was to indicate how it differed from the original card.

At first Feingold looked at some simple factors such as the length of the original exposure, but then a new question arose. What if the second card was shown in a totally different setting, in new surroundings? Specifically, he asked, "Does the feeling of familiarity or strangeness which is aroused by the general environment so color consciousness with its own particular tone as to make a new item appear familiar in the one case, and a previously experienced item appear strange in the other?" (p. 43). Feingold used a procedure similar to the one he had used before except for the fact that some of the recognition tests were conducted in the same environment as the original material while others were conducted in a different environment. The results were clear: the new environment inhibited recognition. Writing over sixty years ago, Feingold felt his work had important implications for police interrogations: "The proper way to obtain successful recognition is not to bring the witness into the police court, but to bring the supposed lawbreaker to the scene of the crime and have the witnesses look at him precisely in the same surroundings and from the same angle at which he saw him originally" (p. 47). While this implication may not be very practical in most cases, Feingold's work is valuable because it can help the police to understand why a suspect whom they are certain is guilty cannot be accurately recognized by a witness who views him in the police station.

Type of Retrieval

Mary Smith, the victim of the hypothetical mugging described earlier, rushed home to call the police. When they arrived, their job was to get as much good-quality information from Mary as they could. They might have asked her open questions, such as "Tell us all you can remember"—questions in which she was free to report any details she wished. Or they might have asked her very specific questions requiring short answers, such as "Give us a description of what your assailant was wearing." The first type of question has been called the narrative or free report form while the second is a controlled narrative question. The police might have posed multiple choice questions to Mary Smith, such as "Did your attacker have dark or light hair?" This has been called the interrogatory report form. Finally, the police might have presented Mary with a set of photographs, asking her to try to recognize the assailant if she could. The form in which a question is put to a witness exerts a strong influence on the quality of the answer.

Compared to other forms of report, narrative reports include fewer errors but they tend to be less complete. Cady (1924) staged a live event before three psychology classes in order to look into this issue. Ten minutes after the lecture had begun, the instructor announced: "A government official will come here this morning to make an announcement. I advise every student to take the test that will be offered by him as preliminary to obtaining a position in government service. One who takes the test is not obliged to go further in this matter." Just then a man came into the room and offered his hand to the instructor. The stranger made an announcement to the class, then gave the instructor two bundles of paper and left the room. His appearance was on the order of five minutes.

The instructor then distributed the papers to the students in the class. One bundle asked the students to "write a detailed account of all that has happened since the representative of the government entered the room today. Include a description of his dress, personal appearance . . . No detail is too small to deserve mention." The other half of the class was told: "Answer each of the following questions in detail. No detail is too small to deserve mention. Quote in quotation marks any words used by either party." There followed a list of forty-two questions, covering all phases of the event. Cady's results were clear-cut: "More errors occur when the [subjects] are forced to answer questions than when they are free to choose their own details" (pp. 111-112).

Other investigators have found this same result using filmed materials rather than a live event. Marquis and colleagues (1972) showed a two-minute color and sound movie to subjects which depicted two college-age boys throwing a football outside of a supermarket while a young man and woman carrying groceries and engaging in conversation leave the store. The man says he has forgotten something and goes off; the woman continues walking toward her car. She is then struck by an automobile and her package spills onto the ground. The woman and driver start yelling at each other, the young man returns and begins scuffling with the driver, and the boys playing football appear. The scene ends with one of the boys running toward the supermarket to call the police.

The subjects who viewed this film — 151 males between the ages of 21 and 64 — were interrogated in a number of different ways. Just as Cady had found, those who were allowed to report freely produced the most accurate reports, but they were the least complete. The investigators also included questions that invited a controlled narrative, such as "Tell me about the traffic and weather conditions." The reports that resulted tended to be less accurate than the totally free reports, but somewhat more complete. Finally, the investigators elicited reports by asking a series of very specific multiple-choice questions, such as "Where did the incidents happen: in a vacant lot, in a street, on a sidewalk?" "What color was the lettering on the sign in the front window of the building: red, blue, green or was it some other color?" These interrogatory reports tended to be less accurate than the narrative forms, but even more complete.

In Lipton's study (1977), subjects saw an 8-mm color film depicting a peaceful scene in a Los Angeles area park in which, suddenly, a man is shot and robbed. Nearly 150 details existed in the film that could be recalled. With a narrative form, subjects were 91 percent accurate in the details they recalled, but they recalled only 21 percent of the details in the film. With the interrogatory form, their accuracy score was only 56 percent but their quantity score rose to 75 percent. Again, we see that a narrative produces much higher accuracy but much lower quantity.

How does one choose the best way to interrogate a witness like Mary Smith? Clearly, if accuracy is important and completeness is not, one should choose the narrative form. If completeness is important but not accuracy, one should choose the interrogatory form. But what if both are important? It might seem obvious that both forms should be used, but which should be used first? This question received substantial attention from psychologists during the early part of this century, and these investigators agree: the narrative report should come first, followed by the interrogatory. That is, let the witness tell the story in his own words, and when he has finished, then ask specific questions.

A study that best illustrates this conclusion was conducted by Snee and Lush (1941). Subjects saw a motion picture color film involving a man and a woman in which there was a transfer of money, followed by an assault, a theft, and an escape. The film lasted one minute. Afterwards, the subjects, all students from three women's colleges, were tested, some in the interrogatory-narrative order and others in the narrative-interrogatory order.

As shown in table 5.1, in the interrogatory part of the test a prior narrative produced no appreciable change in the number of incorrect responses but consistently increased the number of correct responses and decreased the number of "don't know" responses in the subsequent interrogatory. In the narrative portion of the test there were more correct responses when the narrative was preceded by the interrogatory portion, but there were also more incorrect responses.

When a controlled narrative was substituted for the free narrative, nearly identical results were found. However, accuracy was increased somewhat, without unduly increasing the number of errors.

These studies indicate, then, that the witness should first be allowed to report freely, or in a controlled narrative fashion. This free report can be followed by a series of very specific questions so as to increase the range or coverage of the witness's report. For example, suppose a bystander has witnessed a crime, has described everything he can remember in a free report to the police, and is then asked some specific questions, such as "Was the intruder holding a gun?" At that point the witness may remember the gun and may include a description of it, even though he had initially forgotten to mention it. But if the witness is asked specific questions before his free report, such as "Did you see a gun?" he will probably say no if no gun existed, but when later asked to "tell us everything you remember about any weapons," the witness might say to himself: "Gee, I remember something about a gun. I guess I must have seen one. It was probably black." Thus, asking specific questions before the narrative can be dan-

Table 5.1. Narrative-interrogatory testing versus interrogatory-narrative testing. (Data from Snee and Lush 1941.)

Response	Performance on the interrogatory		Performance on the narrative	
	Narrative-interrogatory	Interrogatory-narrative	Narrative-interrogatory	Interrogatory-narrative
Correct	71.8	68.9	21.8	35.8
Incorrect	15.3	15.2	2.3	4.8
"Don't know"	12.9	16.1	—	—

gerous because information contained in those questions can become a part of the free report, even when the information is wrong (see Loftus 1975).

Question Wording

The precise questions asked during the interrogatory are crucial, for small changes in their wording can result in dramatically different answers. Harris (1973) showed that people's answers are affected by question wording. His subjects were told that "the experiment was a study in the accuracy of guessing measurements, and that they should make as intelligent a numerical guess as possible to each question" (p. 399). They were then asked either of two questions such as "How tall was the basketball player?" or "How short was the basketball player?" Presumably the former form of the question presupposes nothing about the height of the player, whereas the latter form involves a presupposition that the player is short. On the average, subjects guessed about 79 and 69 inches, respectively. Similar results appeared with other pairs of questions. For example, "How long was the movie?" led to an average estimate of 130 minutes, whereas "How short was the movie?" led to an average estimate of 100 minutes. This phenomenon is at work in other contexts, such as the recalling of past personal experiences. Several years ago forty men and women in Los Angeles supermarkets and shopping centers were asked to participate in market research about headaches and headache products. Having been told that they would be paid ten dollars for a half hour's time, they came to a conservative-looking office building, where, unknown to them until later, they were being filmed by a hidden camera for a television commercial. I was asked to do the interviewing, and I decided to use this opportunity to collect a few data on the effects of question wording.

I devised two critical questions. One of them asked the respondent about products other than the one currently being used, and two wordings were used: "In terms of the total number of products, how many other products have you tried? 1? 2? 3?" And "In terms of the total number of products, how many other products have you tried? 1? 5? 10?" The 1/2/3 respondents claimed to have tried an average of 3.3 other products, whereas the 1/5/10 subjects claimed an average of 5.2 other products.

The second key question asked about frequency of headaches in one of two ways: "Do you get headaches frequently and, if so, how often?" And "Do you get headaches occasionally and, if so, how often?" The "frequently" respondents reported an average of 2.2 headaches per week, while the "occasionally" respondents reported only 0.7 headaches per week. This miniexperiment indicates that the changing of a single word or so can affect a person's recollection about his past personal experiences. It does not tell very much about *how* the specific words affect memory, for example, whether "frequently" raises the person's estimate above the true level or whether "occasionally" lowers the person's estimate. In order to determine this, one would have to know something about the person's past history. But another way to pinpoint the inaccuracies that particular wordings produce is to have subjects witness an event in the laboratory, on film, and then to answer specially constructed questions about what they remember. Experiments along these lines have shown that memory for recently witnessed events, like memory for past personal experiences, can also be affected by question wording.

In one such study (Loftus and Zanni 1975), one hundred students were shown a short film segment depicting a multiple-car accident: a car makes a right-hand turn into the main stream of traffic, causing oncoming cars to stop suddenly and resulting in a five-car bumper-to-bumper collision. After viewing the film, the subjects filled out a questionnaire containing some critical questions and some fillers. Three of the critical questions asked about items that had appeared in the film, while three others asked about items that had not actually been present. For half of the subjects, the critical questions began with the words "Did you see a . . . " as in "Did you see a broken headlight?" For the rest, the critical questions began with the words "Did you see the . . . " as in "Did you see the broken headlight?" Thus, the two questions differed only in the form of the article, "the" or "a."

There was a good reason to look at "the" versus "a." A speaker uses "the" when he assumes the object referred to exists and may be familiar to the listener. An investigator who asks "Did you see the broken headlight?" essentially says "There was a broken headlight. Did you happen to see it?" His assumption may influence the witness. The other article, "a," carries no such assumption about the existence of the object it precedes. The percentage of "yes," "no," and "I don't know" responses in two of our experiments is given in table 5.2. Witnesses who received the questions using "the" were much more likely to report having seen some-

Table 5.2. Percentage of "yes," "no," and "I don't know" responses to items that were present and not present in the film. (Data from Loftus and Zanni 1975.)

	Present		Not present	
Response	"the"	"a"	"the"	"a"
Experiment I				
Yes	17	20	15	7
No	60	29	72	55
I don't know	23	51	13	38
Experiment II				
Yes	18	15	20	6
No	62	28	69	56
I don't know	20	57	11	38

thing that had not really appeared in the film. In the first experiment 15 percent in the "the" group said "yes" when asked about a nonexistent item, while only 7 percent in the "a" group made that error. In the second study the difference is even more striking: 20 percent versus 6 percent. On the other hand, witnesses who received the question with "a" were more likely to respond "I don't know" both when the object had been present and when it had not. In both studies, "a" witnesses were two to three times as likely as "the" subjects to say "I don't know."

In another experiment using films of automobile accidents (Loftus and Palmer 1974), the purpose was to see whether the substitution of one word for another would affect quantitative judgments—judgments, for example, of speed. Forty-five subjects who saw the film were asked questions. The critical one for some subjects was "About how fast were the cars going when they hit each other?" For other subjects the critical question was the same except that the verb "hit" was replaced with "smashed," "collided," "bumped," or "contacted." Although the words all refer to the coming together of two objects, they differ in what they imply about speed and force of impact. And they differ in terms of the judgments about speed that they elicit from witnesses. Subjects who were queried with the "smashed" question gave the highest speed estimates (40.8 mph); those questioned with "collided," "bumped," and "hit" gave progressively lower estimates (39.3, 38.1, and 34.0 mph, respectively), while those questioned with the word "contacted" gave the lowest (30.8).

Taken together, these experiments show that in a variety of situations the wording of a question about an event can influence the answer that is given. This effect has been observed when a person is reporting his own experiences, describing events he has recently witnessed, or answering a general question (for example, "How short was the movie?") not based on any specific witnessed incident.

The legal system has recognized this in part and as a result has developed the concept of a leading question and has formulated rules indicating when leading questions are allowed (*Federal Rules of Evidence* 1975). A leading question is simply one that, either by its form or content, suggests to the witness what answer is desired or leads him to the desired answer. But a problem remains: While leading questions can be controlled in the courtroom, there is very little control placed on the police during their investigations. Further, some ways of leading are quite subtle and would be hard to detect. Imagine a police officer who asks a witness "How short a distance was he from you when you first saw him?" Or a lawyer who asks before the trial, "Mrs. Jones said the car was speeding; what do you think?" The different ways of influencing a witness's answers are innumerable. And once the answer is given it can be "frozen" into the witness's recollection.

Who Is Asking the Questions

It seems obvious that if a person of high status is conducting an interrogation as opposed to, say, a passerby asking a few questions, the recollections of a witness will be very different. Psychologists in the past have suggested that the authority of the interrogator can matter a great deal.

Marshall's study (1966) in which subjects looked at a 42-second film involving a boy, a baby carriage, and an angry woman investigated this factor. Immediately after seeing the picture, one group of law students were asked to go into a separate room with their law professor, and a group of police trainees were asked to do the same with one of their instructors who was a police captain and who wore his uniform for the occasion. The status figure, whether professor or police captain, made this statement: "It is extremely important that each of you gives us as much of his recollection as he possibly can, both as to what he heard and saw. I am particularly anxious that you do well in this. Very often it is found that the people answering the questionnaire omit simple things which may be important in a trial. For example, there was a tree on the lawn in front of the house. Or that at the very beginning the man put his hand in the carriage and took something out. Or in describing the house, that the door on the right was partly open. Or that the man, at the end, squatted under a mailbox. It is all this kind of detail that we would like to have from you insofar as you can recall what you saw and heard." The status figure remained in the room while the subjects filled out their questionnaires. Control groups of law students and police trainees were not exposed to any status figures.

Marshall found some interesting effects. When the test was conducted in the presence of a high status person, both law and police students produced longer reports than did the control subjects. The law students, but not the police trainees, also tended to include more inferences about the motives of the characters and also about events not directly depicted in the film. Accuracy about specific items that had or had not appeared was not affected by this manipulation (see table 5.3).

It is not surprising that a person of high status would have influence over an eyewitness to a complex event. In other areas of psychology it has been shown that highly credible people can manipulate others more readily. They can persuade others, they can change attitudes, and they can influence the behavior of others in countless ways.

Table 5.3. The influence of a high status interrogator on a witness's recollection. (Data from Marshall 1966.)

Students' responses	No status figure present	With status figure present
Word count		
Law	183	264
Police	135	178
Correct recall		
Law	15.2	14.8
Police	9.5	13.4
Inferences		
Law	6.8	10.5
Police	5.8	5.8

Does it matter whether the interrogator is supportive of the witness rather than challenging? Marquis and colleagues (1972) looked into this issue using their two-minute film of the incident in a supermarket parking lot. Subjects were interrogated about the contents of the film at a later time by trained speech and drama students who conducted the interviews in either a supportive or a challenging manner.

The supportive interviewer praised the quality of the witness's free report narrative. Throughout the interview, the interviewer used head nods, smiles, and prearranged statements to indicate approval of the witness's performance. He said things like: "That's fine. You're being very helpful." "You're doing well. Let's continue." "Good, this information is important."

The challenging interviewer expressed disapproval of the free report. Throughout the interview which followed, the interviewer did not smile, use head nods, or lean toward the witness. At specified points, he inserted a negative statement about the performance of the witness or merely stared at him in silence. On two occasions the interviewer actually challenged a specific piece of testimony given by the witness. Typical comments by the challenging interviewer were: "Well, if that's all you can remember, let's go on to this . . . " "Well, I can see there are a lot of things you don't remember." "Look, this information is important. Try to remember things accurately."

The supportive approach to interviewing a witness makes the simple assumption that if the interviewer is warm and accepting, the respondent will form a positive attitude toward the interview and this, in turn, will result in better performance. The first assumption was confirmed; subjects who were interviewed by a supportive interviewer felt happier and more positive about the interview. However, contrary to expectation, the atmosphere created by the interviewer had no effect on either the accuracy or completeness of the witness's report. While it is often dangerous to accept a no-effect conclusion on the basis of a single experiment, this particular experiment was unusually well designed. The atmosphere variation was powerful in affecting the witness's feelings about the interview, and so its failure to influence performance is rather persuasive.

In sum, it appears that the credibility or status of an interviewer can influence how successful the interview is in terms of accuracy and completeness, but whether the interviewer is a nice guy or not seems to make very little difference.

Confidence in One's Recollection

Return for a moment to the case of Mary Smith, the young woman who was mugged on her way home from work (Woocher 1977). After an initial interrogation during which Mary described her attacker, she helped the police to construct a composite picture. Using a photo-kit containing hundreds of differing types of noses, eyes, mouths, and so on, Mary and the police officer produce a composite photo that satisfies Mary to a reasonable degree.

Some weeks later, a parole officer reports that the composite resembles one of his parolees, Jimmy Jones, who has three prior burglary convictions. His photo is pulled from police files and, along with seven others, is shown to Mary. She picks up the photo of Jimmy Jones and states, "This is the only one it could be." The officer presses her: "Could you be any more positive?" She waffles a bit and then says, "It looks like him, all right." Later, during a lineup conducted at the jail Mary points to Jimmy Jones and says: "Number three looks familiar." "Are you certain that's the man?" asks the detective. Mary announces, "I'm pretty sure . . . Yeah, that's him."

At the showing of the photographs, and again at the lineup, the officer is interested in how positive Mary's feeling is. It is apparently important that she be rather certain. And, indeed, it seems intuitive that a witness is more likely to be correct if the witness is certain. But is this intuition reasonable? Is a person who is confident in a recollection necessarily more likely to be accurate than a person who is not?

The evidence that has come out of many laboratory experiments shows that the amount of confidence a subject has in a response is related to the accuracy of that response. This result has been shown in many traditional memory studies (Murdock 1974) and in some of the studies on eyewitness testimony. An example is the experiment conducted by Lipton (1977), in which subjects were presented with an 8-mm color film depicting a Los Angeles park in which a man is suddenly shot and robbed. Either immediately after the film or else one week later the subjects answered over a hundred questions about the details of the film and then gave a rating of their confidence on a seven-point scale. Lipton found a very strong relationship between confidence and accuracy ($r = +0.44$), indicating that the more accurate the answer, the higher the subject's confidence in it. However, the relationship is far from perfect, indicating that "in many cases a witness may be very certain about his testimony yet inaccurate, or be uncertain and accurate" (p. 94).

The more traditional laboratory studies on human memory have provided further evidence that subjects are aware of what they know and do not know and can predict their performance to a reasonable degree of accuracy (Hart 1967). Despite this, there exist several studies that show no relationship at all between confidence and accuracy—for example, Clifford and Scott's experiment on eyewitness testimony after violent versus nonviolent events (1978). Here no relationship at all was found between the correctness of a witness's response and his confidence in that response. Similarly, the recent work of Wells and colleagues (1978) shows that witnesses who make false identifications of a suspect can be as confident in the correctness of their identifications as are witnesses who make accurate identifications.

There are even some studies which show that under certain circumstances a person can be *more* confident when incorrect than when correct. This happened in the study in which some subjects saw a red Datsun go through a stop sign, while others saw it go through a yield sign (Loftus et al. 1978). During the retention interval these subjects were exposed to misleading information about the sign—those who saw a stop sign were told it was a yield sign, and vice versa. When the misleading information was delayed and introduced just prior to the time that the subject was tested, subjects who were incorrect about the sign they saw were *more* confident than subjects who were correct.

To reiterate, although there are many studies showing that the more confident a person is in a response, the greater the likelihood that the response is accurate, some studies have shown no relationship at all between confidence and accuracy. In fact, there are even conditions under which the opposite relation exists between confidence and accuracy, namely, people can be more confident about their wrong answers than their right ones. To be cautious, one should not take high confidence as any absolute guarantee of anything.

Knew-it-all-along Effect

Research performed by Fischhoff (1975, 1977) reveals a curious phenomenon. If you tell people that an event has already occurred, they tend to believe that they knew all along that it was going to happen. This has been called the "knew-it-all-along" effect, and it has some implications for the eyewitness.

In Fischhoff's 1975 study, subjects read a 150-word description of a historical or clinical event for which four possible outcomes were provided. One of the passages that was used is about a battle between the British and the Gurkhas of Nepal:

> For some years after the arrival of Hastings as governor-general of India, the consolidation of British power involved serious war. The first of these wars took place on the northern frontier of Bengal where the British were faced by the plundering raids of the Gurkhas of Nepal. Attempts had been made to stop the raids by an exchange of lands, but the Gurkhas would not give up their claims to country under British control, and Hastings decided to deal with them once and for all. The campaign began in November, 1814. It was not glorious. The Gurkhas were only some 12,000 strong; but they were brave fighters, fighting in territory well-suited to their raiding tactics. The older British commanders were used to war in the plains where the enemy ran away from a resolute attack. In the mountains of Nepal it was not easy even to find the enemy. The troops and transport animals suffered from the extremes of heat and cold, and the officers learned caution only after sharp reverses. Major-General Sir D. Octerlony was the one commander to escape from these minor defeats.

After reading the passage, the subjects were offered four possible outcomes: British victory, Gurkha victory, military stalemate with no peace settlement, and military stalemate with a peace settlement. They were then asked, "In the light of the information appearing in the passage, what was the probability of occurrence of each of the four possible outcomes?" Each subject assigned a probability value to the outcomes, the sum of which had to equal 100 percent.

The average probability assigned to each outcome by the control group is shown in the top row of table 5.4. Notice that people tended to feel that a British victory was the most likely; it had an average probability of almost 34 percent. A stalemate with no peace settlement was next most likely, with an average probability of over 32 percent. And a stalemate *with* a peace settlement was least likely—about 12 percent.

Other subjects in the experiment were treated a bit differently. They were given a piece of outcome information, told it was the true outcome, and then asked to ignore the outcome and to indi-

Table 5.4. Knowing an outcome can have an effect on the way one interprets the events that led up to the outcome. People think an outcome is more likely when they have been given that outcome than when they have not, as bold type indicates. (Data from Fischhoff 1975.)

Information given	British victory predicted	Gurkha victory predicted	No peace settlement predicted	Peace settlement predicted
None (control group)	33.8	21.3	32.3	12.3
British victory	**57.2**	14.3	15.3	13.4
Gurkha victory	30.3	**38.4**	20.4	10.5
No peace settlement	25.7	17.0	**48.0**	9.9
Peace settlement	33.0	15.8	24.3	**27.0**

cate how they would have responded if they had not known the outcome. So, some subjects were told that the British victory had really occurred, but to ignore this and give their subjective probabilities for the four possible outcomes. Other subjects were told that the Gurkha victory had really occurred, and they too were to predict how they would have responded had they not known this information.

As shown in table 5.4, subjects who were told that a particular outcome occurred tended to think that this outcome was much more likely to begin with. For example, when given no outcome information, people predicted a 34 percent chance of a British victory; when told that the British had won, people predicted a 57 percent chance of a British victory. When given no outcome information, people predicted a 21 percent chance of a Gurkha victory; when given the information that the Gurkhas had won, people felt this outcome was much more likely—now 38 percent.

Fischhoff found this with other kinds of material (1977), which led him to the conclusion that telling people an event has occurred causes them to believe they knew all along it was going to happen, and that people underestimate the effect that information about the outcome of an event has on their perceptions.

In his later research Fischhoff looked for a knew-it-all-along effect using general knowledge questions taken from almanacs and encyclopedias. The subjects were asked questions that had two alternative answers, one of which was correct. For example, "Absinthe is (a) a precious stone or (b) a liquor?" As with his previous experiment, for each item some of the subjects simply assigned a probability of being correct (between 0 and 100 percent) to the alternatives, and other subjects were given the correct answer and were then asked to respond as they would have had they not been told what the answer was. The questions covered a wide variety of content areas such as history, music, geography, nature, and literature. The results showed that for nearly all of the items, the subjects who were given the correct answer and told to ignore it assigned probabilities to the correct alternatives that were from 10 to 25 percent higher than the probabilities assigned by the uninformed subjects.

In explaining his results Fischhoff argued that when a person hears the answer to a question, be it "Who won the battle?" or "What is absinthe?" the answer is integrated with whatever else he know about the topic, in order to create a coherent whole out of all relevant knowledge. Sometimes integration involves reinterpreting previously held information to make sense out of it in light of the reported answer. These processes are so natural that people do not appreciate the effect that hearing the answer has on their perceptions. For this reason, they overestimate how obvious the correct answer would be before its correctness was indicated.

These findings have implications for the legal process. Being told, either directly or in a more subtle way, that a particular culprit had a mustache or that a given car ran through a red light can lead a witness to believe that he knew this fact all along. Thus, a fact that is reported sometime after a critical incident along with the remark "I knew it at the time, but I just forgot to mention it" should be treated with some caution. Hindsight does not equal foresight.

Hypnosis and Recall

On July 15, 1977, a bus filled with twenty-six youngsters from Chowchilla, California, completely disappeared. It would later be discovered that three masked men brandishing guns had kidnapped the children and their bus driver, Ed Ray. The men had driven them all to a gravel quarry one hundred miles away and forced them into an abandoned trailer truck that was buried six feet underground.

For sixteen hours the captives tried unsuccessfully to dig themselves out of their predicament. Soon afterwards they were rescued and questioned by the FBI. The officials, the victims, and the entire country wondered who the abductors were. In an attempt to find this out, the FBI asked an expert to hypnotize the bus driver. In a Fresno motel room Ray fixed his eyes on a spot on the wall, began breathing deeply, and was soon hypnotized. He relived the kidnapping in his mind, and—to the great joy of the law enforcement authorities—he was able to recall all but one digit of the license plate on the kidnappers' white van. Through this crucial information the three suspects were tracked down (*Time*, September 13, 1976).

Since the early 1960s various United States agencies have used hypnosis as an aid to criminal investigation. And some believe that it gives utterly fantastic results, as in the dramatic cases of the Boston Strangler, the San Francisco cable car nymphomaniac, and Dr. Sam Sheppard of Cleveland, accused of killing his pregnant wife, Marilyn (Block 1976).

Despite these apparent successes, the use of hypnosis has critics aplenty. First of all, when it does work, it may not be because of any awesome, mysterious power that it has. Hypnosis may simply encourage a person to relax more, to cooperate more, or to concentrate more than he would otherwise. Theorists have argued that hypnosis is best understood in terms of the interpersonal relationship existing between the hypnotist and his subject. A good relationship results in the subject's behaving in a way that is pleasing to the hypnotist and in a way that the subject perceives a good hypnotic subject should behave (Evans and Kihlstrom 1975). But most troublesome is the fact that authorities in the field of contemporary experimental hypnosis do not agree as to exactly what hypnosis is. Prominent among them is Theodore X. Barber, whose views on hypnosis are the result of twenty years of painstaking research (My 1978).

> What are the facts about hypnosis? What is hypnosis? Everybody knows what hypnosis is; hypnosis is a state of consciousness, something like that . . . The hypnotist puts you into it and once you're in it, you're under his sort of control and you do silly things if he asks you to. You forget what occurred. And there are various levels of it . . . medium, deep, light. I mean, like everybody knows that. It's a fact. Except, it isn't. None of us agrees entirely with the layman. I don't agree at all, I completely disagree. It's nothing like that. It's complete mythology in some very basic way. What's the fact about hypnosis? There's no fact at all! . . .
>
> It's saying let's shift our thoughts in various ways. A hypnotic induc-

tion might help a person do that, but not always. Sometimes it backfires, especially when you say: "Now you're going into hypnosis." That
backfires a lot. How you get a person to let his thoughts go in the direction that you're guiding him or want him to guide himself, that's
the question. One way is to simply tell a person *to think with it, to
imagine with it*. If that's all they mean by "trance," they ought to drop
the word because that's a funny word to use for just thinking. (p. 44)

Barber's summary, then, is that there is no mystery in hypnosis,
no magic, no hocus-pocus. Why it happens is still a bit of a mystery, but how it happens is not. Concentrate hard, stop thinking
about the present, allow your thoughts and your imagination to
go in a different direction, and *viola*!

A second reason for being somewhat suspicious of the use of
hypnosis, one hinted at by Barber, is that when experts have attempted to use it to solve criminal cases, they have sometimes
come up with very peculiar results. Salzberg (1977) reports two
attempts to hypnotize people as part of a criminal investigation.
In the first case, a soldier who admitted accidentally shooting and
killing a missing soldier was unable to remember where he disposed of the body, despite intensive interrogation that lasted for
days. Salzberg attempted to hypnotize the soldier, and after
twenty minutes he began talking about the night of the killing.
The prisoner said that he accidentally shot the other soldier in the
head while inspecting a pistol. Then he panicked, drove several
miles into the country, and disposed of the body in a ravine. He
recalled a few of the landmarks during the drive, and eventually
these led officials to the body. What is peculiar is that the hypnotist did not believe that the soldier was in a deep trance and the
soldier told other authorities that he had not been hypnotized at
all.

The second case involved a woman who had been sexually assaulted. She was awakened in her bed by a man who held a knife
at her throat and told her that if she screamed her children would
be killed. The assailant blindfolded the woman, forced her to
undress and to put on high-heeled shoes. She was then led into
the living room, where she was forced to perform fellatio. This
woman was one of twenty who had been assaulted in a similar
way. She was an extremely cooperative hypnotic subject and went
into a very deep trance. But she could not identify her assailant in
any way except for remembering an odor about his clothes which
reminded her of either a garden store or a bowling alley. Even

this lead turned out to be of no use. Nothing whatsoever came out of the interview that was useful in apprehending the assailant. (He was, however, later found and convicted on circumstantial evidence.)

These two cases indicate that hypnosis does not always work, even when a deep trance state is achieved, and that valuable information can be obtained even when an individual is not really hypnotized. But there is a third reason why many researchers, including two of the country's leading experts, Ernest Hilgard and Martin T. Orne, have strong objections to the legal applications of hypnosis except by court order and with medical supervision and videotape records. "People can flat-out lie under hypnosis, and the examiner is no better equipped to detect the hypnotic lie than any other kind. Even more serious, a willing hypnotic subject is more pliable than he normally would be, more anxious to please his questioner. Knowing even a few details of an event, often supplied in early contacts with police, may provide the subject with enough basis to create a highly detailed 'memory' of what transpired, whether he was there or not" (*American Bar Association Journal*, February 1978, p. 187). In other words, even people who are mesmerized by hypnosis can fantasize, make mistakes, even lie.

One recent study (Putnam in press) shows how suggestible subjects who have been hypnotized can be. Subjects were shown a videotape of a car-bicycle accident. After a delay subjects received a questionnaire containing some objective questions and misleading information. Some of the subjects were later questioned under hypnosis while others were not. The hypnotized subjects were told that "under hypnosis it would be possible for them to see the entire accident again just as clearly as they had seen it the first time, only this time they would be able to slow it down or zoom in on details if they chose to." Putnam found that more errors were made by subjects in the hypnosis condition, particularly on the leading questions. His results were interpreted as indicating that hypnosis does not necessarily allow subjects to retrieve a veridical memory. On the contrary, subjects appeared to be more suggestible in the hypnotic state and therefore more easily influenced by the leading questions.

These observations about the impact of hypnosis should present a cause for concern about court cases in which hypnosis plays a role. A frightening example is the recent case of two Filipino nurses, Filipina Narciso and Leonora Perez, who were convicted in July 1977 of poisoning nine patients, two of whom died, at the Ann Arbor, Michigan, Veterans Administration Hospital (Jones 1977). There was little doubt that a muscle-paralyzing drug called Pavulon had been injected into the victims, causing instant suffocation, but the FBI had difficulty finding evidence that would link anyone, including their two suspects, to the crime. Victims and staff members were hypnotized to "refresh" their memories. Early on, one witness under hypnosis remembered two different nurses as being in his room, but well before his attack. Pressed to recall more relevant memories, particularly those involving Filipino nurses, this witness finally guessed that he had seen a Filipino nurse and eventually became more certain that he had seen one lurking in his room when his breathing stopped. Perhaps his memory had been truly refreshed, but it is also possible that certain suggestions, subtle or not, could have caused those changes in his memory. Although we can never know this for sure, it is of some interest that the judge in this case ordered a new trial for the nurses, and the prosecution decided not to retry the case.

The proponents of hypnosis are not worried. They insist that they use the information they get only as a lead, and then attempt to verify it. Once it is corroborated, they argue, hypnotic evidence, along with the corroboration, should be allowed in court. Martin Reiser, Director of the Los Angeles Police Department's behavioral sciences services, is a great supporter of hypnosis as a tool: "If an officer has missed some important aspect, or a terrible attack has left a victim in shock, or a witness has turned numb, we see no reason not to help them help themselves" (Stump 1975).

The battle over hypnosis will continue to be fought both among the experts in the field and within the legal profession. As the battle continues, hypnosis will continue to be used in probably a handful of cities, and the critics of its use will continue to criticize. Any conclusions about hypnosis must await the outcome of further research.

The conditions prevailing at the time information is retrieved from memory are critically important in determining the accuracy and completeness of an eyewitness account. Some of the more important factors that operate during this stage are whether the retrieval environment is changed, what types of questions are used to obtain information, how these questions are worded, and who is asking them. Confidence in one's memory and the accuracy of that memory do not always go hand in hand: people are often confident and right, but they can also be confident and wrong. The value of hypnosis in enhancing recall is still a murky area, and more research needs to be done.

Most people, including eyewitnesses, are motivated by a desire to be correct, to be observant, and to avoid looking foolish. People want to give an answer, to be helpful, and many will do this at the risk of being incorrect. People want to see crimes solved and justice done, and this desire may motivate them to volunteer more than is warranted by their meager memory. The line between valid retrieval and unconscious fabrication is easily crossed.

6

Theoretical Issues in the Study of Memory

HOW IS KNOWLEDGE represented in memory? This is one of the most important but one of the toughest questions facing psychology today. Competing theorists are currently waging something of an intellectual battle in this area, and as yet there are no clear answers. However, several quite detailed proposals have been offered, and they seem to fall into two major categories.

Some theorists have argued that the information we gain from our environment is represented as a complex network of propositions (Anderson and Bower 1973; Kintsch 1974; Norman and Rumelhart 1975). Suppose a person has witnessed an accident, one portion of which involved a red Datsun stopped at a stop sign, as in figure 4.2. According to the propositional view, this scene would be stored in memory as a series of ideas comparable to "The car was red," "The car was a Datsun," "The car was stopped at a traffic sign," "The sign was a stop sign," "There were trees all around," and so on. A variation in this "propositional" view is that information is stored in memory in some very abstract way but is then transformed into propositions before it is retrieved.

Other theorists have argued that there are types of memory representations that are specific to vision, hearing, and the other senses (Paivio 1971; Shepard et al. 1975; Kosslyn 1975). When we see something complex, this is tied to the visual system. When we hear or touch something, the information we take in makes contact with different systems. Information that comes in from the various senses is not stored in a common propositional format, but in a format that depends on how it originated. This we might call the "nonpropositional" view of memory.

Unfortunately, the distinction between a propositional and a nonpropositional memory is complicated by the fact that these two positions are actually very difficult to distinguish (Pylyshyn 1973). They sound quite different, but upon second glance they are not. When the theorists on either side of the battleground are pressed on such issues as "What is a proposition?" and "How is a proposition different from a modality-specific representation for a piece of information?" the issue becomes clouded. A more general reason that scientists have as yet been unable to disentangle this issue is that they cannot directly observe the mind. Because it is not possible to have direct access to a witness's "true" experience, scientists normally make decisions about what is going on in the mind by examining how a person behaves — what he says and what actions he takes. These external indicators are then used to make inferences about the mind and how it functions. As more and more is learned about brain function, less and less will need to be inferred.

While skirting the issue of precisely how information is represented in memory, some psychologists have argued that in order to comprehend an event that we witness, various aspects of the event must be interpreted by us. Only part of this interpretation is based upon the environmental input that gave rise to it; that is, only part comes from our actual perception of an event. Another part is based on prior memory or existing knowledge, and a third part is inference. We store in memory not the environmental input itself, nor even a copy or a partial copy, but the interpretation that we gave to the input when we experienced it. In fact, we probably store only fragments of that interpretation (Rumelhart and Ortony 1976).

Why only fragments? Perhaps the pressure of time or the complexity of the experience itself affords time sufficient only for an incomplete interpretation. Or perhaps the interpretation was relatively complete soon after the experience, but after the passage of time whatever was stored initially is subject to decay and only fragments of it remain. An attempt to recall the experience, then, would involve reconstructing the original interpretation using the fragments of it that are available at the time. The steps involved in the comprehension and retrieval of an experience, according to this position, are shown in figure 6.1.

To apply these notions to a specific eyewitness situation, suppose a person sees an automobile accident. The witness is presumed to interpret the accident by calling upon (1) portions of the initial input, that is, the accident itself; (2) ideas from his store of general knowledge (about accidents, intersections, and pedestrians, for example); and (3) inferences. The inferences are likely aspects of the situation which have not actually been observed; thus, upon realizing that an accident occurred, a person might infer that some damage was done either to the car or to the pedestrian. Fragments of this interpretation are then stored in memory.

Postevent Information

In addition to determining how information is stored in memory, researchers are equally interested in determining how the memory for an experience — whatever its structure — is altered by information to which a person is subsequently exposed. Suppose that after the accident referred to above is over, the witness is exposed to some misleading information concerning the event. For example, the witness is asked a question which presumes that the main car involved in the accident ran through a red light. What must the witness do to answer this question? First, he must comprehend the question, which involves an interpretation process similar to that used to comprehend the initial event. This may involve visualizing that portion of the accident needed to answer the question. If the witness accepts the information about the red light, he introduces it into his visualization, calling upon his general knowledge about red lights (their color, location, and so on) to do so. He answers the question, and the entire process results in a set of fragments being stored in memory. Finally, at some later time, the witness is asked to retrieve some information about the initial event. His choice will depend upon his reconstruction of the event, which in turn is based on available fragments. This process is diagrammed in figure 6.2.

Fragments were presumably stored at two different times, once at the time the event was observed and again when subsequent information about it was encountered. A crucial question arises at this point: At the time the intervening information occurs, does the witness simply store a new set of fragments, leaving the

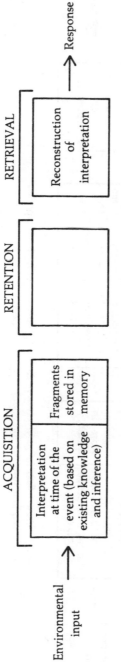

Figure 6.1. Steps involved in the comprehension and subsequent retrieval of an experience.

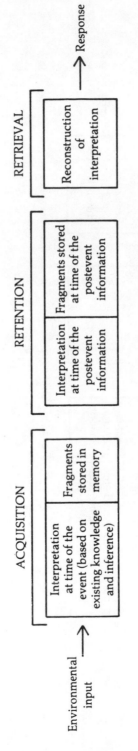

Figure 6.2. Steps involved in the comprehension of both an experience and subsequent information about that experience.

earlier set unchanged, or does the storage of the second set of fragments result in an alteration of the first set? This is a major theoretical issue--the coexistence-alteration issue.

Coexistence versus Alteration

Suppose a hit-and-run accident has occurred in which a green car knocks down a pedestrian and quickly drives off. A witness to the accident overhears someone say that the car was blue, and believes this to be true. Has the "blue" information essentially erased any traces of "green" from the witness's memory, or do green traces reside somewhere in the recesses of the witness's mind? Has the new information altered the old, or do both really coexist in memory?

Many people believe that everything one has ever learned is buried somewhere deep in memory, but this may not be true at all. People cling to highly suspicious evidence to support this belief, evidence of various sorts. For example, the apparent remembering of childhood experiences under hypnosis and the occasional successful use of hypnosis in criminal investigations lead people to believe that memories are in some sense permanent. But many investigators believe that hypnosis is unreliable and unpredictable, and is just as likely to create new memories as to recover old ones. And despite occasional highly publicized successes, the accounts that are produced under hypnosis cannot ordinarily be verified. The apparent improvement in recall that can occur under the drug sodium pentothal, and that is brought about during psychoanalysis using free-association techniques, is subject to the same criticism. Vivid memories may be produced, but who can say whether these have or have not been altered by subsequent experiences to which a person has been exposed.

Perhaps the most impressive evidence for the notion that everything one ever learns is permanently stored in the memory comes from a technique involving electrical stimulation of certain regions of the human cortex. During the 1940s Wilder Penfield, a neurosurgeon, was operating on epileptic patients and removing the damaged areas in their brains. To guide him in pinpointing the damage, he stimulated the surface of the brain with a weak electric current in hopes of discovering, in each patient, a region in the brain that was related to the epileptic attacks. He would then destroy these areas. During this electrical invasion of their brains, Penfield's patients were completely conscious; however, their scalps had been anesthetized so as to be insensitive to pain. Penfield discovered that stimulation of certain areas of the brain caused a patient to feel strange sensations on the skin, while stimulation of other areas caused a patient to see flashes of light or swirling colored forms. But most interesting of all, when Penfield moved his stimulating electrode near a portion of the brain called the hippocampus, some patients reexperienced events from their past life (Penfield and Roberts 1959; Penfield 1969), as Blakemore (1977) vividly describes: "One of Penfield's patients was a young woman. As the stimulating electrode touched a spot on her temporal lobe, she cried out: 'I think I heard a mother calling her little boy somewhere. It seemed to be something that happened years ago . . . in the neighborhood where I live.' Then the electrode was moved a little and she said, 'I hear voices. It is late at night, around the carnival somewhere—some sort of traveling circus. I just saw lots of big wagons that they use to haul animals in' " (p. 88). According to Blakemore, "There can be little doubt that Wilder Penfield's electrodes were arousing activity in the hippocampus, within the temporal lobe, jerking out distant and intimate memories from the patient's stream of consciousness."

Penfield himself, in his 1969 writings, seems to suggest a belief in the relatively permanent nature of memory:

> It is clear that the neuronal action that accompanies each succeeding state of consciousness leaves its permanent imprint on the brain. The imprint, or record, is a trail of facilitation of neuronal connections that can be followed again by an electric current many years later with no loss of detail, as though a tape recorder had been receiving it all.
>
> Consider now what happens in normal life. For a short time, a man can recall all the details of his previous awareness. In minutes, some of it has faded beyond the reach of his command. In weeks, all of it seems to have disappeared, as far as voluntary recall is concerned, except what seemed to him important or wakened in him emotion. But the detail is not really lost. During the subconscious interpretation of later contemporary experience, that detail is still available. This is a part of what we may call perception. (p. 165)

On what does Penfield base these conclusions? Apparently on his observation of "flashback" responses.

> The flashback responses to electrical stimulation are altogether different. They bear no relation to present experience in the operating

room. Consciousness for the moment is doubled, and the patient can discuss the phenomenon. If he is hearing music, he can hum in time to it. The astonishing aspect of the phenomenon is that suddenly he is aware of all that was in his mind during an earlier strip of time. It is the stream of a former consciousness flowing again. If music is heard, it may be orchestra or voice or piano. Sometimes he is aware of all he was seeing at the moment; sometimes he is aware only of the music. It stops when the electrode is lifted. It may be repeated (even many times) if the electrode is replaced without too long a delay. This electrical recall is completely at random. Most often, the event was neither significant nor important. (p. 152)

Yet by Penfield's own admission these responses occurred in only 40 cases out of a total series of 1,132 cases surveyed, or only 3.5 percent of the time (1969, p. 154).

The phenomenon of spontaneous recovery—the reappearance of items that have been forgotten—sometimes constitutes evidence for the notion that memories are stored permanently. Yet it is plausible that under some circumstances the memory for some detail might not be permanently available. One could reasonably assert that under some conditions, the fragments resulting from the comprehension of an experience might be altered by what follows that experience. Irrevocable transformations of memory could occur on occasion, just as caterpillars become butterflies and cheese turns to mold.

It is possible to design experiments that might demonstrably show that one's original memory for an event has remained intact. It is *not* possible to design an experiment that can conclusively prove that an alteration in memory has occurred. For example, suppose we used the strongest available technique to induce a witness to reveal an intact original memory. If the witness did so, evidence for coexistence would be provided; if the witness failed to do so, we have not proven that the original trace is altered, for it can always be argued that we have not used a sufficiently strong technique, that we did not dig deep enough. This is similar to the "lost coin" problem. Suppose Harry has a theory that his lost lucky penny is somewhere in his house. Mary, on the other hand, believes it is not in the house. Harry can prove he is right by finding the penny in some nook or cranny. Mary will not be able to prove she is right. If she searches everywhere and fails to find the coin, Harry can say, "Maybe it is stuck in the shag rug." If Mary then vacuums the rug and still fails to find the coin, Harry can say, "Maybe it is lodged in a doorway." If Mary then unhinges all the doorways and still fails to find the coin, Harry can say . . . and so on.

With these preliminary remarks behind us, let us concern ourselves with a person who has witnessed one detail (for example, a green car, a stop sign) and is later exposed to the new information (a blue car, a yield sign). Suppose that the witness now believes that he has actually experienced the new information and has absolutely no recollection at all of the true detail. Experiments have shown that such persons are reasonably easy to come by. My colleagues and I have used a number of different techniques to try to induce such witnesses to reveal evidence of any traces of the original information. In all of these cases, we have been unable to provide any evidence that an intact original memory remains.

Techniques for Digging

Incentives. Recall the experiments in which subjects viewed a series of thirty color slides depicting an auto-pedestrian accident. Half of the subjects saw the car stopped at a stop sign while the other half saw the same car stopped at the yield sign. When given misleading information about the sign during the retention interval, many subjects indicated that they thought they had seen the opposite sign when tested later on. In one study, slightly over half of the subjects chose the wrong sign when tested soon after the incident, whereas when the test was delayed for a week and the misleading information was introduced toward the end of that week, over 80 percent of the subjects believed they had seen the wrong sign.

It could be argued that the reason so many people went along with the misleading information is that they were not highly motivated to be accurate. If high incentive was provided for accurate responding, perhaps the subjects would show evidence that their memories were accurate. If a person was offered a dollar, or five dollars, or even twenty-five dollars for responding correctly, would he still choose the yield sign that he had read about over the stop sign that he had actually seen?

We designed an experiment to find this out. Subjects saw a series of thirty color slides; some saw a slide with a red Datsun stopped at a stop sign while others saw the Datsun at the yield sign. The subjects returned to the laboratory two days later and filled out a questionnaire consisting of twenty questions. For all subjcts, the seventeenth question presupposed the existence of the sign opposite from the one actually seen. Shortly after completing the questionnaire, the subjects participated in a forced-choice test. Fifteen pairs of slides were presented, and for each pair the subject selected the slide that he recognized as having seen before. The critical pair, of course, was a slide depicting the red Datsun at a stop sign and a nearly identical slide depicting a yield sign.

At the beginning of the forced-choice test, twenty subjects were told that one of the pairs had been selected randomly to be the "reward" pair. When the reward pair appeared, the subject would be told, and he would be given a dollar if he performed correctly on this pair. The reward pair was always the stop sign/yield sign pair. Twenty other subjects were told that they would be given five dollars for accurate performance on the reward pair. Twenty additional subjects were told that the person in the experiment who scored the highest would receive twenty-five dollars. And finally, the last group of twenty subjects were told nothing about a reward. All rewards were paid when they were deserved but they did not influence the likelihood that the subject would perform correctly on the critical pair, as table 6.1 shows.

To account for the fact that monetary rewards are not motivating to everyone, a second kind of incentive was used with twenty additional subjects. These people were told at the beginning of the forced-choice test that "most intelligent people can accurately choose the slide they have seen before, despite any distracting information they have been exposed to." Only 25 percent of these subjects performed accurately on the critical pair.

In sum, we did not find more accurate performance when incentive was provided. This study indicates that the subject truly

Table 6.1. Number of subjects who correctly selected the slide they had seen before when offered monetary incentives.

Reward	Number of subjects who were correct	Percentage of subjects who were correct
None	5	25
$1	4	20
$5	6	30
$25	3	15

believes he has seen the incorrect sign, thus providing incentive has no effect on performance.

Second-guessing experiments. A second-guess technique is particularly suited for investigating the coexistence-alteration issue. The logic of this technique is as follows: At the time a subject is asked for his recollection of an event, he first guesses among fixed alternatives, and if he guesses incorrectly, he chooses among the remaining uncommitted alternatives. If he chooses correctly on the second guess at a level higher than chance, then he must have had some information available about the correct response in spite of the error on the first guess. A variation of this technique has been used successfully in the study of psychophysical thresholds (Swets et al. 1961), tachistoscopic recognition (Bricker and Chapanis 1953), and paired-associate learning (Bregman 1966). For example, in the Bregman study, subjects were presented with a list of word pairs or letter pairs, and subsequently provided with all of the stimuli and responses which they were to attempt to match. The subjects were then asked to give a second guess by rearranging the pairings which they had guessed (matched) incorrectly. They were correct at a better-than-chance level on the second guess, indicating that they must have known something about the correct answer even though they at first gave the incorrect answer.

My colleagues and I first performed a second-guess experiment using memory for colors. In one study, subjects viewed a series of slides depicting a complex incident involving several people. Some subjects saw one slide that showed a man sitting down and reading a book with a green cover. Subsequently, these individuals were exposed to the information that the cover was blue. Previous work had indicated that many of these subjects would later indicate that they had seen a blue cover rather than a green one. But the earlier work was silent on the issue of whether the original "green" information remains anywhere in memory. A second-guess procedure could detect it.

Before describing the experiment in more detail, it is important to note that in a study of memory for colors, one must pay careful attention to the precise colors used. For example, suppose that a person was shown a green book, was subsequently told that the book was blue, and finally was asked whether the book that had been seen was yellow, green, or blue. If the person incorrectly chooses blue, we might ask for a second guess. However, the person is likely to choose green, the correct color, no matter what, because green is between yellow and blue in the color spectrum. The coexistence hypothesis (that traces of green still exist) predicts green will be chosen because it assumes that the subject has both pieces of information in memory. The alteration hypothesis (that the "blue" information altered the memory trace so that the original does not exist) also predicts that the second guess will be green because green is closer to the altered memory (blue) than is yellow.

But by changing colors slightly, we can cause the two hypotheses to make different predictions. Suppose that a subject is shown a yellow book and is subsequently told that the book is blue. Finally the person is asked whether the book that had been seen was yellow, green, or blue. The person is also asked to pick a second choice, assuming that his first choice is incorrect. The coexistence hypothesis predicts that the second guess will be the correct color, yellow, since it assumes that the subject has both pieces of information in memory. The alteration hypothesis predicts that the second guess will be the incorrect color, green, because green is closer to the altered memory than is yellow.

In our first experiment, two hundred subjects saw a series of twenty color slides, depicting a couple of people taking a walk and talking, arguing, scuffling, reading, entering buildings, and engaging in other ordinary activities. One of the twenty slides was critical and was shot in three versions. One version showed a person reading a book with a green cover, while nearly identical versions showed the same person reading a book with either a yellow or a blue cover. Each subject saw only one version.

After viewing the slides, the subjects participated in a filler activity, and finally were given a series of twelve questions. The critical question was "Did the pedestrian who was reading the book with a _____ cover have a hat on?" Either the word green, yellow, or blue was inserted in the space. Finally, a color test was administered. The subjects were given a list of fifteen descriptions of objects shown in the slides (one of which was the book that the man was reading), along with three possible color names associated with each object. Their task was to pick the color name that best represented their recollection of the object. They were also told to indicate their second choice, assuming that the first choice was incorrect. They were urged to report only on the basis of what they had actually seen, and to leave the question blank if they had absolutely no recollection.

Fifty subjects actually saw the green cover and their question presupposed it was blue (GB), fifty saw blue while their question presupposed green (BG), fifty saw yellow while their question presupposed blue (YB), and finally fifty saw blue while their question presupposed yellow (BY). On the final color test all subjects were asked to indicate their recollection of the color of the book that the man was reading by choosing among the colors yellow, green, or blue. They also indicated their second choices.

The GB and BG subjects are similar to each other in that the new misleading color was adjacent on the color spectrum to the original color. The YB and BY subjects are similar in that the two colors are separated by an intervening color, green. When the new color was adjacent, 44 percent of the subjects believed they had seen it; and 82 percent of these chose the true color as their second choice. This finding is predicted by both the coexistence and the alteration hypotheses.

What is more interesting is what happens when the new color is separated from the original color by an intervening color—for example, the subject sees yellow and is told that it is blue. Now 26 percent of these subjects incorrectly chose the misleading color as their first choice, and of these, 77 percent *incorrectly* chose green as their second choice, while only 23 percent chose the correct color. Thus, subjects chose the incorrect color on their second guess significantly more often than would be expected by chance. This is predicted by the alteration hypothesis, but is the reverse of the prediction of the coexistence hypothesis.

In a further second-guessing experiment, ninety subjects were asked to recognize the actual colors rather than color names. They viewed the series of twenty slides; half saw the green book cover while the other half saw blue. After viewing the slides, the subjects participated in a short filler activity and were then given a series of twelve questions, one of which gave them the wrong color—that is, if they saw blue, they were told that it was green, and vice versa. Finally, a color test was administered. The subjects were shown a color wheel containing thirty color strips, each of which was numbered. Numbers 1-5 corresponded to shades of violet, 6-10 corresponded to blue, 11-15 to green, 16-20 to yellow, 21-25 to orange, and 26-30 to red. Thus, all the colors in the spectrum were used, as well as some intermediate shades. The subjects were given a list of ten objects, and for each object their task was to pick the color that best represented their recollection of the object and to write down the color number next to the name of each object. They were also asked to indicate their second choice, assuming that the first choice was incorrect. Once again they were urged to report only on the basis of what they had actually seen, and to leave the question blank if they had absolutely no recollection.

As in previous studies, subjects' initial choices tended to be a compromise between what they actually saw and what they were told on their questionnaire, that is, they selected a bluish-green. However, the important data were the second guesses, because if their second guesses were in the direction of the correct color at a better-than-chance level, they would show that some information about the correct response was available in memory. Of those subjects who were incorrect on their initial choice (72 out of 90 subjects), 47 percent indicated a second guess that was in the direction of the correct color, while 53 percent indicated a second guess that was in the opposite direction. Thus, the hypothesis that these subjects have retained some information about the original color is not supported.

We conducted another second-guessing experiment to see if our results would extend beyond the domain of colors. In this experiment we used the stop/yield sequence. The subjects looked at the thirty slides, one of which contained either a stop or a yield sign. They returned to the laboratory after one week and were given a questionnaire which subtly told them that they had seen either a stop sign, a yield sign, or a no parking sign. After a fifteen-minute filler activity, they were given a test. The critical item asked them to indicate their recollection of the type of sign that they had seen on the corner by choosing among the signs: stop, yield, and no parking. They also indicated their second choices.

In this experiment, too, we found that when subjects were initially wrong (and nearly 90 percent of them were wrong), their second guesses did *not* tend toward the correct alternative. In 44 percent of the cases, the subjects chose the correct alternative for their second choice, and in 56 percent of the cases they did not. The pattern of responses in this experiment, like the others, suggests that subjects did not have information about the correct alternative available to them.

Unfortunately, these experiments, while suggestive, cannot conclusively prove that an alteration in memory has occurred. Nonetheless, they could have shown the opposite, namely that the original information had remained intact, if the subjects had shown highly accurate second-guessing performance. But the subjects showed a low level of second-guessing accuracy. The reason that the experiments cannot definitely prove the alteration case is that it could still be argued that we have not used a sufficiently strong technique to uncover the true memory, and if we had such a technique we would be able to uncover it. Until such time as science provides us with a direct method of distinguishing between an event that is temporarily unavailable and one that does not exist in the memory system, indirect methods must suffice.

Blatantly false information. What happens when a witness receives some information that is blatantly contradictory to what was actually seen? An experiment I conducted indicates that witnesses will reject such information; furthermore, an attempt to introduce it can increase the likelihood that the witness will resist any misleading suggestions about other items that would ordinarily not be particularly immune to suggestion. I will describe this experiment in some detail because the follow-up to it bears on the coexistence-alteration issue.

Forty-six subjects saw a series of twenty-four color slides at a five-second rate depicting a wallet snatching. The slide sequence opens with a young woman walking down a busy street. She meets a friend and stops to talk for a moment. As the woman continues down the street, she is approached by a man wearing a cowboy hat who bumps into her, causing her to drop her shopping bag. The man and woman both stoop to pick up some articles that have fallen out. When the woman is looking the other way, the man reaches into her shoulder bag and takes her wallet. The woman does not notice and the two part. Soon, the victim becomes aware that her red wallet is missing, at which point two other women cross the street toward her and gesture in the direction of the fleeing man. A scene from this sequence, showing the man taking the wallet, is shown in figure 6.3.

After a short filler activity, the subjects answered a questionnaire designed to determine accuracy. The questionnaire consisted of thirty items that addressed diverse details of the wallet snatching incident. It asked about major details such as information about the central characters, their clothing and actions, and it asked about minor details such as the surrounding environment, extraneous people, buildings, and traffic. The thirty items

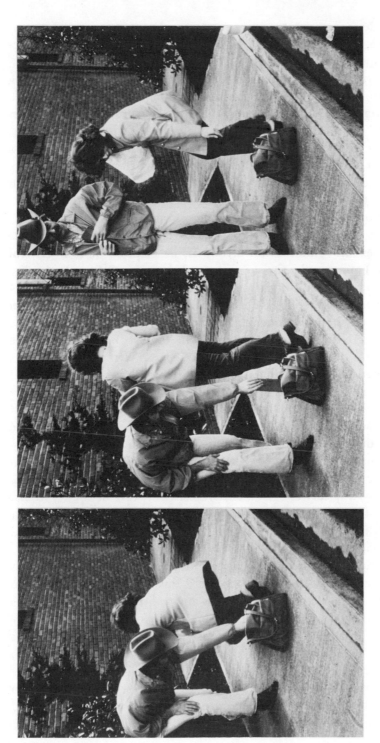

Figure 6.3. Black and white reproductions of three of twenty-four color slides depicting a wallet snatching.

were declarative sentences requiring a phrase or word to be completed. To complete these sentences, a five-alternative multiple-choice test was given. For example, one question was "The victim's friend was carrying _____. (a) a newspaper (b) a shopping bag (c) a notebook (d) an umbrella (e) none of the above."

After completing the questionnaire, the subjects left and returned the following day. At the beginning of this second session, they were given "suggestibility" paragraphs to read. These were a version of the incident that was allegedly written by a psychology professor who had seen the slides for thirty seconds each, much longer than the subjects had. To conceal the purpose of this task, the subjects were asked to rate the paragraphs on certain attributes such as clarity of writing. Two versions were constructed. One version contained an erroneous description of four critical items. For example, the slides showed the victim's friend carrying a green notebook, but the paragraph referred to it as blue. A second version of the suggestibility paragraph contained, in addition to the four items, erroneous mention of a very obvious object. It referred to the red wallet taken by the thief as being brown. We knew this detail was blatantly false because virtually all subjects who had been tested in another experiment correctly identified its color, and 98 percent of the subjects in this experiment correctly identified its color on the accuracy questionnaire. One half of the subjects received a suggestibility statement containing the four subtly erroneous items plus the blatant one whereas the other half of the subjects received a suggestibility statement containing only the four subtle errors. A short filler activity followed, and the subjects were given a final test consisting of twenty items, each of which was a declarative sentence lacking a phrase or word. These were to be completed with one of three choices listed with each.

In examining the results, we found that our initial expectations were supported. Subjects who were given a blatant suggestion tended to be better able to resist suggestions on other items to which they would not ordinarily be immune to suggestion. Having the professor call the obviously red wallet brown made it harder to sway witnesses' recollections about other objects, such as the color of the notebook carried by the victim's friend. Further, subjects were better able to resist a suggestion about an item if they had initially been accurate on that item than if they had not (fig. 6.4).

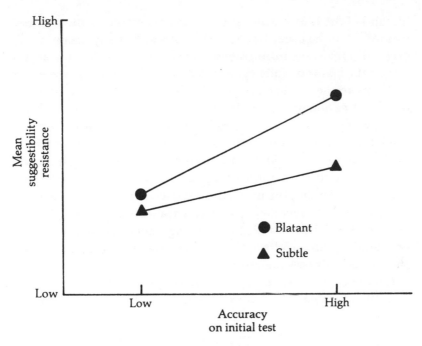

Figure 6.4. Mean suggestibility resistance on an item as a function of initial accuracy on that item, presented separately for subjects given a blatant suggestion and those given only subtle (no blatant) suggestions.

The followup experiment to this one bears on the coexistence-alteration issue. In this second experiment, the blatantly errone-ous information—that the wallet was brown—was not presented along with the initial misleading information—that the notebook was blue—but was delayed for some subjects. The rationale for this experiment is as follows: Suppose a witness sees a person car-rying a green notebook and later hears that the notebook is blue. Ordinarily many witnesses will come to believe that they saw a blue notebook. However, if along with the information that the notebook is blue the witness also hears some blatantly false infor-mation, many fewer witnesses will accept the misleading blue in-formation. This was shown in the previous experiment. Suppose instead we introduced the misleading blue information soon after the incident but delayed the blatantly false information for a day or so. The witness is likely to accept the misleading blue informa-tion when it is introduced, but the question is, what happens a day or so later when the witness is confronted with the blatantly false information? If the memory has truly been altered, then the blatantly false information should have no effect on the witness's memory. On the other hand, if the witness has any access to the original (green) memory traces, the witness may be able in the face of the blatantly false information to resist the blue suggestion and stick to the correct green. In other words, delaying the blatant information would produce the same effect as introducing it early, along with the other pieces of suggestive information.

The results, shown in figure 6.5, are quite clear-cut. Delaying the blatant information eliminates the effect that it has on a witness's ability to resist misleading suggestions. This is consistent with the notion that the misleading suggestions were incorporated into the witness's memory, effectively transforming what the witness had previously stored. Introducing a piece of blatantly false information cannot affect these items now since they are now a part of the witness's memory.

Response speed. It turns out that the speed with which a witness responds to a question can often be used to make inferences

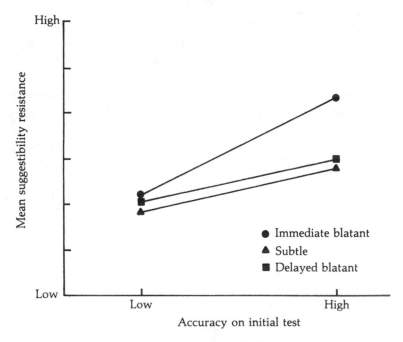

Figure 6.5. Mean suggestibility resistance on an item as a function of initial accuracy on that item, presented separately for subjects given a blatant suggestion along with other misleading suggestions, a blatant suggestion that is delayed for two days, and only subtle (no blatant) suggestions.

about the mental processes that went into comprehending and answering the question. We decided to use response times as a way of exploring the issue of what people do with new information to which they are exposed (Cole and Loftus in press). The rationale behind this experiment is relatively straightforward. Suppose a person sees a car pass through a stop sign and later hears that it was a yield sign. Still later the person is asked to testify as to whether the sign said stop or yield. As we know, many individuals will, under these circumstances, come to believe and report that they have actually seen the yield sign. Assuming that the stop sign was perceived in the first place, when the "yield" information is first presented it must produce a conflict at some level, a conflict that needs to be resolved. When does this conflict resolution take place? Does it occur at the moment the new information about the yield sign is introduced? Or does the resolution take place only later when the person finally is asked to comment upon the traffic sign?

These two notions — resolution of conflict at time of comprehension of new information, versus resolution at time of final report — lead to very different predictions about the speed of answering a later question. Suppose the two pieces of information remain in memory until the time of the final report when the witness is asked "Stop or yield?" A conflict must then be resolved, and the witness should take longer to respond, compared to a condition in which no misleading information was received. On the other hand, if a person resolves any conflict at the time the misleading information is first introduced — prior to the final test — then the time to respond "Stop or yield?" should be no longer than it would be if the subject had received no misleading information. Furthermore, the response might even be quicker, if the decision at final report was a repetition of a recently made decision and if such a repetition could now be made more quickly.

We conducted this experiment with forty-eight subjects, who saw a long series of slides. Following this phase, they were given misleading information about some of the items in the slides. Finally, they were tested for their recollection of the items in the slides, and their speed of responding to the questions on this final test was measured.

While many measures were taken in this experiment, the one that is important to the current discussion is the comparison between speed of responding in the face of misleading information versus no information. We found that the response times were not different from each other. This result is inconsistent with the hypothesis that the old and new information coexist in memory, producing a conflict that is resolved at the time of final test. Such a hypothesis predicts that response times would be lengthened. The data are in accord, however, with a model in which any conflict produced by the two pieces of information is resolved prior to the test at the time the new information is introduced. To be more specific about how this might happen, suppose our witness has seen a red Datsun stopped at a stop sign. He is now asked a question: "Did another car pass the red Datsun while it was stopped at the yield sign?" What must be done to answer this question? In answering it, the subject may "visualize" or "reconstruct" in his mind that portion of the accident needed to answer the question, and, if he accepts the misleading information, he introduces it into his visualization. When interrogated later "Stop or yield?" he responds on the basis of his earlier reconstruction. In other words, he "sees" the yield sign that he has himself constructed.

Did they notice it in the first place? A question arises in all of these experiments as to whether the original critical piece of information entered memory in the first place. Did the stop sign actually get in? Did the witness actually notice the green car, or whatever it is that we are attempting to mislead him about? We have clearly shown that it is more difficult to alter a person's recollection about an object if the person originally noticed the object and indicated this to us. In the experiment on blatantly false information, if a witness correctly told us that the victim's friend was carrying a notebook (as opposed to an umbrella or some other object), it was more difficult to mislead the witness about the color of the object — but not impossible.

In another experiment subjects viewed the slide series containing either a stop sign or a yield sign. Subsequently, some subjects were asked to "describe in your own words what you just saw and include as many details as you can remember." Here is an example of the descriptions that resulted:

> A young man and a young woman walked together conversing from a building along a sidewalk. A red Datsun passed and came to a stop sign as a bus went by. The woman stopped to lean on a post as the man began to step off the curb. At the stop sign, the Datsun moved toward

the walking man. The pedestrian appeared to trip and fall before the car reached him. The woman walked over to him lying on the street as a police car pulled up in front. Only after the policeman and female pedestrian approached the fallen man did the two in the car get out to look. (They had stopped after he fell.) The passenger was a male in his 20's. He wore a red shirt and blue pants. After looking at the guy in the street he turned and ran back along the sidewalk toward the white building and toward the right side. The fallen man wore a striped t-shirt, plaid wool shirt and red pants. The woman with him wore jeans, a striped shirt, and a hat.

Other subjects were given a sheet of paper with an intersection outlined on it and were instructed to fill in as many details as they could remember. A sample drawing is shown in figure 6.6. In both of these samples, the subjects indicated that they had seen the stop sign or yield sign. When subjects returned a day later and were exposed to misleading information about the sign, then tested for their recollection of the sign, those who had indicated that they noticed the sign were harder to mislead. However, they too could be influenced. On the basis of experiments such as these, we know that introducing misleading information into a witness's memory can be done not only when a witness has not noticed a particular critical object, but also when the witness has noticed it.

Coexistence-Alteration: A Final Remark

In this section I have provided several examples of techniques used to explore the issue of whether new information transforms the old, or whether they coexist in memory. These experiments, while suggestive, cannot conclusively prove that an alteration in memory has occurred. But they could have shown the opposite, namely that the original information remained intact: incentive could have led to improved memory for the original material; second-guessing could have shown a greater-than-chance ability to recover the original material; delaying blatant information could have continued to help a subject resist misleading suggestions in favor of the true original material. None of these things happened. Those who believe that memories are permanent would still argue that we have not used a sufficiently strong technique to uncover the true memory; if we would only submit our witnesses to hypnosis, or to a polygraph, or to the stimulating electrode of Wilder Penfield, we would see the true memory

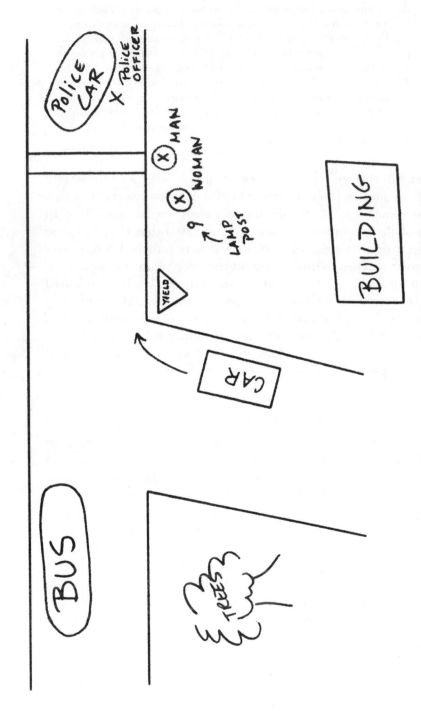

Figure 6.6. Sample drawing made by a subject who viewed the thirty-slide sequence of an automobile-pedestrian accident. One slide showed a red Datsun stopped at a yield sign.

emerge. I can almost guarantee that if these all were tried and if the true memory still failed to appear, the critics would still argue that we had simply not gone far enough. For the moment, however, it seems just as reasonable to assume that some of these memories no longer exist as to assume that all of them are only temporarily unavailable.

Whether new information alters a previously acquired representation or coexists with it, the phenomenon discussed here has enormously important practical implications. The person's response has changed, no matter what theory of memory is subscribed to. However, the two theories have different implications for how one would induce a witness to return to his original (true) representation. Under the coexistence theory, one would simply remove the interfering information (assuming one could find the right technique) and the original information would become available. Under the alteration theory, one could only return a witness to his original memory by realtering the version currently in memory.

7

Recognizing People

WHEN DAVID WEBB was released from a Washington state penitentiary in February 1978 he said he felt as though "God was working a miracle in my life." His miracle came after he had already spent ten months in jail and prison for crimes he never committed: rape, attempted rape, and attempted robbery. Webb was arrested for these crimes in the first place because he resembled a composite picture of the rapist constructed after the crimes. Eyewitnesses at his trial identified Webb as the man who had raped one of them and attempted to rape and rob the other in separate incidents in two grocery stores in Everett, Washington. Despite some inconsistencies in the testimony of the eyewitnesses and despite the testimony of alibi witnesses, Webb was convicted and sentenced to up to fifty years in prison.

Months later another man confessed to the crimes for which Webb had been convicted. But the police still had to investigate this confession. Both Webb and the man who confessed were placed together in a lineup. According to newspaper reports, the victims could no longer identify Webb as the man who assaulted them (*Seattle Post-Intelligencer*, February 3, 1978). Some law enforcement officers had commented that the two men looked similar, although Webb commented after seeing the other man for the first time in the lineup, "I don't think he looks at all like me."

David Webb suffered immeasurable pain on account of the errors of a couple of eyewitnesses. Other innocent persons have similarly suffered after the mistakes of one, sometimes two, occasionally as many as ten or twenty eyewitnesses. Psychologists have attempted over the years to delve into the problem of mistaken identification by conducting experiments in which witnesses are exposed to some particular individual and then asked to make an identification at some later time. One of the most disquieting of these investigations was one conducted in 1974, in which nearly two thousand witnesses were wrong (Buckhout 1975). This large-scale study was possible with the cooperation of a New York television station. On December 19, 1974, the television viewers of the nightly news on channel 4 (NBC) were treated to a specially staged purse-snatching incident filmed by an NBC production crew. This was to be a part of a short documentary piece on the topic of eyewitness reliability. The film showed a young woman walking in a hallway. A man wearing a leather jacket lurked in the doorway and suddenly ran toward the victim, grabbed her purse, and knocked her down. For a second or so he ran face forward into the camera. The entire incident lasted twelve seconds. Following this, the announcer presented a lineup of six men who resembled the assailant. The viewers were told that the attacker might be in the lineup, but he also might not be. Any viewer who wished could call a special number, flashed on the screen, to indicate whether he recognized the assailant in the six-person lineup.

Over two thousand calls came in. Each respondent indicated either recognition of one of the six men in the lineup or else said the assailant was not in the lineup. The real attacker was in the lineup in position number two. The results from this demonstration are shown in table 7.1. Overall, only 14.1 percent of the viewer-witnesses made a correct identification of the attacker. This is the same result as would be expected if the witnesses were merely guessing: someone who had not even seen the incident but guessed would have one chance in seven of picking the correct person, number two. (The reason the odds are one in seven, given a six-person lineup, is that the response "not in the lineup" is counted as a possible choice that a witness could have given.) The data in table 7.1 also indicate that men and women witnesses did not respond differently from one another. Taking men and women together, their data produced a striking result: 1,843 mistaken identifications.

When a witness to a crime must later identify the person who was seen before, various psychological factors can play an impor-

Table 7.1. "Nearly 2,000 witnesses can be wrong." Distribution of responses to a six-person lineup by 2,145 eyewitnesses to a televised crime.[a] The actual attacker was number 2. (Data from Buckhout 1975.)

	Lineup positions						
Viewers	1	2	3	4	5	6	"Not in lineup"
Males	15.2%	15.3%	9.8%	13.5%	14.2%	7.5%	24.5%
Females	14.5	13.3	10.5	12.8	14.7	5.9	27.9
All viewers combined	14.7	14.1	10.1	13.0	14.3	6.6	25.0

a. The chance level for the lineup was 14.2%.

tant role. Many of these factors have already been discussed: the retention interval, or period of time between the crime and the identification; the exposure time, or the amount of time that a witness had to look at the assailant; prior knowledge and expectations; misleading suggestions; stress. All of these will operate to reduce the accuracy of an identification just as they affect the accuracy of any kind of testimony. In fact, in many of the studies that have already been described, subject-witnesses were asked to recognize faces that they had seen before. And in one example, it was shown that the perceptual activity that a witness engages in while looking at a face can affect later recognition.

However, recognizing people can be fraught with its own set of difficulties. There are certain phenomena that take place when one person attempts to recognize another that do not occur with other kinds of eyewitness testimony. For example, many criminal situations involve a cross-racial identification, where a member of one race attempts to identify a member of a different race. These are notoriously difficult. Secondly, an unconscious transference can take place, where a person seen in one situation is mistakenly remembered by a witness as being seen in a different situation. Third, in order to obtain an identification, police often rely on lineups and photo arrays — procedures which are delicate and difficult to perform fairly.

Cross-Racial Identification

It seems to be a fact — it has been observed so many times — that people are better at recognizing faces of persons of their own race than a different race. How do psychologists know this? From a series of studies, a classic of which was conducted by Malpass and Kravitz (1969). These investigators used subjects from the University of Illinois, a predominantly white university, and Howard University, predominantly black. The experimental materials consisted of photographs of forty black and forty white males of college age. Each subject saw a random arrangement of ten black and ten white faces, presented for about a second-and-a-half. After the faces had been presented, the subjects were shown the forty black and forty white faces, randomly ordered, and they indicated on a response sheet which faces they had seen before. The results, shown in table 7.2, led the researchers to conclude that subjects recognized faces of their own race better than faces of the other race. Over the years, this study has been repeated again and again. For example, Luce (1974) replicated the result, but also included Orientals in his study. Luce's subjects were 75 blacks, 72 whites, 65 Chinese-Americans, and 60 Japanese-Americans. The blacks, who attended a university in the southwest, reported a good deal of contact with whites and none with Asian-Americans. The whites, at another university in the southwest, reported a good deal of contact with blacks and no previous contact with Asian-Americans. In contrast, the Asian-Americans attended a multiethnic state university in San Francisco and had friendships with all four ethnic groups.

Each subject went through the experimental procedure separately with an experimenter of the same race. First the subject studied a page of twenty photographs, all persons of one racial group. After one minute passed, the subject was given a test sheet

Table 7.2. Cross-racial identifications. (Data from Malpass and Kravitz 1969.)

Subjects	Mean number of correct identifications		Mean number of incorrect identifications	
	Black faces	White faces	Black faces	White faces
Illinois				
Black	7.38	6.77	5.69	3.61
White	6.08	7.92	4.85	3.46
Howard				
Black	6.14	7.14	2.43	3.00
White	5.57	6.14	5.86	2.14

containing nine photographs from the original twenty and eleven new ones, and he marked the faces he recognized. Each subject went through this procedure with four sets of photographs, one for each ethnic group.

The results are clear: Subjects recognized members of their own race most easily. The black subjects had more difficulty recognizing all photographs except those of blacks, even though they had had extensive contact with whites. The white students, who had no previous contact with Asian-Americans, recognized them almost as easily as they did white faces, but they had trouble identifying blacks, in spite of their previous association with them.

These two studies were not the first ones to investigate the cross-racial problem nor will they be the last. Nearly all of the studies have used black and white subjects, although occasionally a different group, such as Asians, is used. One study used students from India—with the same results (Scott and Foutch 1974). A recent investigation by Brigham and Barkowitz (1978) points out three assumptions that are commonly made about ethnicity and accuracy of identification. These are:

(1) Both blacks and whites are more accurate in identifying members of their own race than in identifying members of the other race.
(2) Highly prejudiced persons will be less accurate in their cross-racial identifications than more egalitarian persons will be.
(3) People who have had more experience with members of another race will be more accurate in their cross-racial identifications than will persons who have had fewer cross-racial experiences.

As it happens, the first assumption has received ample support in psychological experimentation, but the second and third have not. But can this be? It makes good sense to hypothesize that the reason people have difficulty in recognizing members of another race is because they have had relatively less experience with members of another race. It is even reasonable to suppose that persons who are prejudiced against members of another race might look at them less often, distort their images more often, and, on the whole, be less able to recognize them. As we shall see, these explanations don't hold water.

Brigham and Barkowitz used 72 black and white facial photographs selected from high school yearbooks. There were 18 photos in each of these four groups: white males, black males, white females, black females. The photographs were converted to slides, and 24 of them were shown to each subject. Each slide was seen for almost two seconds; then, after a five-minute break, the subjects viewed all 72 slides, randomly ordered, and indicated which they had seen before. The subjects also took a test designed to measure their racial attitudes and experience.

The results showed the usual interaction: both whites and blacks performed significantly better at identifying pictures of their own race than pictures of the other race (fig. 7.1). But, contrary to widely held assumptions, racial attitude and amount of interracial experience were not related systematically to recognition accuracy for subjects of either race.

These findings and those of the previous studies discussed leave us with this conclusion: People have greater difficulty in recognizing faces of another race than faces of their own race. This cross-racial identification problem is not due to the fact that people have greater prejudices or less experience with members of the other race.

What then causes it? Psychologists do not really have the answer. One reasonable hypothesis is that members of a different race often have distinctive features in common. For example, most Orientals have distinctive eyes, and most Indians are dark-complexioned. It is possible that when a white person sees an Oriental for a few brief seconds, the distinctive eyes stand out, are attended to, consume a good deal of the white witness's processing time. Later on, when the white witness is confronted with an array of Orientals and is asked to pick the one that was seen before, the distinctive feature that the witness concentrated on will not be helpful at all in discriminating an Oriental who was seen before from several who were not.

One problem that has been raised about the cross-racial identification studies is that most of them have used photographs. There is a large conceptual leap between viewing of photographs in an experimental laboratory and viewing a criminal during a real-life incident. For this reason, Brigham has designed some "field" experiments—experiments in which actual witnesses see actual people. The work, which is in its early stages, delves into the accuracy of eyewitness identifications by clerks working in

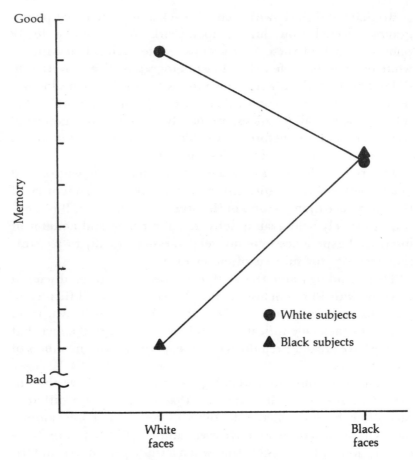

Figure 7.1. Whites and blacks are both more accurate at identifying photographs of faces of their own race than faces of the other race. (Data from Brigham and Barkowitz 1978.)

over fifty small convenience stores in the Tallahassee, Florida, area. Most of the stores are open from early in the morning until nearly midnight, although some are open all night. These stores are the victims of numerous robberies and robbery attempts. Typically, a robber enters the store and approaches the one cashier, demanding money; often these cashiers are later called upon to make eyewitness identifications.

The plan for the experiment is to have the stores visited by both a black and a white "customer" (or suspect) who enter the store about fifteen minutes apart from each other. What is needed, then, is some sort of interaction that each customer can engage in with the cashier, an interaction that is reasonably long so that it would be possible for the cashier to make a subsequent identification but not so bizarre that all realism is lost. Preliminary testing has uncovered two fairly decent interactions.

One customer enters the store, waits until no one else is speaking to the cashier, and then purchases some cigarettes. The cashier must reach behind the counter and hand these to the customer. The customer then indicates, with great apology, that he must pay for the cigarettes with pennies, about seventy of them. The cashier must then count the pennies. Finally, the customer asks the directions to a local shopping mall, hospital, or airport.

A second customer enters the store, waits until the cashier is alone, and then carries a single item (about $1.50 in value) to the cashier, apparently to purchase it. After the cashier has rung up the item, the customer discovers that he only has $1.00, and he asks the clerk to let him have the item for $1.00. When the clerk indicates his agreement to or refusal of the idea, the customer then asks for directions to some local spot.

Just a few hours later, the identification phase takes place. (The original pilot work used a twenty-four-hour retention interval, but it was found that with an interval this long, the cashier could not identify anyone.) The identification is conducted by two persons who enter the store, present the clerk with two photographic arrays containing seven photographs each, and ask whether any of them has been seen within the last twenty-four hours. One array contains only blacks and includes the black customer; the other contains only whites and includes the white customer. The photographic arrays were developed in close consultation with the Tallahassee Police Department, who helped construct the arrays as they would have in a real case. The seven males in each array were highly similar to each other in skin color, hair style, and general appearance.

It is too early to tell what the outcome of this experiment will be. But I believe that the usual cross-racial identification difficulty will be observed; cashiers will be more accurate in identifying customers of their own race than of the other race. The value of this study is that it is so realistic, so close to a real situation. Of course, it is not perfect. The cashiers in this study will not be experiencing the kind of stress that real crime victims or witnesses would be expected to feel; in the ideal study, a stress situation would be created so that the cashiers would feel arousal similar to that felt during the real crime. However, ethical and practical concerns preclude the use of techniques that would provide enormous stress for unsuspecting cashiers.

Unconscious Transference

A ticket agent in a railroad station who was held up at gunpoint subsequently recognized a sailor in a lineup as the culprit. The sailor had an iron-clad alibi, however, and was eventually released from custody. The ticket agent, who was later interviewed in an attempt to determine why he had misidentified the sailor, said that when he saw the sailor in the lineup, his face looked familiar. As it happened, the sailor's base was near the railroad station and on three occasions prior to the robbery, he had purchased tickets from this agent. It appears, then, that the ticket agent mistakenly assumed that the familiarity related back to the robbery when it undoubtedly related back to the three times the sailor bought train tickets (Wall 1965).

This is an example of unconscious transference, the term used to refer to the phenomenon in which a person seen in one situation is confused with or recalled as a person seen in a second situation. In the clerk-sailor example, an unconscious transference took place, since the person who bought the tickets was confused with or recalled as the person who committed the robbery.

There is a possibility that unconscious transference occurred in an experiment cited by Buckhout (1974), in which students witnessed a staged assault on a professor. Seven weeks later, when they were asked to pick out the assailant from a group of six photographs, 40 percent of the witnesses chose the right man; the other 60 percent either failed to make any identification or else they chose the wrong man. Of the five photographs that did not depict the culprit, one was a photograph of a person who had been at the scene of the crime, but only as an innocent bystander. If the tendency to pick the bystander was no greater than the tendency to pick one of the other non-culprits, then 20 percent of those who made a mistake (or seventeen people) should have picked the innocent bystander. However, over 40 percent (thirty-five people) in fact picked the person who had been standing near the scene of the assault but had not committed it. This may be an instance of unconscious transference: a person who is at the scene of the crime is confused with the person who committed the crime. However, there is another interpretation of this result. It is possible that when a witness made an incorrect identification, the bystander was picked most often simply because he looked most like the culprit. The design of the study does not permit elimination of this interpretation.

In another experiment designed to investigate unconscious transference (Loftus 1976), fifty students were presented, via tape recorder, a story concerning six fictitious college students. The introduction of each character was accompanied by a photograph of that character presented for approximately two seconds. Only pictures of white males, with medium-length brown hair and no glasses, were used. After three days the subjects attempted to identify the criminal in the story from a set of five faces presented to them. For half of the subjects, the criminal's face was not among the five, but the face of an incidental character in the story was included. The experiment was designed so that one particular photograph was the criminal for some subjects, was the incidental character for other subjects, and was only in the identification set for still other subjects (that is, he was not one of the six students in the story).

Of interest are the data from the subjects who were tested with an identification set that did not include the face of the criminal but did include the face of an incidental character. Of those subjects, 60 percent chose the incidental character, 16 percent chose a different incorrect man, and 24 percent refused to make a choice. If the tendency to pick the incidental character was no greater than the tendency to pick one of the other non-culprits, then 20 percent of those who made a selection should have picked the incidental character. In fact, 79 percent of those making a selection picked the incidental character.

How is it that a person seen in one context can be confused with a person seen in another context? Unconscious transference is a byproduct of the integrative, malleable nature of human memory. It appears that a brief exposure to a person can cause that person to look familiar when he is seen later. For example, an incidental character seen prior to a crime may look familiar to a witness who is attempting to identify the perpetrator of a crime from a set of photographs. The character looks familiar and this familiarity is interpreted as being due to the perception at the time of the crime, when in fact the familiarity is due to a time prior to the crime. The familiar trace of the incidental character becomes integrated into the witness's memory for the crime.

One fact about unconscious transference is that in any given case it is nearly impossible to tell whether it has occurred or not. A witness says the defendant committed a crime. The defendant says he did not, but admits he was at the scene of the crime, either at the time of the crime or on a prior occasion. Or perhaps the defendant and the witness live near one another and have in the past chanced upon each other at the local laundromat. Without other information, no one can say for sure that an unconscious transference either has or has not taken place. All that can be said is that the phenomenon of unconscious transference exists, and that there are situations in which it is more or less likely to occur.

Photospreads and Lineups

A crime has been committed and the police are anxious to obtain an identification. Many times they will rely on what is called a "recognition" test. Witnesses are presented with one or more human faces and asked if they recognize a face as one that was seen before. Sometimes a single photograph is shown or a single person is shown to a witness, and the witness essentially says yes or no to indicate that this person is or is not the one who committed the crime.

More often the police will present several photographs to a witness, or they will conduct a lineup. In either case the witness is in essence taking a multiple-choice recognition test. The witness must look through the alternatives and see if anyone looks familiar. Although in theory witnesses know that the culprit may not be in the set, in practice many witnesses believe that the police would not be conducting the test unless they had a good suspect. Thus, they try hard to identify the true criminal, but failing that, they often indicate the person who best matches their recollection of the criminal.

The composition of the lineup is a matter of great importance; how many people are in it, what the people look like, what they are wearing — all these are crucial issues that can influence the degree to which the lineup is free from suggestive influences and thus determine its value. Whereas the situation is not usually quite as bad as that depicted in figure 7.2, it is important that the persons other than the suspect be similar to the suspect in appearance. Otherwise the "distractors" can be immediately rejected as implausible and the true suspect picked by default.

Figure 7.2. Example of a biased lineup. (From Loftus and Loftus 1976.)

Detecting Unfair Lineups

When the suspect in a crime is a large, bearded man, most lineups do not include little kids, older ladies in wheelchairs, or blind men with canes. Note that I have said *most* lineups. Wall (1965) has provided some examples of lineups that are nearly as ludicrous. In one case a suspect who was a member of one race or nationality was placed among members of a noticeably different race or nationality. Of course, such lineups are grossly suggestive, and the identifications they produce are practically worthless.

But occasionally there are biases in a lineup which are a bit more subtle, though not undetectable. Psychologists have used a fairly straightforward procedure to investigate the success that the police have had in constructing a lineup composed of people who all fit some minimal description of the defendant. Say the lineup has six persons, including the suspect. If it is truly fair (that is, not constructed with any suggestive influences), then the probability that a person who did not even witness the crime will identify the defendant is one in six. (This probability could be one in seven if the alternative "I choose no one" is included as a possibility.) Also, if the lineup is fair, a person who did not witness the crime but who has read a brief description of the culprit, say in a police report, should still identify the suspect with only a 1/6 probability. To test a specific lineup for bias, a psychologist goes out to interview a random sample of people who are not witnesses. The brief description of the culprit is read, a photograph of the lineup is shown to them, and they are asked to select the person whom they think committed the crime. If these randomly selected subjects choose the suspect significantly more often than 1/6 of the time, the lineup can be declared unfair. This would mean that the distractors, or other participants in the lineup, simply did not sufficiently resemble the description to provide a valid test of the inaccuracy of the actual witness's identification of the suspect.

I performed such a test in connection with an actual case in Santa Clara, California, several years ago. The case was relatively straightforward: William Soto was arrested and charged with the armed robbery of a gas station. A witness-victim, Richard Quinones, originally stated to the police that the robber was a male, twenty-one to twenty-three years of age, five feet seven to five feet eight inches tall, 150 to 160 pounds, with black hair of medium length. Later, Quinones identified Soto from a six-person photographic lineup in which only one person (possibly two) could be said to have medium-length hair. I performed an experiment on the photographic lineup: I read the description given above to twenty people individually and then asked them to look at the photos and pick out the person they thought had committed the crime. If the lineup were truly unbiased, about three to four people should have picked out the photograph of William Soto (1/6 of the nonwitnesses). Thirteen people picked him. Thus, even people who had not witnessed the crime at all had a tendency to pick Soto's photo, indicating that the photospread was not fair. Yet the prosecution in Soto's trial placed a police officer on the stand who testified that in his opinion the photo array was extremely fair.

A similar test was performed in connection with an actual case in Canada by Doob and Kirshenbaum (1973). The case was *Regina v. Shatford*, one in which eyewitness testimony was critical in convicting the defendant. Shatford was accused of being one of two men who robbed a department store of $7,000. The cashier who was robbed could not remember very much about the criminals except that "they were very neatly dressed, and rather good looking and they looked enough alike to be brothers." Three days after the robbery, she and several other witnesses spent over six hours with a police artist drawing a composite picture of the suspects. She did not remember much about their physical characteristics and so could not add much to the drawings, but still she was able to pick the accused out of a lineup consisting of twelve persons.

How could the witness be so vague and uncertain about her description, and yet pick out the accused from the lineup? Doob and Kirshenbaum argued that she was able to do this because she remembered the partial description she had made to the police: that the culprits were neatly dressed, looked like each other, and were rather good-looking. Being neatly dressed and looking like each other are two pieces of information that are not particularly useful in picking out one man from a set of twelve neatly dressed men. But the fact that the culprit was recalled as being rather good looking could have been used as a clue. If the witness recalled this description, she might simply have picked from the lineup the person who best fitted this description.

Doob and Kirshenbaum interviewed other people who had not witnessed the crime, and these people rated the suspect as the most attractive person in the lineup. Thus, the investigators' contention that the cashier in the robbery case simply remembered her partial description and then picked the best-looking man in the lineup seems quite reasonable.

They conducted one more test, however, and its results supported their idea that the lineup was inherently biased. They showed the picture of the lineup to twenty-one subjects and said: "Imagine that you were a witness to a crime. All you can remember about the criminal is that *he was rather good looking*. The police then arrest someone whom they think committed the crime, and they place him in a lineup. Imagine that you are shown this lineup and asked by the police to identify the guilty person. The police seem certain that they have the right person, but they need your identification. You try your best to pick out the guilty man. In the picture below, whom would you pick?" Under these conditions, eleven of the twenty-one subjects picked the suspect. Four others said the suspect was their second choice. By chance you would expect that the suspect would be chosen 1/12 of the time. That means fewer than two out of twenty-one subjects should pick him. The fact that eleven subjects chose him indicates he was chosen significantly more often than one would expect by chance.

What this study shows is that the suspect in the lineup was different from the distractors, or other participants. He was not different in some obvious way, such as height or weight, which are easily amenable to physical measurement, but he differed in terms of his attractiveness, and this cue may have been used by the witness in making her identification. This study also demonstrates that people arranging lineups should take pains not only to have all participants in the lineup be the same sex, race, and approximately the same age, height, weight, and manner of dress, but to have the participants match, as much as is possible, any characteristic that was verbalized by a witness.

The Functional Size of a Lineup

In a grossly unfair six-person lineup, say where the suspect is a youth of eighteen and the distractors are all over thirty, it is clear that while the actual size of the lineup is six, the functional size is much less than that. Eyewitnesses might as well be presented with the single eighteen-year-old and asked if this is the one. Experimental demonstrations with nonwitnesses would undoubtedly yield a huge percentage picking the suspect rather than the 17 percent that would be expected by chance alone.

Wells and colleagues (1977) have developed a procedure for calculating the functional size of a lineup. The procedure is quite similar to the ones that have already been discussed for detecting inherent bias in a lineup. A group of experimental subjects (nonwitnesses) are shown a photograph of the actual lineup, along with a description of the suspect's gross physical characteristics. If the lineup is fair, the choices of these nonwitnesses should be reasonably equal across the participants in the lineup. On the other hand, if the suspect is distinctive for some reason, that is, if the suspect is the only person who matches the gross description of the criminal, then the suspect would receive a relatively larger proportion of the choices.

The procedure for calculating functional size is simple. It is the proportion N/D where N is the number of nonwitnesses, each of whom gets a single choice, and D is the number of nonwitnesses who choose the suspect. Thus, suppose forty nonwitnesses are involved in the experiment and twenty of these choose the defendant. In this case, the functional size of the lineup is two, irrespective of how many people were actually in the lineup. If the functional size of a lineup is found to be two, and there were only two persons in the lineup, one could conclude that there were not obvious clues as to whom the police suspected. On the other hand, if the functional size is found to be two but the lineup actually contains six persons, this would suggest that there were considerable clues available to actual witnesses as to whom the police suspected.

The issue of how many nonwitnesses must be used in an experiment is important. There are no definitive answers. However, there must be enough nonwitnesses for the investigator to be fairly confident that the functional size observed is reasonably close to the true functional size. (In the standard parlance of psychology, the investigator should use enough nonwitnesses to produce a 0.95 confidence limit of ± 0.5 on the functional size. Thus, an investigator who finds a functional size of three could claim with 95 percent confidence that the true functional size is closer to three than it is to two or four. With this requirement in mind, most psychologists could calculate the needed sample size quite easily.)

Ostrom and his colleagues used this procedure in an actual case, the case of the *United States v. Mills*. The case arose out of a bank robbery incident in which the robber was described by three witnesses as being "black, male, short, full beard and thin but not skinny." Mills was arrested for the crime and placed in a lineup that included six persons. The psychologists presented a photograph of this lineup to sixty students, along with the general description of the robber and a description of the crime. The nonwitnesses (subjects) were asked to pick the person they thought to be the suspect and were allowed to pick "none of the above." All of the nonwitnesses were tested individually. Of the sixty nonwitnesses, forty-one made a choice and nineteen picked "none of the above." The defendant, Mills, was the most frequent choice, with 61 percent of the nonwitnesses who made a choice picking him. The distribution was as follows: 2, 1, 2, 8, 3, 25 (Mills was in the last position). The investigators then calculated the functional size: $N/D = 41/25 = 1.64$ members. Thus, even though the lineup actually contained six persons, its functional size was only 1.64 persons.

In sum, there exist techniques for assessing the fairness of a lineup or photospread. Current discussions of lineup fairness are highly subjective, with no empirical or scientific base. But these techniques do provide specific criteria which law enforcement officials can use to decide logically whether a lineup is fair or not.

Functional size is easy to measure, and one can then declare as unfair any lineup whose functional size is far below the number of people in the lineup. Further, with enough knowledge, the police investigators can improve their ability to conduct lineups with reasonable functional sizes.

Photo-Biased Lineups

When a crime has been committed, and the police have an available eyewitness, it is common procedure for them to first present the witness with an array of photographs. If an identification is made, an in-person lineup often follows. Such a lineup identification has serious problems, since almost invariably only one person is seen in both the photographs and the lineup. It is unlikely that a witness will identify in the lineup anyone other than the person who was chosen from the photospread. The chances of a mistaken identification rise dramatically in these situations, and so such lineups have been referred to as "photo-biased lineups."

A study showing the dangers of viewing a photograph during the interval between an incident and a lineup was conducted by Brown and colleagues (1977). In one of their experiments, subject-witnesses viewed two groups of five "criminals" (total strangers) for twenty-five seconds each. The subjects were told to scrutinize the criminals carefully since they might have to pick them out from mugshots later that evening and from a lineup the following week. About an hour and a half later the subjects viewed fifteen mugshots, including some people who were "criminals" and some people who were not. One week later several lineups were staged and the subjects were asked to indicate whether each person had been seen at the original "crime" scene.

The results were dramatic. Of the persons in the lineup who had never been seen before, 8 percent were mistakenly "identified" as criminals. However, if a person's mugshot had been seen earlier, his chances of being falsely identified as one of the criminals rose to 20 percent. None of these people had committed a crime or had ever been seen in person before, but were now "recognized" in the lineup because their photograph had been seen.

In a second experiment in this series, subject-witnesses viewed the criminals under conditions in which they did not think they would have to remember them — the criminals were the people who handed out the midterm examination taken by all students in a class. As in the previous study, the subject-witnesses looked at mugshots two or three days later and then witnessed lineups about four or five days after the mugshots were seen.

The results were even more dramatic: 18 percent of the persons in the lineup who had never been seen before were mistakenly identified. However, if a person's mugshot had been seen in the interim, this percentage rose to 29 percent. Both of these experiments show clear evidence of mugshot-induced biases, and they bear on questions of admissibility of testimony in situations where procedures such as mugshots may bias such testimony.

The photo-biased lineup problem is similar to the general problem of unconscious transference. When a witness goes to a lineup, a person whose photograph was seen before will look familiar. This familiarity may be mistakenly related back to the crime rather than back to the photographs where it properly belongs. Thus, the photo-biased lineup is actually one particular type of unconscious transference.

Along these same lines, when a witness constructs a composite photograph of a suspect, this too can affect the accuracy of subsequent in-person lineup identification. In a study by Hall and Ostrom (1975) subjects were presented with a facial photograph and were later asked to try to identify the person from a lineup. However, during the interval between the exposure to the face and the lineup, some subjects worked with an artist to create a composite drawing of the person whose face had been viewed before. The results indicated that the subjects who made the composite drawings made more errors at a subsequent lineup than did subjects who had not made composite drawings. The former group averaged 50 percent errors while the latter group averaged only 31 percent errors. These lineups resulted in errors irrespective of whether the person to be recognized was present in the lineup or not.

In summary, when a witness to a crime is later called upon to identify the culprit who committed the crime, many psychological factors come into play. Some of these factors, such as the retention interval, the quality of the lighting, and the amount of stress that a witness was experiencing during the crime, will affect the accuracy of any kind of testimony, including testimony about person recognition. However, some phenomena are peculiar to the case in which a witness attempts to recognize people. The cross-racial identification problem is a perfect example: people make more errors in attempts to recognize faces of another race than they do in attempts to recognize faces of their own race. A second phenomenon is unconscious transference, where a person seen in one situation is mistakenly remembered by a witness as being seen in a different situation. It is conceivable that there could be unconscious transference of objects other than faces — for example, an automobile that was seen in one place could mistakenly be recalled as having been in a different place. However, the term "unconscious transference" has usually been reserved to refer to the case in which the to-be-remembered object is a face. Finally, those influential legal creatures, lineups, are important for the crucial role they play in affecting the accuracy of an identification and for the potential they hold for contributing to a mistaken identification. As we begin to better understand these special situations, we will surely bring about more justice by reducing the chances that one person will mistakenly identify another.

8

Individual Differences in Eyewitness Ability

I F A HUNDRED PEOPLE were to see the same automobile accident, no two reports would be identical. Granted, there would be some similarities, but people would vary a great deal in terms of the accuracy and completeness of their reports. Why is this? As we saw in chapter 3, poor witnesses may suffer more stress and arousal than reliable witnesses. Poor witnesses may enter the situation with expectations that bias their perception. Perhaps they are not paying as close attention or are engaged in some perceptual activity that interferes with acquiring good information. These would all be expected to matter.

But other, more enduring factors that differentiate people could conceivably affect eyewitness ability—the sex of the witness, the age, the amount of general anxiety or unhappiness the witness is experiencing in life, the amount of training the witness has had. In this chapter we examine the research on some of these characteristics that the witness possesses long before the incident ever occurs, with an eye toward determining which, if any, of them can be used to predict who will be a good witness and who will not.

General Anxiety

The stress produced by the experience of a very unpleasant event is likely to affect nearly all of us. But there is another more general kind of anxiety that some people experience more than others. Does a higher level of this general anxiety cause one to perform more poorly in a test of eyewitness accuracy? Siegel and I hypothesized that this was the case, and set out to design an experiment to test our hypothesis. One way to proceed would have been to administer a standardized test to our subjects—such tests have been developed by psychologists to measure general anxiety. But in an actual legal proceeding it would be somewhat awkward or impossible to determine a witness's general anxiety by administering a standardized test, so we felt that it would be desirable to have a way of tapping anxiety indirectly. Several studies have suggested that the accumulation of undesirable life changes, or life stress as it has been called, is associated with anxiety and depression—changes such as the death of a close friend, loss of a job, and so on (Sarason et al. 1978). Therefore Siegel and I (1978) designed our experiment to determine whether life stress and the resulting anxiety are negatively related to performance on a test of eyewitness ability. Should such a connection be observed, this factor might be very useful in a legal proceeding for deciding which witnesses are more likely to be reporting accurately.

Our experiment was conducted with eighty-four students. Each student completed a test of anxiety, a test of life stress, an eyewitness testimony task, and then a test designed to measure self-preoccupation. The anxiety test—the Multiple Affect Adjective Checklist (Zuckerman and Lubin 1965)—consisted of a list of 132 mood adjectives (for example, agitated, calm, desperate). Subjects responded by endorsing the adjectives that were descriptive of how they were feeling at the present time. Twenty-one of these are relevant for determining how anxious the person is.

The life stress test, called the Life Experiences Survey (Sarason et al. in press), is a 57-item self report inventory to which subjects responded by indicating those events they had experienced in the past year (death of a close friend, marriage, new job). Respondents rated both the desirability (positive and negative) of each event and the extent to which they felt affected by the event. On the basis of these responses, we gave each student a score indicating the undesirable life changes that had been experienced in the last year.

The eyewitness testimony task was designed to measure subjects' ability to perceive and recall a complex event. The subjects were shown the sequence of twenty-four slides depicting a wallet-snatching incident in a small town (described in chapter 6). About one minute after viewing the slides, the subjects filled out a questionnaire designed to determine accuracy. The questionnaire consisted of thirty items that addressed diverse details of the wallet-snatching incident. For example, one question was "The thief wore a (a) heavy shirt, (b) long winter coat, (c) short winter coat, (d) light jacket, (e) down vest."

The self-preoccupation scale (Sarason and Stoops 1978) measured the degree to which an individual was preoccupied by task-irrelevant thoughts. The scale yields two scores: scale 1 consists of the subjects' responses to items dealing specifically with fears about performance (for example, I thought about how poorly I was doing), and scale 2 consists of the subjects' judgments concerning how much their minds wandered during the previous task.

Examining the test results, we found that the average score on the eyewitness task was 14.6 items correct. Some subjects did much better, some did worse. Of central interest to us was the relationship between eyewitness ability and the other individual measures. We performed simple tests of correlation and found, as predicted, that performance on the test of eyewitness ability was negatively correlated with anxiety and with the two preoccupation scales. (The correlation coefficients were -0.20, -0.24, and -0.26, respectively.) In other words, persons who are highly anxious and preoccupied tend to do worse on the eyewitness task. Although the results for life stress were suggestive, the correlation did not quite reach statistical significance; it was -0.12, indicating that there is a slight tendency for people who are experiencing great life stress to perform more poorly on a test of eyewitness ability.

This study suggests that anxiety and preoccupation tend to result in somewhat less efficient performance by an eyewitness. This may be due to the fact that highly anxious persons do not attend adequately to important cues in their environment, and thus they may miss some of the information that is crucial for performing effectively.

In addition to general anxiety, a closely related personality trait — neuroticism — was also found to be related to eyewitness ability. This relationship was observed by Zanni and Offermann (1978) in a study in which subjects looked at a film depicting a man taking a journey. Following this, the subjects answered forty written questions, five of which pertained to items that were not present in the film. Appended to the questionnaire was the

Eysenck Personality Inventory (Eysenck 1967), for the purpose of measuring neuroticism. The investigators suspected a relationship with neuroticism because this personality trait is usually conceptualized in terms of arousal—individuals scoring high on a scale of neuroticism function at a higher level of arousal than individuals scoring low on the scale. Highly neurotic subjects perform more poorly than their less neurotic counterparts on complex cognitive tasks; therefore the researchers assumed that the neurotic subjects would make more errors than other people when interrogated about some witnessed event since this can be a relatively complex task.

And that was exactly what they found. Defining an error as a yes response to one of the five critical items that were not present in the film, the researchers discovered that highly neurotic persons made an average of 3.3 errors, whereas less neurotic persons made an average of 2.8 errors. In a second experiment a correlation between neuroticism scores and error rates was found to be 0.41, indicating that those subjects who were higher in neuroticism tended to make more errors on an eyewitness test.

Another study has shown that anxiety affects facial recognition (Mueller et al. 1978). Ninety-six students, half men and half women, took a test designed to measure anxiety, and then participated in a facial recognition task. Subjects looked at a set of fifty black-and-white slides of male and female faces presented at a rate of one every five seconds. Immediately after this phase, these fifty slides were randomly mixed with fifty new slides and then shown one at a time. Subjects indicated on an answer sheet whether they thought each slide had been shown before.

The researchers found that high-anxiety subjects did worse on the facial recognition test than did low-anxiety subjects. Again, the reason for this deficit is that the high-anxiety subjects do not use as much of the information as they could be using when they initially look at the faces.

In sum, psychological research has shown that people who are generally anxious, neurotic, or preoccupied tend to make slightly worse eyewitnesses than those who generally are not. High arousal apparently causes the witness to concentrate on certain details to the neglect of others.

Sex

All things equal, who makes a better witness, a man or a woman? Psychological research on the effects of sex differences on eyewitness ability has produced results that are equivocal. Some studies of sex differences have shown that females perform better than males (for example, Ellis et al. 1973; Lipton 1977; Witryol and Kaess 1957), while others have shown that males perform better than females (Clifford and Scott 1978; Trankell 1972); still others indicate no differences in the accuracy of women and men (Bird 1927; Cady 1924; McKelvie 1976).

With this colossal variety of results to contend with, what are we to believe? Recent work conducted by my colleagues and me suggests a possible answer, namely, that both women and men pay more attention to items that catch their interest and consequently store more or better information in memory about those items. If a subsequent test asked about female-oriented items, women would outperform men. The converse would be true if testing concerned male-oriented details (Powers et al. 1979). The results of several studies support this contention.

In one experiment, fifty subjects looked at a sequence of twenty-four slides depicting a wallet-snatching incident (see description of slides in chapter 6) and then filled out a thirty-item questionnaire designed to measure the accuracy of their memory. The following day, the subjects were given one of two "suggestibility" paragraphs to read—versions of the incident allegedly written by a psychology professor who had seen the slides for much longer than had the subjects. The two versions of the paragraph differed only in their description of four critical items. The control version contained an accurate description of these four items, while the other version contained erroneous information about them. Thus, the control version might correctly refer to the green notebook that was being carried by the victim's friend, while the experimental version erroneously called it a blue notebook.

After a short filler activity, the subjects took a final test consisting of twenty items that was designed to measure the extent to which the misleading information was incorporated into the witness's recollection. The accuracy scores ranged from 9 to 24, with a mean score of 16.7. Overall, females were slightly, but not significantly, more accurate than males. However, significant differences in accuracy for males and females were found when specific questions were looked at. Women were more accurate than men on questions dealing with women's clothing or actions, whereas men were more accurate on questions concerning the thief's appearance and the surroundings. It was also found that females were more suggestible than males; they were more likely to incorporate the misleading information into their final recollections. However, this sex difference in suggestibility could be explained by the specific critical items about which the subjects were misled. As it happened, three of the four critical items about which false information was supplied were details about the surroundings. Women were less accurate on these key items, indicating that they gave less attention to them and were consequently more open to suggestion about them.

A subsequent experiment (Powers et al. 1979) confirmed that systematic sex differences in accuracy and suggestibility might be a result of special item peculiarities. Men and women participated, one hundred of each sex. Fifty of them participated in a preliminary procedure designed to select a set of items that were likely to be noticed by men and a second set likely to be noticed by women. They saw a series of slides that opened with a group of people sitting together on the grass. A man and a woman leave the group and begin walking through a parking lot, where they spot two people who are apparently fighting with each other. The man rushes in to stop the fight while the woman goes off to a phone booth, apparently to call for help. After viewing these slides, subjects took a twenty-five-item accuracy test, and from the responses to this test, four critical items were selected, two on which male respondents were substantially more accurate than women and two on which females outperformed males.

The remaining 150 subjects, half men and half women, participated in an experiment nearly identical to the one previously described. The overall procedure included four phases: viewing the slides, filling out an accuracy questionnaire, reading a suggestibility paragraph that contained four pieces of misleading information, and taking a final test.

The results were clear: women were more accurate and less suggestible on the two female-oriented items, whereas the reverse was true for the two male-oriented items. This indicates that females and males tend to be accurate on different types of items, perhaps indicating a difference in their interest in particular items and a correspondingly different amount of attention paid to these items. One consequence is that the ease with which misleading information can be supplied to men and women about these specific items also varies. This reasoning is in accord with the experts in the field who have written about sex differences in more traditional laboratory tasks. Maccoby and Jacklin (1974), in a thorough review of the sex differences in accuracy, concluded that stable differences do not exist in common laboratory memory tasks, while Eagly (1978), in her review of sex differences in susceptibility to influence, concluded that people "are more readily influenced to the extent that they lack information about a topic or regard it as trivial and unimportant" (p. 96).

Age

Does a person's age affect the accuracy and completeness of an eyewitness account? In the ideal world a researcher would conduct a longitudinal study, that is, a set of individuals would be studied when they are very young, when they are adolescents, when they are in their twenties and thirties, when they are middle-aged, and when they are older. Obviously, this would take a great deal of time, and so it is not ordinarily the way most research is conducted. Rather, it is common to take groups of people at various ages and test their ability simultaneously—a cross-sectional study.

Numerous cross-sectional studies have compared the eyewitness ability of children of various ages. The results from one such study are fairly typical. Ellis and colleagues (1973) selected a group of boys and girls, half of whom were twelve years old and half of whom were seventeen, and showed them twenty color slides of undergraduate students, half men and half women. Four hours later the twenty slides were mixed with forty others and shown one at a time to the subjects. The subjects were required to indicate for each slide whether it had been shown earlier or not.

Seventeen-year-olds remembered more faces than twelve-year-olds—79 percent versus 72 percent. This result is similar to others: twelve- to fourteen-year-olds have been found to outperform six- to nine-year-olds (Goldstein and Chance 1964, 1965), and eleven-year-olds demonstrated superior recognition accuracy over eight-year-olds, who were, in turn, better than five-year-olds (Kagan et al. 1973). In most of these studies, then, older children outperform the younger ones. Oftentimes this improved ability is due to the fact that the older children make many fewer false identifications. This could be due, in part, to the fact that older children are less likely to guess when they are uncertain, but it could also represent a genuine improvement in ability to discriminate what was seen before from what was not.

At the upper end of the age continuum, the situation is a bit more complicated. Some studies have shown that people over the age of sixty or so perform more poorly than do somewhat younger people (Smith and Winograd 1977), and many tasks have shown some decrease in performance between the ages of forty and sixty (Schaie and Gribbin 1975). One might be tempted to conclude from these results that after a certain age (perhaps fifty or sixty) eyewitness reliability will decline somewhat with age. This generalization would not be correct. As leading experts in the field are now stressing, although performance on some tasks, for example, memory for details, may weaken a bit with age, other cognitive skills are maintained with advancing age. Furthermore, there are great individual differences among people; one person may show some decline with advancing age while another shows no decline (Baltes and Schaie 1976). Thus, investigators in this area have begun to dispel the myth of an overall decline with advancing age. It seems safe only to conclude that performance on some tasks may decline somewhat, but performance on others, such as memory for logical relationships and ability to make complex inferences, will not.

While the precise function relating recall and recognition ability to age cannot be drawn, since it will depend upon the exact task that a witness is trying to accomplish, a tentative function would basically indicate that recall and recognition ability improves with age up to a point, say about fifteen or twenty years old, and that a decline may begin to occur in the later years, perhaps about the age of sixty years.

The age of a witness is important in another way. Age *may* be related to the susceptibility of a witness to potential biases and misleading information. The child, as a witness, has always been regarded as not only particularly inaccurate but also highly suggestible. This view has been fairly widespread: "Create, if you will, an idea of what the child is to hear or see, and the child is very likely to hear or see what you desire" (Brown 1926, p. 133).

A dramatic piece of evidence for this view can be found in the work of Varendonck (1911, reviewed in Whipple 1913), who was one of the first psychologists to be used in the courtroom as an expert witness on testimony. The case occurred in Belgium in 1910, where Varendonck was asked to evaluate the information obtained from two young girls under suggestive questioning in a preliminary examination. He devised a series of ingenious experiments incorporating questions similar to those which had been asked of the two young witnesses. The responses obtained from children of the same age as the two witnesses demonstrated to Varendonck's satisfaction that the original testimony could have resulted from the suggestive questions. For example, when eighteen seven-year-old students were asked to report on the color of the beard of one of the teachers in their building, sixteen answered "black," and two did not answer. In fact, the teacher did not even have a beard. When twenty eight-year-olds were asked the same question, nineteen reported a color; only one correctly said the man had no beard. In another experiment, a teacher visited a class, stood before the students for five minutes while talking to them, and kept his hat on. Immediately after he had left the room, the teacher of the class asked: "In which hand did Mr. ____ hold his hat?" Seventeen claimed it was in the right hand, seven said the left hand, and only three gave the correct answer. These compelling results convinced Whipple that "children are the most dangerous of all witnesses" (1911, p. 308) and "are well known to be more open to suggestion than adults" (1918, p. 245).

Other social scientists shared Whipple's view. Stern (1910) showed pictures to adults and children and then interrogated his witnesses with questions of varying suggestiveness. He concluded that "the power of the 'suggestive' question showed itself to be dependent in large measure on age" (p. 272). Lipmann (1911) also concluded that "younger children prove to be very much more suggestible than older children or adults" (p. 258). Whipple summarized Lipmann's interpretation of the unreliability of reports of children in these words: "First, the child does not distribute his attention the same way as the adult . . . secondly, the child is uncritical in filling out gaps in his memory and uses freely material supplied through custom, through his own imagination or through suggestion. It follows that the training of the child in correct report must transform his distribution of attention to one corresponding to that of the adult and must develop a critical attitude toward misstatements in filling out gaps" (Whipple 1912, p. 266).

Years later, the firm belief in the suggestibility of children had not let up. McCarty (1929) stated, "There is a very common impression that children are more suggestible than adults" (p. 270), and went on to suggest that a devious lawyer, if he so desired, could control the testimony of a child by means of suggestion and could elicit from a child evidence that is wholly false and unreliable. Rouke (1957) reviewed the extensive literature on the ability of witnesses to recall material from either pictures or actual events and concluded that "children were in every respect poorer than adults" (p. 52). In sum, it appears to be a strong belief that one can "create, if you will, an idea of what the child is to hear or see, and the child is very likely to hear or see what you desire."

My colleagues and I investigated one method of "creating an idea of what the child is to see," namely, that of varying the wording of the questions used to interrogate a child about some event he has recently witnessed (Dale et al. 1978). We showed boys and girls some short films and then asked them some questions about the events in the films. Some of the questions were leading, for example, "Didn't you see some bears?" whereas others were neutral. Would these children pick up the suggestive information contained in the leading questions? Although very young children may be highly suggestible, it is not clear that their relatively short experience with the language is sufficient for them to learn the force of very subtle changes in language. Our results were straightforward: When a question was asked about an entity which was not present in the film, the form of the question significantly affected the probability that a child would falsely respond with yes. Leading questions such as "Didn't you see some . . . ?" were more likely to be answered yes than other, more neutrally worded questions.

In sum, the preponderance of research indicates that not only are children relatively inaccurate but they are also highly suggestible. They can be influenced by very subtle changes in the wording of questions that are put to them. In light of what we know, the response of the legal profession has been unusual. It is recognized that the suggestive powers of the leading question are, as a general proposition, undesirable. However, numerous exceptions have been permitted by the courts. The witness who is hostile, unwilling, or biased can be asked leading questions. And so can the child. In other words, the witness who might be most easily misled by suggestive questions is one to whom these questions may be directed.

The Honorable Charles F. Stafford has pointed out that "a child is" often in the right place at the right time to see people, things, and events that are never witnessed by adults . . . it will be necessary to determine whether his testimony will enhance or stay the cause of justice" (1962, p. 303). In the state of Washington, nine-year-old children have been considered competent witnesses, and there are even cases in which children as young as five have testified. Such testimony has been admitted into evidence in cases ranging from indecent liberties to murder and rape. But in other cases children within this same age have not been allowed to testify. Usually it is the judge who decides whether the child may testify, and he usually does so on the basis of the child's intelligence or ability to truly relate the facts rather than upon the basis of age. Is there any minimum age below which judges tend to feel a child should not be allowed to testify? Yes, in most states the appellate courts have held that four years of age is about the absolute minimum at which a child will be considered competent to testify.

Witnesses at the upper age range have not received as much attention. But here, given the great individual variability, the procedures probably ought to be similar in some respects, but not in others. The judge can again assume the burden of determining whether the aging witness has the intelligence and ability to understand and relate the truth. But it is likely that there is not a maximum age at which a person will be considered competent to testify.

Training

In many courtrooms a police officer who has witnessed a crime is called upon to testify as a "trained observer." People seem to have the intuitive feeling that a trained observer will give a more accurate eyewitness account than a layperson. Is there anything to this feeling?

Certainly a witness's prior knowledge and expectations can influence perception and memory. Even telling a witness what type of incident will be viewed can affect memory. In a study by Thorson and Hochhaus (1977) sixty students viewed an eight-second scene involving two cars in an accident at an intersection. Half of the subjects were told "You are about to see a videotape of an 8-sec. event. Watch carefully." The other half were told "You are about to see an 8-sec. scene of an automobile accident. After you view the tape we are going to ask you certain qustions about the event. First, what kind of cars were involved? Second, how many people were in each car? Third, how fast was each of the two cars going? Fourth, which car was at fault? Now would you repeat the four questions?" Ten minutes after the videotape, the subjects answered questionnaires, some subjects being given leading questions while others were given neutral questions.

When the results were analyzed, they showed two major effects (fig. 8.1). Subjects who had answered the leading questions produced higher estimates of speed than subjects who had not. Furthermore, subjects who were informed about the procedure to follow produced higher estimates than those who were uninformed. Note also that subjects in the leading-uninformed and in the neutral-informed categories tended to give accurate estimates of speed (about 30 mph). Those in the leading-informed tended to overestimate, while those in the neutral-uninformed tended to

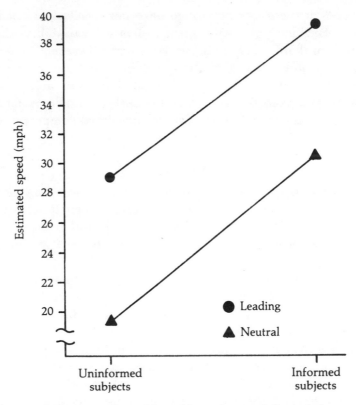

Figure 8.1. Estimate of speed for subjects who were informed about what they would see and those who were uninformed. The results also show that leading questions lead to higher estimates than neutral questions. (Data from Thorson and Hochhaus 1977.)

underestimate. But what is important for the present question is the fact that a greater proportion of informed over uninformed subjects were accurate. While this study might indicate that "a person trained to give an accurate estimate of speed may be a very poor witness when faced with a leading question" (p. 456), it does not really get at the crucial question of whether police officers, who are presumably trained, are in general capable of giving better testimony then laypeople.

One of the few studies to really explore this issue was conducted by Tickner and Poulton (1975). Twenty-four police officers and 156 civilians were shown a film of a street scene which had been made from a first floor window of a building which faced the end of a street. The cameras, looking along the street from its end, showed the usual movement of traffic and pedestrians, and also a number of additional people and actions which were inserted deliberately (fig. 8.2). The subjects' main task was to watch for particular people in the film, people whose photographs the subjects had previously been shown. Some subjects were asked to also report any instances of a certain act, such as petty theft, and others were asked to watch for more than one person.

Some of the results were unsurprising; for example, both people and actions were detected reliably more often when they were near the camera than when they were further away. But comparing the performance of police officers with civilians, the researchers found that the officers reported more alleged thefts (false detection of thefts) than did the civilian observers, but on the number of *true* detections of people and actions, there were no significant differences between the police and the civilians.

Can it really be that police officers are no better in their eyewitness accounts than laypeople? Is it possible that the extensive training that certain groups undergo makes them no better prepared to accurately perceive and recall complex events? Are our intuitions in this area dead wrong? It may be that the answer to these questions is yes.

Various training procedures have been developed that emphasize attention to facial features. These programs are based on the recommendations of Penry (1971), who advocates that the best way to remember a face is to treat it as a collection of features. Breaking the face down into its components allows better discrimination among faces and better remembering of a face later on. Penry argues that "the reliable clues to facial identity are to

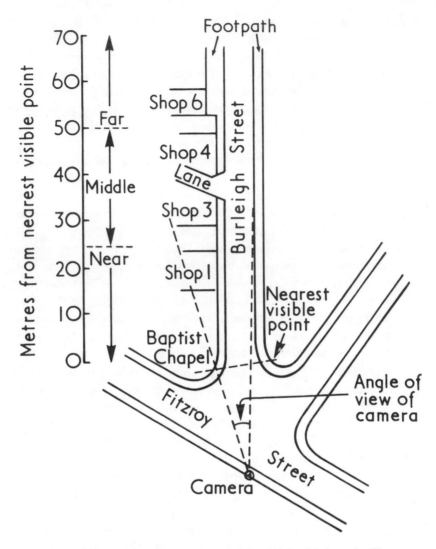

Figure 8.2. Diagram of the street in Cambridge, England, where the films were made that compared the eyewitness abilities of police and civilians. (From Tickner and Poulton 1975.)

be found in the basic formation, first of the face-outline as a whole, then of its separate parts" (p. 13). The best way to "register" a face is to ignore any movement in the facial pattern. Yet never has any evidence been presented for the validity of a feature-oriented training system.

Three British psychologists attempted to test the feature approach by evaluating an ongoing training course that used this technique as a basic guide for recognizing people (Woodhead et al. in press). The training program had been under way for months prior to the study. Between eight and twenty men attended the course with the hope of improving their general standards of recognition. During three days of intensive training the trainees heard lectures, saw slides and film demonstrations, participated in discussions, handled case history materials, and performed field exercises. Although the teaching was imaginative and enthusiastic, no examinations were given to find out if the training actually led to any improvement.

In their first experiment the three psychologists presented twenty-four photographs of faces of white males to trainees who were signed up for the course and to control subjects who were not. The faces were differentiated by various poses, expressions, and disguises, similar to those shown in figure 8.3; the disguises used were easy to adopt: changes in hair style, or the addition of a beard, mustache, or glasses.

The twenty-four faces were shown one at a time, for ten seconds apiece. All subjects were urged to take a "good hard look" at each face because later on they would be asked to remember the faces they had seen. They were warned that later certain faces might appear in disguise. About fifteen minutes after the faces

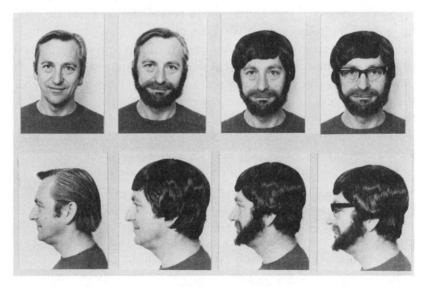

Figure 8.3. Poses, expressions, and disguises used in an experiment to test the effectiveness of face-recognition training. (From Patterson and Baddeley 1977.)

had been viewed, a larger set of seventy-two faces was presented and for each face the subject had to indicate whether it was a "new face" or one that had been "seen before."

During the next three days, the twenty-six trainees attended the course on improving recognition, while the twenty-two control subjects spent the days on their normal work. Finally, all subjects were again tested on their ability to recognize previously seen faces. The results were striking. They show absolutely no evidence for any effect of the training course on the ability of subjects to remember photographed faces (fig. 8.4). For both groups of subjects, changes in the appearance of a previously seen face did make a tremendous difference. For unchanged faces, recognition was quite good—about 80 to 90 percent of the time, a subject said yes to a face that had actually been seen before. When the faces assumed a change in either pose or expression, recognition dropped off to about 60 to 70 percent, and when the faces were disguised, performance was extremely poor at about 30 percent. Note that a subject who was merely guessing would have a 50 percent chance of being correct.

Occasionally in real law enforcement practice it is not necessary to rely on memory in order to recognize a face. Oftentimes investigators carry photographs that they can use to match to a suspicious face. However, many times a wanted person is in view for just a second or two and he looks very different from the way he looks in a photograph. With these ideas in mind, these investigators sought to explore whether recognition training improved the ability to match nonidentical versions of a given face. Their procedure was similar in many ways to the previous experiment; the performance of trainees who were about to take the improvement course was compared with the performance of control subjects who were not. All subjects were tested for their "matching" ability twice, once before the course, and again three days later.

The results of this follow-up research indicated that the recognition training provided in the course did not produce any improvement whatsoever in ability to match different versions of the same face. The fact that the course did not improve either matching ability or memory ability was surprising and unexpected to the investigators. Subjectively, they had found the course to be well organized and quite convincing. Why no improvement?

One possibility is that the course is based on faulty ideas of how people recognize faces. The course emphasized the importance of

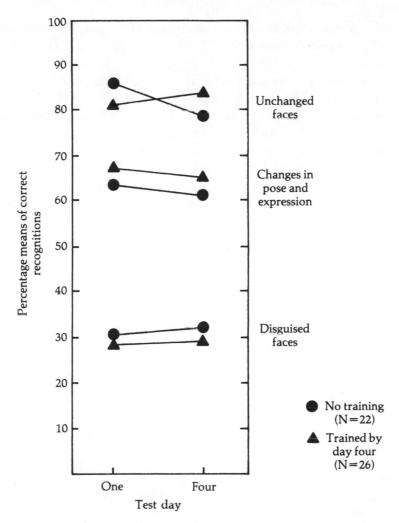

Figure 8.4. Trainee and control subjects were equally good at recognizing faces. Changes in appearance caused drastic reductions in performance. (Data from Woodhead et al. in press.)

selecting individual facial features, rather than considering the face as a whole. Perhaps the basic face framework and arrangement is even more important than the individual physical features. There is some evidence for this. Many investigators have found that people are less good at recognizing faces when their attention is drawn to a specific feature of the face than when their attention is focused on some holistic assessment. A course approach that recognizes the whole/part distinction might see an improvement in ability.

There are many factors other than anxiety, sex, age, and training that could prove to be good predictors of eyewitness ability. For example, the education and intelligence of a witness could matter, and his health might make a difference, but these have not yet been explored sufficiently to allow us to draw reasonable conclusions. Researchers will continue to explore these topics and ultimately we will have a far better understanding of who makes a good witness.

9

Common Beliefs about Eyewitness Accounts

SEVERAL YEARS AGO a widely publicized trial, known as the San Quentin Six Trial, took place in Marin County, California. It resulted from an incident at San Quentin prison on August 21, 1971, in which black prison leader George Jackson was shot along with three white guards and two prison trustees. Six prisoners housed in the cell block where the violence erupted were charged with murder and conspiracy to escape.

The evidence implicating Willie Tate, one of the defendants, consisted of the testimony of a single eyewitness, Charles C. Breckenridge, a guard who first discovered that a rebellion was in progress when he returned a prisoner to the cell block. According to Breckenridge, one inmate, Hugo Pinell (nicknamed Yogi), escorted him to a particular part of the cell block and turned him over to two other inmates, Willie Tate and David Johnson. Johnson and Tate allegedly put Breckenridge in a cell, bound his hands and feet, and blindfolded him. Subsequently, Breckenridge's throat was cut, purportedly by Pinell.

At the trial Tate's lawyers attempted to call me as an expert witness to testify about the factors present in this situation which would have reduced the accuracy of an identification, in particular Breckenridge's identification of Tate. Many of the factors that are known to affect the accuracy of eyewitness testimony existed in the San Quentin incident. For example, a cross-racial identification was involved: Tate was a black defendant; Breckenridge was a white guard. There was a stress factor: Breckenridge, whose throat was cut, could be assumed to be experiencing extreme stress. Several other factors were also relevant.

The judge did not permit the testimony, arguing, in effect, that a psychologist could not tell the jury anything the jury did not already know. This reaction prompted me to wonder just what people in general, and jurors in particular, know about the factors that affect eyewitness testimony. Are people generally aware that there is a cross-racial identification problem — that people are less good at recognizing faces of another race than faces of their own race? Do people understand how stress can affect the memory of an eyewitness to a serious event? Susan Porietas and I conducted a study to find out.

During the years 1977 and 1978, we collected information from over five hundred registered voters in the state of Washington, all of whom were students at the University of Washington. We asked them to simply fill out a questionnaire designed to sample their knowledge of some of the factors that affect eyewitness testimony. Each of the questions was to be answered by selecting one of four alternative answers that were listed with the question. The subjects also indicated their confidence in their answers by circling a number ranging from 1 (guessing) to 6 (very sure).

Cross-Racial Identification

One of the questions we asked was:

"Two women are walking to school one morning, one of them an Asian and the other white. Suddenly, two men, one black and one white, jump into their path and attempt to grab their purses. Later, the women are shown photographs of known purse snatchers in the area. Which statement best describes your view of the women's ability to identify the purse snatchers?

(a) Both the Asian and the white woman will find the white man harder to identify than the black man.
(b) The white woman will find the black man more difficult to identify than the white man.
(c) The Asian woman will have an easier time than the white woman making an accurate identification of both men.
(d) The white woman will find the black man easier to identify than the white man."

The percentage of subjects giving each of the answers is shown in table 9.1. Only 55 percent of the subjects gave the correct

Table 9.1. Percentage of subjects that gave each of the responses to the questionnaire designed to tap common beliefs about eyewitness testimony. The percentage giving the correct answer is indicated in bold type. Mean confidence ratings are in parentheses.

Topic	Answer			
	a	b	c	d
Cross-racial identification	16	**55**	16	13
	(3.29)	(3.38)	(3.17)	(3.06)
Stress	12	3	**67**	18
	(4.00)	(2.00)	(3.95)	(3.95)
Violence of event	66	**18**	6	10
	(4.06)	(3.62)	(3.11)	(2.40)
Weapon focus	2	20	39	**39**
	(2.67)	(3.90)	(4.00)	(3.82)
Question wording	4	1	**90**	5
	(3.60)	(1.50)	(4.94)	(3.88)
New information[a]	7	26	38	29
	(3.91)	(3.03)	(3.57)	(4.09)

a. No correct answer.

answer (b). Forty-five percent were wrong. It is of some interest that 13 percent of the subjects checked alternative (d), indicating that they thought the white woman would find the black man *easier* to identify than the white man.

Stress

The Yerkes-Dodson Law says that extreme stress and arousal interfere with a person's ability to process information. Do people know this? One of our questions was designed to find out:

"When a person is experiencing extreme stress as the victim of a crime, he will have:

(a) greater ability to perceive and recall the details of the event.
(b) the same ability to perceive and recall the details of the event as under normal conditions.
(c) reduced ability to perceive and recall the details of the event.
(d) greater ability to recall the details of the event, but less ability to perceive the details of the event."

About two-thirds of the subjects questioned correctly believed that extreme stress interferes with eyewitness ability, while one-third did not believe this to be true (table 9.1). It is curious that 18 percent felt that ability to recall the details would be enhanced while ability to perceive was reduced. If poor information gets into memory in the first place, it is hard to imagine how good information could be pulled out.

Violence of the Event

People find it harder to recall information about a violent event than a nonviolent one, as shown by Clifford and Scott (1978). Our questionnaire included a question that was designed to find out how much people understood about this factor. It was here that our subjects performed most poorly. The question was:

"Suppose that a man and a woman both witness two crimes. One crime involves violence while the other is nonviolent. Which statement do you believe is true?

(a) Both the man and the woman will remember the details of the violent crime better than the details of the nonviolent crime.
(b) Both the man and the woman will remember the details of the nonviolent crime better than the details of the violent crime.
(c) The man will remember the details of the violent crime better than the details of the nonviolent crime and the reverse will be true for the woman.
(d) The woman will remember the details of the violent crime better, and the man will remember the details of the nonviolent crime better."

Only 18 percent of our subjects checked the correct choice, (b). Most people incorrectly believed that the opposite was true, namely, that memory for the details of a violent event is better. Sixteen percent believed that the sexes behave differently (table 9.1).

Weapon Focus

When a person witnesses a crime involving a weapon, that weapon captures a good deal of the witness's attention, takes up a portion of the witness's processing time, and leaves less time available for focusing on other details. One result is a reduced ability to later recognize the face of the person who was holding the weapon. Some people appear to understand this phenomenon while others do not. We asked our subjects this question:

"Consider a situation in which a person is being robbed. The robber is standing a few feet from the victim and is pointing a gun at him. The victim later reports to a police officer, "I was so frightened, I'll never forget that face." Which of the following do you feel best describes what the victim experienced at the time of the robbery?

(a) The victim was so concerned about being able to identify the robber that he didn't even notice the gun.
(b) The victim focused on the robber's face and only slightly noticed the gun.
(c) The victim got a good look at both the gun and the face.
(d) The victim focused on the gun which would interfere with his ability to remember the robber's face."

Close to 40 percent chose response (d), indicating that they had some knowledge of the fact that the gun might interfere with facial recognition (table 9.1). But just as many people believed that the victim would typically get a good look at both the gun and the face under these situations.

Question Wording

Are people aware of the fact that small changes in the wording of a question can affect the answer that a witness gives? Do they know that "Did you see the broken headlight?" is more likely to yield a "yes" answer than "Did you see a broken headlight?" Our results indicate that most people have some awareness of this fact. We asked this question:

"Suppose a person witnesses a car accident and he is later asked questions about it. (1) "Did you see a broken headlight?" or (2) "Did you see the broken headlight?" Would it make any difference which question the witness was asked?

(a) No, since the witness would know whether or not he had seen a broken headlight.

(b) No, there is no difference between the two questions.
(c) Yes, since question 2 assumes that there was a broken head-light.
(d) No, the witness would disregard the distinction between *a* and *the*."

We found that 90 percent of our subjects chose answer (c), indicating that they believed it would make a difference whether the word "the" or "a" was used. The remaining 10 percent thought it would not make a difference, either because the witness would know what he had seen or because the distinction would simply be disregarded (table 9.1).

New Information

Our last question was designed to determine the extent to which people believe that a witness who is exposed to new, conflicting information will come to believe that he actually witnessed that new information. We asked this question:

"Suppose that a very serious auto-pedestrian accident occurred in front of ten witnesses. The witnesses were upset but thought they saw the car run a red light. The witnesses later read about the accident in the newspaper. The newspaper account mistakenly reported that the light had been green. How many of the witnesses do you think would now believe they had seen a green light rather than a red one?

(a) None.
(b) One or two.
(c) About half.
(d) More than half."

The percentage of subjects giving each response is indicated in table 9.1. None of these responses is in bold type because there is no way of knowing what the precise correct answer is. The information is useful in that it tells us what people *think* the correct answer is. Only 7 percent felt that no one would come to believe the information that was provided in the newspaper, 26 percent claimed that just one or two persons would be persuaded, while 67 percent of the subjects felt that half or more of the witnesses would come to believe they had actually witnessed the information in the newspaper account.

Confidence

When the subjects in this experiment answered each question, they also indicated their confidence in their answer by circling a number from one to six, where one indicated guessing and six indicated the subject was "very sure." The average confidence rating given by the subjects who chose each alternative is indicated in parentheses in table 9.1. For cross-racial identification and question wording, people who gave the correct alternative tended to have higher confidence than those who were incorrect. For the questions on stress, weapon focus, and violence of the event, this was not the case. Confidence was highest for an incorrect answer.

To summarize, our experiment showed that sometimes the common beliefs held by people regarding eyewitness ability conform to the psychological research, but in other cases these beliefs do not. The percentage of subjects who answered correctly ranged from a low of 18 for the question about weapon focus to a high of 90 for the question about question wording. These percentages are an overestimate of how much people actually know, since they have not taken into account the fact that some people could have been correct simply by guessing. In a multiple-choice question with four alternatives, a person who is merely guessing has a one-in-four chance of answering correctly; some of these correct answers were undoubtedly produced by people who were only guessing.

The study was designed to sample people's knowledge of some of the factors that affect eyewitness testimony. More research on this issue is badly needed to correct the mistaken notion that an experimental psychologist cannot tell the jury anything it does not already know.

10

The Eyewitness and the Legal System

ON NOVEMBER 23, 1937, three men held up a clothing store in a small town in Michigan. The owner of the store was shot and killed, and when his twenty-one-year-old daughter rushed to his aid, she was slugged with a revolver by one of the robbers. Charles Clark was later identified by the girl in a lineup as the man who shot her father. Despite the fact that Clark's landlady testified that he was home the entire day of the murder, and one of the other defendants said that Clark had no part in the murder, the man was convicted. His conviction was based solely on the identification testimony of the young daughter, and Clark was sentenced to prison for life.

Several times during his thirty years of imprisonment, Clark tried for a new trial, but was denied each time. Clark was a model prisoner and for this reason he was later offered a pardon; he refused, claiming that to accept would have been an admission of guilt.

In 1968, the case was assigned to the Legal Aid and Defenders Association of Detroit. Attorneys for Clark pored through early transcripts and discovered that the victim's daughter had at one time said that she could not identify Clark as one of the robbers. She finally admitted that when she could not identify Clark, he was pointed out to her before the lineup and she was told by the authorities that he was the guilty man.

Charles Clark was granted a new trial in 1968, thirty years after his initial conviction. The prosecutor moved to dismiss the case, and Clark was freed. In 1972 the governor of Michigan signed into law the following:

> Sec. 1. There is appropriated from the general fund of the state the sum of $10,000.00 to Charles Lee Clark, born October 17, 1899 at Americus, Georgia, residing at 238 E. Mount Vernon, Detroit, Michigan, for mental suffering incurred in state prison for an offense of which he was found innocent upon later trial after 30 years of confinement.
> Sec. 2. The money appropriated under the provisions of this act is not made in payment of any claims for damages, but is provided solely out of humanitarian consideration.
> Ordered to take immediate effect.
> Approved January 28, 1972.

There are no official reports printed in the case of Charles Clark. This account was put together as part of a court opinion in Michigan from newspaper reports of the case (*People v. Anderson*, 1973). The problem is clear: the unreliability of eyewitness identification evidence poses one of the most serious problems in the administration of criminal justice and civil litigation. The seriousness of the situation was stated clearly as long ago as 1932 by Borchard, who reviewed the criminal prosecutions and convictions of sixty-five innocent persons:

> Perhaps the major source of these tragic errors is an identification of the accused by the victim of a crime of violence. This mistake was practically alone responsible for twenty-nine of these convictions. Juries seem disposed more readily to credit the veracity and reliability of the victims of an outrage than any amount of contrary evidence by or on behalf of the accused, whether by way of alibi, character witnesses, or other testimony. These cases illustrate the fact that the emotional balance of the victim or eyewitness is so disturbed by his extraordinary experience that his powers of perception become distorted and his identification is frequently most untrustworthy. Into the identification enter other motives, not necessarily stimulated originally by the accused personally—the desire to requite a crime, to exact vengeance upon the person believed guilty, to find a scapegoat, to support, consciously or unconsciously, an identification already made by another. Thus doubts are resolved against the accused. How valueless are these identifications by the victim of a crime is indicated by the fact that in eight of these cases the wrongfully accused person and the really guilty criminal bore not the slightest resemblance to each other, whereas in twelve other cases, the resemblance, while fair, was still not at all close.

Some members of the legal profession are beginning not only to understand the hazards involved in eyewitness testimony but to respond to those hazards. Laypersons, on the other hand, have given every indication that they do not have this understanding. Rather, most continue to place great faith in an eyewitness account, even one that is weak. This chapter will examine some of the Supreme Court's decisions regarding eyewitness accounts and will discuss alternative solutions that offer some legal protection against mistaken identification.

Supreme Court Decisions

On June 12, 1967, the United States Supreme Court decided a trilogy of landmark cases, *United States v. Wade, Gilbert v. California*, and *Stovall v. Denno*. All three dealt with the constitutionality of police practices and procedures in obtaining eyewitness identifications. The three decisions concern one specific part of criminal procedure. Whenever a crime is committed, a witness may be either the victim of that crime or an innocent bystander. Soon afterward, the witness is typically questioned by the police and usually asked to describe the offender. Occasionally the witness will view photographs and attempt to make an identification. Later, if the police have a suspect, the witness may be asked to view the suspect either by photograph or in person, and either alone or as part of a group. Once the witness identifies a particular person as being the perpetrator of the crime, the witness will ordinarily testify to this at the trial. This last part of the process must be qualified, however, since only a small percentage of criminal cases actually come to trial (Levine and Tapp 1973). Most of them are settled before the trial, for example, by the defendant agreeing to plead to a lesser charge. Thus, more often than not, the eyewitness is not challenged by cross-examination during the trial. Mistaken identifications have very little chance of being revealed.

The Wade-Gilbert-Stovall decisions are concerned only with those cases where the police had arranged a pretrial confrontation between the eyewitnesses and the defendant for the purpose of seeing whether the witness could recognize him. They apply only to those crimes where the police had to establish the identity of the perpetrator by means of a photo identification, a showup (that is, the presentation of the suspect alone to the witness), or a lineup (the presentation to the witness of several choices, including the suspect).

The Wade case produced the most famous of the three decisions. The accused, Billy Joe Wade, was indicted and arrested for the robbery of a federally insured bank. A defense attorney was appointed to represent him, but an FBI agent arranged, without notifying the attorney, to have two bank employees observe a lineup of the accused and five or six other prisoners. All those in the lineup were required, like the robber, to wear strips of tape on their faces and to say "Put the money in the bag." The bank employees identified Wade.

At the trial the witnesses both indicated that it was Wade who had committed the robbery. The defense attorney appealed on the grounds that there had been a pretrial identification at which Wade's lawyer had not been present. The United States Court of Appeals for the Fifth Circuit reversed Wade's conviction on the ground that holding the lineup in the absence of the accused's counsel violated his Sixth Amendment right to counsel.

The Supreme Court heard Wade's case. The Court indicated an awareness of the problems of mistaken identification when it stated that a confrontation between an accused and the victim or witnesses to a crime to elicit identification evidence "is particularly riddled with innumerable dangers and variable factors which might seriously, even crucially, derogate from a fair trial" (388 U.S. 228). It cited some examples of gross abuse: "In a Canadian case . . . the defendant had been picked out of a lineup of six men, of which he was the only Oriental. In other cases, a black-haired suspect was placed among a group of light-haired persons, tall suspects have been made to stand with short nonsuspects, and, in a case where the perpetrator of the crime was known to be a youth, a suspect under twenty was placed in a lineup with five other persons, all of whom were forty or over" (388 U.S. 232).

The Court wound up by recognizing that a pretrial lineup (or showup) is a critical stage of a criminal proceeding at which the suspect is entitled to have the aid of counsel. The purpose of requiring counsel is to have someone present who would prevent unfairness in the composition of the lineup. The presence of counsel reduces the chances of suggestiveness in police conduct at the lineup. Further, if the witness identifies the wrong man, counsel will know and this cannot be kept secret at future hearings and at any future trial.

If the police have held a lineup without counsel, any subsequent in-court identification must be preceded by a hearing (out of the presence of the jury) at which the prosecution must clearly show that the in-court identification has a basis independent of the illegal lineup. Thus, for example, if the prosecution could show that the witness and the suspect had known each other for years, this would constitute evidence that the in-court identification had an independent basis.

In Wade's case, the Court sent the case back to the trial court for a hearing to determine whether the in-court identifications had an independent basis. If the trial court was convinced of the independent basis, then the conviction would be reinstated. Otherwise, a new trial would take place in which the jury would not be allowed to hear the bank employees' courtroom identifications.

Gilbert v. California was a companion to the Wade case. Jesse James Gilbert was convicted in the Superior Court of California of the armed robbery of a savings and loan and of the murder of a police officer who entered during the course of the robbery. Prior to his trial, the police had required Gilbert to participate in a lineup conducted without notice of his counsel sixteen days after indictment and after appointment of counsel. At his trial the court admitted in evidence the in-court identifications of the accused by witnesses who had observed him at the lineup. He was convicted of armed robbery and murder and was sentenced to death.

The Supreme Court of California affirmed Gilbert's conviction and his case was next considered by the United States Supreme Court. The Court applied the Wade decision to this state prosecution. Specifically, it said that it was an error to admit the in-court identifications without first determining that they were not tainted by the illegal lineup but were of independent origin. Gilbert's case was slightly different from Wade's, however, in one important way. In the Wade case the prosecution had not yet tried to introduce the evidence of the pretrial lineup, and the Court ordered that the prosecution must show an independent basis before allowing its introduction. Depending upon the ability of the prosecution to show this, the trial judge could decide whether Wade got a new trial or not. In the Gilbert case the prosecution had already introduced the evidence of the pretrial lineup, and thus the Court decided to automatically grant Gilbert a new trial. The Court essentially decided that whenever the prosecution is so unfair as to introduce a tainted lineup into a trial, they will not be allowed a later opportunity to show that the testimony had an independent source. This was necessary, the Court thought, to ensure that law enforcement authorities will respect an accused person's constitutional right to the presence of an attorney at the critical lineup.

The third case was *Stovall v. Denno*. An assailant had entered the home of a New York doctor and fatally stabbed him. The doctor's wife was also stabbed eleven times and required major surgery to save her life. Two days later a black suspect was brought to the victim's hospital room where he, the only black in the room, was handcuffed to one of the officers and was directed to say a few words for voice identification. The victim identified Theodore Stovall from her hospital bed. At his trial the doctor's wife made an in-court identification and also testified to the hospital identification. Theodore Stovall was convicted and sentenced to death.

The Supreme Court held that the principles of the Wade and Gilbert cases would not be applied retroactively. Thus, these principles would only apply after June 12, 1967, the date when the three decisions were announced. But the Court also commented upon the identification procedure used by the police in the Stovall case, noting that a showup is inherently suggestive since the witness has basically only one choice. But the Court found that this particular showup was absolutely imperative because of the specific circumstances. The Court held that the showing up was suggestive, but not unnecessarily so.

The Court, in reviewing the practice of showing a single suspect for purposes of identification, agreed that the showup procedure was not a good one, but concluded that "a claimed violation of due process of law in the conduct of a confrontation depends on the totality of the circumstances surrounding it" (p. 302). Because the witness in the Stovall case was critically ill, showing Stovall under these circumstances was imperative. Although the jail was near the hospital, taking the witness to a police station lineup was out of the question. Bringing Stovall to the hospital room was the only feasible procedure.

In sum, in *Stovall*, the Court said that any *unnecessarily* suggestive procedures that are conducive to irreparable misidentification deny due process. It recognized, however, that some circumstances may make suggestive procedures necessary. The due process test was made applicable to any pretrial identification procedure, either before or after June 12, 1967.

Thus, in 1967, the trilogy of Supreme Court cases afforded some safeguards against mistaken identifications:

(1) They required the presence of counsel at all pretrial lineups and showups taking place after June 12, 1967.
(2) Even if counsel is present, the identification procedure may not be so unnecessarily suggestive as to be conducive to a mistaken identification. Otherwise, there is a violation of due process.
(3) If these safeguards are violated, various sanctions will be imposed.

Through these cases, the Supreme Court exhibited an awareness of the possible weaknesses of any identification obtained without defense counsel present and acknowledged that a suggestive pretrial confrontation could taint any subsequent identifications. However, it allowed the prosecution to introduce evidence if it could be demonstrated that the identification was accurate.

One year after the Wade, Gilbert, and Stovall decisions, the Court heard *Simmons v. United States* (1968). In this case the Court said that an identification obtained from a photographic spread, viewed by the witness the day following the robbery but prior to the apprehension of the accused, did not violate a due process right. Here the due process test was worded slightly differently. In the Stovall case any confrontation that is "so unnecessarily suggestive and conducive to irreparable mistaken identification" is a violation of due process. In the Simmons case a violation of due process would be found if the identification procedure was "so impermissibly suggestive as to give rise to a very substantial likelihood of irreparable mistaken identification." Although worded differently, the test was, the Court felt, the same. At that time the Court discussed the need for prompt identification procedures in certain situations, observing that such procedures are a protection for a suspect whose innocence is thereby established. The defendant, Simmons, was not helped much by this decision, for the Court found that the facts indicated little likelihood that the wrong man had been identified, and therefore due process had not been violated.

In 1972 the court heard *Kirby v. Illinois*. Thomas Kirby was arrested along with a companion and brought to a police station. The police found certain items among their possessions and learned that some of them had been stolen in a recent robbery. The robbery victim was brought to the police station and immediately identified Kirby and his companion as the robbers. No attorney was present when the identification was made. Several weeks later both were indicted for robbery. At their trial in an Illinois state court, they were identified by the robbery victim. Both were convicted, and when the case reached the Supreme Court, the conviction was affirmed.

This was the beginning of the gradual dismantling of the constitutional safeguards that had been provided by the Wade, Gilbert, and Stovall cases. In the Kirby case the court held that the right to counsel was applicable only after "adversary judicial criminal proceedings" have begun. In other words, the right applies only after the suspect has been indicted. The result: the police now often delay formal charges until after the identification has been made (*Time*, April 1, 1973).

The same year as the Kirby case, the Court heard *Neil v. Biggers* (1972). In this case a woman was confronted by her attacker in her dimly lit kitchen, was taken to a moonlit area, and raped. Biggers was convicted in a Tennessee court of rape, on evidence consisting in part of the victim's visual and voice identification of the defendant at a police station showup held seven months after the crime. The victim in this case claimed to have gotten a very good look at her assailant, first indoors and then under a full moon outdoors, and to have no doubt at all about her identification. The Supreme Court held that based upon the totality of the circumstances, the identification was reliable despite the suggestive procedure; thus, due process was not violated.

The Court found the identification to be reliable after examining five factors: the witness's opportunity to observe the defendant; the witness's degree of attention; the accuracy of the witness at the confrontation; the certainty of the witness at the confrontation; and the time lapse between the crime and the confrontation. The Court agreed that the confrontation was suggestive, that no circumstance such as the need for a prompt identification justified it, but still decided that the identification testimony was admissible. It placed almost exclusive emphasis on the reliability of the identification and retreated from the right to due process afforded by the earlier cases.

This new trend culminated in the case of *Manson v. Brathwaite*

(1977). Nowell Brathwaite was convicted of possession and sale of heroin in a Connecticut court under these circumstances: Jimmy Glover, a black, full-time trooper of the Connecticut State Police, purchased heroin from a seller through the open doorway of an apartment while standing for two or three minutes within two feet of the seller in a hallway. A few minutes later Glover described the seller to another police officer as being "a colored man, approximately five feet eleven inches tall, dark complexion, black hair, short Afro style, and having high cheekbones and a heavy build." The other police officer, suspecting from the description that Brathwaite might be the seller, left a police photograph of Brathwaite with Glover, who viewed it two days later and identified it as the picture of the seller.

The defendant appealed, arguing that the evidence as to the photograph should have been excluded from the trial, regardless of reliability, because the examination of the single photograph was unnecessary and suggestive, and that the identification was unreliable. The Supreme Court disagreed. It stated that reliability is the linchpin in determining the admissibility of identification testimony for all confrontations, before or after 1967. The Court felt that the factors to be weighed against the corrupting effect of the suggestive procedure in assessing reliability were set out in the Biggers case, and included the witness's opportunity to view the criminal at the time of the crime, the witness's degree of attention, the accuracy of his prior description of the criminal, the level of certainty demonstrated at the confrontation, and the time between the crime and the confrontation. When the Court examined the "totality of the circumstances" in this case, it did not find "a very substantial likelihood of irreparable misidentification." Glover was not a casual observer, the Court noted, but a trained police officer. He had ample opportunity to view the suspect, he accurately described him, he positively identified Brathwaite's photograph as that of the suspect, and he made the photographic identification only two days after the crime.

Thus, although the Supreme Court once provided some constitutional safeguards to help protect against faulty convictions, it later dismantled this protection. The court began with an emphasis upon due process and held that the identification procedures should be void of suggestive influences. But it ended by saying that the totality of the circumstances must be taken into account, and placed particular emphasis on the reliability of the identification itself rather than the procedures used to obtain it. (See Sobel 1972, 1976, for a more detailed analysis of these cases.)

Woocher (1977) has argued that the safeguards imposed by the Supreme Court have offered little protection in practice against wrongful conviction of the innocent due to mistaken identification. The decision in the Kirby case was particularly powerful in rendering its predecessors meaningless because the court decided that the right to counsel applied only after the suspect had been indicted. It reached this conclusion despite the fact that in cases in which there is no evidence other than an eyewitness identification, the police would need to have a lineup or showup in order to justify bringing formal charges against a suspect. This is the time at which it is most crucial for counsel to be present, and the Kirby decision removes this protection. Furthermore, if the police wish to hold a lineup without the presence of defense counsel, they may delay formal charges until after the lineup. Because of these problems, Woocher has argued that other safeguards are needed to reduce the potential for conviction of the innocent on the basis of a mistaken identification.

What measures can be taken? Four possibilities have been suggested by Woocher (1977):

(1) Exclude unreliable eyewitness evidence.
(2) Prohibit convictions based solely on eyewitness identification evidence, that is, required corroborating evidence.
(3) Insist that cautionary instructions be given to jurors.
(4) Present expert psychological testimony on the unreliability of eyewitness identification.

Unreliable Eyewitness Evidence

One possible solution is to exclude identification testimony whenever it is so unreliable as to be likely to cause unfair prejudice, confuse the issues, or mislead the jury. For example, if the witness has unusually poor eyesight or claims to have observed the assailant when it was pitch-black outside, or if he saw the assailant from some extraordinarily far distance, the testimony might be excluded outright by the judge. This solution has at least two problems.

First, there would be cases in which a defendant who was actually guilty would not be convicted if the eyewitness testimony was excluded. Even if a witness sees an assailant from some extraordinarily far distance, there is some probability that an accurate identification can be made, although it is smaller than if the assailant were closer to the witness. A jury could decide that it had faith in such an identification, despite the large distance, and the jury's decision might be a reasonable one; even difficult identifications are sometimes accurate. In other cases, there is evidence in addition to the difficult eyewitness identification which links the defendant to the crime. These two pieces together could lead a jury to convict, and this might be reasonable. Excluding all eyewitness evidence that might be deemed unreliable would certainly cause some decrease in the number of justified convictions.

A second problem is the question of who is going to decide whether an identification is so unreliable that it should be excluded. Even experienced judges would have difficulty carrying this burden. Should one jury do it while another decides the case? Probably not, in light of the lack of skepticism with which the jury typically receives eyewitness testimony. A jury should probably hear all information necessary to reach a proper decision and judge its adequacy for themselves.

Corroborating Evidence

A second solution is to prohibit convictions based solely upon eyewitness identification evidence — that is, to require some piece of corroborating evidence. Thus, the law might require, in addition to eyewitness testimony, some information such as the fact that the victim's wallet was found in the apartment of the defendant, or that the victim's fingerprint was found in the trunk of the defendant's car. Without this additional evidence, the eyewitness identification would not be allowed to be brought into trial.

But this solution runs into some of the same problems as the previous one. A corroboration requirement removes the decision from the hands of the jury, rather than presenting the case to the jury and allowing the jury to consider all the relevant evidence. Furthermore, someone would have the tough job of deciding what constitutes adequate corroboration. And finally, this solution would present a problem for a case in which an identification was highly reliable (for example, the victim and defendant had known each other for years), but no corroborating evidence was available. The guilty would go free.

Instructions to the Jury

To minimize the danger of a faulty conviction, the court could give special cautionary instructions to the jury in cases in which eyewitness identification testimony is introduced. This was done in a case that occurred in 1972 in Washington, D.C. (*United States v. Telfaire*). The original Telfaire instruction has been modified many times, quite recently by a special committee of the Michigan State Bar Association (1977). These instructions were designed to focus the jury's attention on the identification issue by stressing several of the factors affecting witness perception and memory that the jury should consider.

(1) One of the questions in this case is the identification of the defendant as the one who committed the crime. The prosecution has the burden of proving beyond a reasonable doubt, not only that the crime was committed, but that the defendant was the person who committed it.

(2) In considering whether the prosecution has proved beyond a reasonable doubt that the defendant is the person who committed the offense, you should consider the following:

(3) The witness's opportunity to observe the criminal acts and the person committing them, including the length of time available for observing; whether the witness had occasion to see or know the defendant before the incident; the distance between the various parties; the light or lack of light at the time; the witness's state of mind at the time of the offense; and other circumstances affecting the witness's opportunity to observe the person committing the offense.

(4) The identification made by the witness after the offense must be the product of his own memory. You may take into consideration any subsequent identification, the circumstances surrounding the identification, the certainty or lack of certainty expressed by the witness, the state of mind of the witness at the time, and other circumstances bearing on the reliability of the identification. You may also consider the length of time that elapsed between the occurrence of the crime and the time the witness saw the defendant as a factor bearing on the reliability of the identification.

(5) [You may take into account any occasions on which the witness failed to make an identification of defendant or made an identification that was inconsistent with his identification at trial, and any other circumstances which you find affect the identification.][1]

USE NOTE: 1. Use (5) only when there is supporting evidence.

These instructions provide some protection and are certainly a step in the right direction. But by themselves the instructions do not supply the jury with any information that it can use in the task of evaluating the reliability of any particular eyewitness account. Judges cannot be asked to go further, however, for two reasons. First, they are not experts on the subject of the capacity of eyewitnesses, and second, they might be forced into commenting upon the evidence itself, something that judges are not supposed to do.

An additional problem with this solution is that often jurors do not give careful consideration to the instructions given them by judges. Judges' instructions tend to be long and tedious and much of the research on them indicates that they are not adequately comprehended (Charrow and Charrow 1978; Sales et al. 1978). An instruction on eyewitness identification would be embedded in a long, difficult list and, even if written in simple language, would not receive the careful attention that it deserves.

It is of interest that the judicial establishment of Great Britain recently squarely confronted this problem. Astonished by the recent pardons of two individuals who had both, independently, been convicted on the basis of erroneous identification, the Home Secretary appointed a committee to investigate this area of criminal law and police procedure, and the committee made the following recommendations (Devlin 1976, pp. 149-150):

> We do, however, wish to ensure that in ordinary cases prosecutions are not brought on eyewitness evidence only and that, if brought, they will fail. We think they ought to fail, since in our opinion it is only in exceptional cases that identification evidence is by itself sufficiently reliable to exclude a reasonable doubt about guilt. We recommend that the trial judge should be required by statute
>   a. to direct the jury that it is not safe to convict upon eyewitness evidence unless the circumstances of the identification are exceptional or the eyewitness evidence is supported by substantial evidence of another sort; and
>   b. to indicate to the jury the circumstances, if any, which they might regard as exceptional and the evidence, if any, which they might regard as supporting the identification; and
>   c. if he is unable to indicate either such circumstances or such evidence, to direct the jury to return a verdict of not guilty.

The Devlin recommendation is, in a sense, a combination. It recommends that the trial judge give a special instruction to the jury, but in addition, it recommends that convictions based solely upon eyewitness testimony not be allowed unless that testimony is exceptional.

Expert Psychological Testimony

What shall be done to protect against the danger of a mistaken identification? The Supreme Court decisions are concerned only with the properness of a pretrial confrontation, and do not address inherent unreliability in eyewitness testimony itself. Outright exclusion of unreliable testimony and requirement of corroboration are not ideal solutions because they take the decision out of the hands of the jury and might prevent the conviction of many who are truly guilty. Special jury instructions, although a step in the right direction, do not go far enough. They offer no guidance to the jurors on how to evaluate eyewitness testimony.

Another solution would be to allow the judge and especially the jury to hear an expert witness present psychological testimony about the factors that affect the reliability of eyewitness accounts. The psychologist could describe the studies that have been conducted on people's ability to perceive and recall complex events, and report the results. Factors that may have affected the accuracy of the particular identification in the case at hand could be related to the jury. In this way the jurors would have enough information with which to evaluate the identification evidence fully and properly. Such expert testimony, although relatively new, has already been allowed in numerous states around the country.

Recall from chapter 4 the case of Aaron Lewis, who was arrested after leaving a grocery store carrying bottles of wine and beer for which he had allegedly not paid. The arrest occurred after a clerk in a small grocery store in the state of Washington called the police and stated that the man leaving was the same man who robbed him at knifepoint seven weeks earlier. The police picked up the defendant a few blocks from the store and arrested him. Lewis denied having committed the armed robbery, arguing that the clerk had made a mistaken identification. The only piece of evidence against the defendant offered at his trial for armed robbery was the word of a single eyewitness. The clerk may have been making a correct identification, but then again he may have been wrong.

At the trial the defense counsel attempted to introduce the testimony of a psychologist for two reasons: to discuss the nature of human memory and the mental processes involved in an eyewitness identification, and to discuss those factors known to influence the accuracy of an identification that were present in the criminal incident for which the defendant was being tried. The first major factor was a long retention interval — approximately seven weeks had passed between the incident and the subsequent identification. The second major factor was unconscious transference — the defendant claimed he had been in the grocery store a number of times when the clerk was on duty, and the clerk must have confused him with the robber. The psychologist described some of the laboratory research that had been conducted on both the retention interval and the phenomenon of unconscious transference.

The deputy prosecutor argued against permitting the testimony of a psychologist, claiming that it would be an invasion of the province of the jurors. It is the jurors, he argued, who have the responsibility of deciding what weight to give to the eyewitness testimony. Nevertheless, the Superior Court judge admitted the testimony. The jury deliberated only two hours before reaching a verdict of guilty. They apparently decided that the eyewitness had not made a mistake. One juror was later interviewed, and when asked "What did you think about the eyewitness testimony?" his response went something like this: "We believe that the passage of time can have a serious effect on a person's memory. We believe that an unconscious transference can sometimes take place. And yet . . . we felt that the experience of a subject in a psychology experiment and the experience of a person with a knife at his throat . . . they just aren't the same!"

In another case, on June 3, 1977, a Specialist Four, United States Army, Fort Seward, Georgia, was assaulted. According to the victim's testimony before an investigation, the incident began early in the morning, at approximately 5:00 a.m. The victim, who had gone to sleep about 3:30, woke up when he was hit in the mouth. He brushed his hand against his mouth and saw that he was bleeding. "I then looked up and saw this guy holding a pistol pointed at my head. I then told him 'Don't shoot, I'll do anything you say!' " The assailant told him to take off his pants, to get onto the bed, to roll over. Then, the culprit tried to insert his pistol into the victim's rectum. A struggle and considerable yelling followed, and finally, the victim managed to grab the pistol and run outside of the building.

On the night of the incident, the victim signed a statement claiming that "I never saw this guy before, but I feel I could identify him if I saw him again." He went on to describe his assailant as 5'11" to 6' tall, medium build, dark complexion, with a me-dium-sized Afro. The victim appeared to be intoxicated. "There wasn't anything outstanding I remember except he sure looked ugly to me."

On June 9 the victim attended a lineup. At this time he identi-fied Paul Powers as his assailant. One day later the victim was in-volved in an automobile accident with a sergeant, Sam Franklin, and at this time he claimed to recognize Franklin as his assailant. The victim's passenger at the time of the accident confirmed that Franklin had been in the barracks on the morning of June 3. The victim did not report this to the authorities because he had heard that Franklin had already been picked up. A lineup occurred on June 14 containing both Franklin and Powers, and this time the victim picked Franklin.

The following September, at Franklin's court-martial, defense counsel attempted to introduce the testimony of a psychologist to discuss the mental process involved in an eyewitness identification and some of the factors known to influence the accuracy of an identification that were present in the criminal incident at hand. The first major factor was cross-racial identification: the witness was white and the defendant was black. The second factor was the stress experienced by the victim. Third, there was the phe-nomenon of weapon focus. Fourth, the victim, by his own admis-sion, had been drinking prior to the incident. These factors, when taken alone and especially in combination, would tend to reduce a person's perceptual abilities and memory. Finally, the phenomenon of unconscious transference was described to the jury. When the victim saw Franklin at the time of the automobile accident, he may have looked familiar. The familiarity could have been due to a chance encounter someplace on the military base, as the two men often inhabited the same places. The famil-iarity that the victim experienced could have been incorrectly re-lated back to the incident, causing the victim to believe that it was Franklin who had committed the assault.

Sam Franklin was acquitted. While it is difficult to know pre-cisely the reasons for any single jury verdict, it is likely in this case that the jury came to believe that the identification was suffi-ciently difficult that they could not convict beyond a reasonable doubt.

These two cases indicate what sorts of factors might be de-scribed to a jury, and they also show that some juries will hear this expert testimony and acquit the defendant while others will convict. In nearly all cases in which psychological expert testimony is offered, the procedure is relatively simple. The witness, in describing the incident and subsequent identification, enumerates many of the factors that were present in the case. The expert then explains how those factors operate to affect the reliability of the identification. Ideally, the psychologist relates the relevant research findings to the corresponding elements of the case. Thus, stress, or postevent information, or cross-racial identification is related when it is relevant to the case at hand.

Legal Cases and Issues

The basic purpose of any evidence, including the testimony of a psychologist, is to facilitate the acquisition of knowledge by the jury, or trier of fact, thus enabling it to reach a final determination. The system of evidence used in American courts rests on two axioms: only facts having rational probative or evidential value are admissible, and all facts having such value are admissible unless some specific policy forbids.

The trial judge has the broad discretion to decide whether a particular piece of evidence, including expert testimony, has sufficient probative value. The judge must weigh the value against the prejudicial effects that the evidence might have and make a decision as to its admissibility in a particular case. The judge is the one to decide whether the jury can receive appreciable help from the expert testimony of a psychologist.

These principles were re-enunciated in a leading appellate decision on the subject of admissibility of expert psychological testimony, *United States v. Amaral* (1973). The defendant, Manuel P. Amaral, was charged in 1973 with the robbery of two national banks. Later that year, at Amaral's trial, defense counsel moved to introduce the testimony of a psychologist in regard to the effect of stress on perception and, more generally, to the unreliability of eyewitness identification. The trial court refused to admit the testimony on the grounds that "it would not be appropriate to take from the jury their own determination as to what weight or effect to give to the evidence of the eyewitness and identifying witnesses and to have that determination put before them on the basis of the expert witness testimony as proffered" (p. 1153). Amaral was found guilty and appealed his conviction on several grounds, one of which was the refusal of the trial court to admit the expert testimony.

The U.S. Court of Appeals for the Ninth Circuit held that the court did not err in excluding the testimony. The appeals court noted that defense counsel had uncovered no confusion or uncertainty as to identity in any of the various witnesses. And, while it acknowledged that stress might affect perception, it noted that not all the witnesses were under similar conditions of stress. One witness saw the robber as he sat in his car blocking the exit from the bank parking lot, another saw him from the safety of her house as he returned from robbing the bank, and another saw him as he entered the bank and approached the teller. Further, this court felt that defense counsel could use cross-examination to inquire into the witness's capacity and opportunity for observation, his attention and interest, and his distraction or division of attention. Amaral stood convicted.

The Amaral decision is important in that it reiterates the general principles regarding expert testimony:

(1) the witness must be a qualified expert;
(2) the testimony must concern a proper subject matter;
(3) the testimony must be in accordance with a generally accepted explanatory theory;
(4) the probative value of the testimony must outweigh its prejudicial effect.

Additionally, the court noted that the trial judge has broad discretion in the admission of testimony. In the Amaral case the judge simply exercised proper discretion when he excluded the testimony.

In his analysis of the Amaral decision Woocher (1977) remarks that the appellate court failed in one important way: it did not establish any guidelines to aid the trial judge in exercising discretion. How is the trial judge to decide whether the expert witness is truly qualified, or whether the testimony concerns a proper subject matter, or whether it conforms to a generally accepted explanatory theory? What standards should the judge use to weigh its probative value against its potentially prejudicial effects? Woocher offers some answers to all of these questions.

In terms of the first criterion, namely, that the expert be qualified, the judge can examine the evidence for the knowledge, experience, training, or education of the proffered expert. In addition to holding an advanced degree in the general field of experimental psychology, an expert should have conducted research and published in that area.

Deciding whether the testimony is a proper subject matter for expert testimony has been a more troublesome task. To be proper, it must be beyond the knowledge and experience of the average layperson. Of course many jury members have some commonsense knowledge of the factors that may cause mistakes in identification. Most people, for example, know that the longer the period of time between an incident and one's recollection, the worse the memory. But there is ample evidence that jurors lack complete knowledge. In many instances, their intuitions about the reliability of eyewitness accounts are unsupported by scientific research—for example, a substantial percentage of people are not fully informed about the problems of a cross-racial identification. In addition to being beyond the common knowledge of the jury, expert testimony, to be proper, should not invade the province of the jury. Those who have argued that it does invade the jury's province are saying, in essence, that the expert testimony relates to the credibility of another witness, and it is the jury that is to make determinations about a witness's credibility. However, the expert testimony that is being proposed does not involve an opinion on the credibility of any particular witness's testimony. The psychologist does not say whether he believes a particular piece of testimony to be accurate or not. Rather, the expert's task is to review the relevant psychological findings and enumerate the various factors affecting the reliability of eyewitness accounts. The psychologist is speaking about the powers of observation and recollection of the typical witness. The jury then decides what weight to give both the eyewitness testimony and the expert testimony.

The third criterion is that the expert testimony should conform to a generally accepted explanatory theory. This test has been used in determining the admissibility of such techniques and devices as the polygraph, voiceprints, breathalyzers, and "truth serum." However, it has not typically been applied to the testimony of medical and psychiatric experts. This distinction led Woocher to conclude that the requirement of a "generally accepted explanatory theory" has been used selectively. It has been used in cases in which the jury is likely to mistakenly regard a particular device, such as the polygraph, as being able to magically reveal the truth. Only if the scientific community accepts and agrees about the device will the jury be allowed to hear about it. Using this standard, there has been reasonable agreement about, say, the breathalyzer, but general controversy surrounding the polygraph. The psychologist, however, is not testifying about magical devices but is simply discussing the extensive research that has been conducted on eyewitness ability. This testimony more properly belongs in the category with medical and psychiatric testimony, where the "generally accepted explanatory theory" criterion for admissibility has not been an issue.

The fourth criterion is that the probative value of the testimony must outweigh its prejudicial effects. Woocher's analysis of this criterion goes something like this: Any testimony has probative value if it is important to the determination of guilt or innocence. When eyewitness identification plays a major role in a case, there is some danger of convicting the wrong person, and thus the eyewitness's testimony and psychologist's testimony are certainly probative. If the expert testimony relates to the factors in the case being tried, it is probative. Since jurors rarely regard eyewitness testimony with any skepticism, the expert testimony will increase the likelihood of this happening. This is its value. In terms of its being prejudicial, there is always the possibility that scientific evidence will bias or mislead the jury. Yet the judge can take steps to minimize this possibility. A caution to the jurors that the expert testimony forms only one piece of the evidence that they should consider, and an insistence that the expert's statements be based on solid scientific data and cover only those studies bearing on the case will minimize any prejudicial effects that the testimony might have.

After a careful analysis of the four criteria that the court in the Amaral decision felt must be met for any expert testimony to be admissible, Woocher has concluded that expert testimony on the credibility of eyewitness identification satisfies this standard.

After the federal courts decided the Amaral case, they confronted the issue again, one year later. *United States v. Brown* (1974) and *United States v. Nobles* (1975) arose out of a robbery on February 6, 1973, of the Crocker National Bank in Los Angeles. Three men were brought to trial later in 1973, two of whom were Tommie Brown and Robert Nobles. The prosecution argued that Brown had jumped behind the tellers' windows and moved down the line of cages collecting money from the cash drawers, while the other robbers guarded the customers and personnel from various positions. Eyewitness identification constituted part of the evidence against both Brown and Nobles. An attempt was made to introduce testimony on the weaknesses of eyewitness identification, but the trial court refused to admit the testimony, reasoning that such evidence would invade the province of the jury, that the time needed to hear the testimony would outweigh its probative value, and that the defense counsels did not adequately argue why such testimony should be admitted. The appellate court, which had just recently decided the Amaral case, concluded that the trial judge had not made an error by his decision to refuse admission. The Supreme Court commented on the issue of psychological testimony, saying, "We in turn cannot conclude that the trial court was in error" (pp. 150-151).

People v. Johnson (1974) is one of the earliest state cases to deal with this issue. The crime: murder, robbery, and assault with a deadly weapon. According to prosecution evidence, three men, including Welvie Johnson, Jr., entered a liquor store in a small town in California. During the robbery the proprietor was fatally shot, a customer was wounded, and $2,000 in paper money was taken. At the trial there was no physical evidence to identify Johnson but there was an eyewitness identification. The defense counsel attempted to introduce the expert testimony of a doctor of psychology on the ability of witnesses to accurately perceive, recall, and relate, and on the effects of excitement and fear on perception and recollection. The trial court refused to admit this testimony, declaring in effect that the testimony would take over the jury's task of determining the weight and credibility of the witness's testimony. The appellate court ruled that the trial judge was well within the range of his discretion. Since the Johnson decision, other California courts of appeal have upheld the discretion of the trial court to refuse to admit testimony of a psychological expert because it would trespass on the jury's domain. Similarly, appellate courts in other states, such as New York and Washington, have applied the same reasoning, affirming a trial judge's refusal to allow such an expert to threaten the jury's function.

The same issue has also been considered recently by the higher court in Canada. The case of *Regina v. Audy* (1977) is an exam-

ple. The charges arose out of a bank robbery in Ottawa that occurred in October 1974. During the robbery a man named Ga-
briel Guerin was forcibly seized by the robbers as they were leaving the bank. He was taken as a hostage, but released a few blocks
away from the bank. Guerin, along with a couple of other people,
was a witness at Audy's trial.

The defense sought to introduce the testimony of a psychologist
to speak generally about identification, about the ability of an
eyewitness to perceive and recall in a stress situation, and about
the particular lineups and photospreads from the case being
tried. The trial judge refused to admit the testimony. He had
many reasons: the testimony would add little to what laypersons
already know; it was fraught with difficulties; the expert would
be cautioning the jury on the dangers of identification evidence,
a task that is traditionally reserved for the trial judge. The court
feared that science was wishing to assume the role of the jury.

Audy was convicted of armed robbery and abduction, and his
conviction was affirmed by the higher court, which agreed with
the opinion of the trial judge. But this court seemed to be indicating that such expert testimony might, under certain circumstances, be admissible. "In our view of the facts of this case, the
ruling of the trial judge was correct. There were no facts elicited
on cross-examination or otherwise which made it necessary for
the jury to be assisted, in arriving at its verdict, by the expert evidence tendered. We are not to be taken as saying that there cannot be a case in which evidence of this kind would be admissible.
We simply hold that this was not such a case" (p. 236).

In all of these cases the Supreme Court, the state appellate
courts, or other higher courts have decided that the judge has the
broad discretion to refuse expert testimony. Most trial judges
have done so on the grounds that it invades the province of the
jury, although occasionally other reasons are given. As Woocher
has shown, one can reasonably argue that this basis for refusing
to admit expert testimony is without merit.

It may, at first glance, seem peculiar that there are so few cases
in this area, and that they are all decided in the same direction
(namely, the trial judge refuses the testimony and the higher
court agrees). The reason for this is that defendants in general
only appeal their cases on this issue when the expert testimony has
been excluded and the defendant has been convicted. If the trial
judge admits the expert testimony and the defendant is convicted

anyhow, no basis exists for an appeal on this issue. If the defendant is found not guilty, there is similarly no appeal. Thus the higher courts have always been handed cases in which the testimony has been excluded and the defendant convicted. This tends to bias the posture of reported cases on the issue of expert psychological testimony because higher courts will rarely reverse the trial judge's exercise of discretion.

Problems with the Expert Testimony

Wells (1978) has suggested that expert psychological testimony may involve a faulty supposition. It assumes that judges and jurors currently believe that witnesses are less fallible than they really are. Yet, according to Wells, there is no empirical evidence to support the assumption that jurors and judges are overbelieving of witnesses. Perhaps the psychologists' expert testimony will create jurors and judges who are *less* believing of witnesses than they should be.

In response to this criticism it can be argued that the issue should not be whether the triers of fact are more or less believing of eyewitnesses than they should be. Rather, the issue is whether triers of fact understand how various environmental and internal factors operate to affect the perception and memory of witnesses. Here there is evidence that people in general do not fully understand the operation of these factors and thus could benefit from the expert testimony.

Wells also argues that any expert witness who came into court to offer an opinion about whether the eyewitness was likely to be right or wrong could be badly mistaken. He says, for example, that an expert, after examining the details of a particular case, might suggest to the court that the conditions of the lineup were so biased that the witness is quite likely to be wrong. But in an actual case, argues Wells, there are so many factors involved (lighting, exposure time, retention interval, and so on) that the probability of accuracy could be 0.95 without a biased lineup and 0.92 with a biased lineup. Biased lineups may have consistently debilitating effects, but likelihood of accuracy depends on too many factors in a given case for any semblance of reasonable estimation. Here again, Wells is right and wrong. Any psychologist who attempted to offer an exact probability for the likelihood that a witness was accurate would be going far beyond what is possible. But a psychologist can show the operation of a relevant factor, such as bias in a lineup, and can point out the usual debilitating effect without giving an opinion as to the magnitude of the effect in the case being tried.

Woocher (1977) has indicated a different kind of problem. After the defense introduces expert psychological testimony, the prosecution may find that it must deal with the problem by countering with its own expert. The prosecution's expert would attempt to impeach the qualifications of the defense psychologist or attack the analyses and emphases. The defense might counter with another expert. The battle of the experts would have only just begun. The court would then need to choose some stopping point so that the situation did not lead to one of ridiculous delay and massive confusion for the jury. Since this can be done with relative ease, the problem is not so great as to warrant a general exclusion of expert psychological testimony on eyewitness identification.

The number of mistaken identifications leading to wrongful convictions, combined with the fact that eyewitness testimony is accepted too unquestioningly by juries, presents a problem for the legal community. The Supreme Court addressed a portion of the problem when it decided to consider the issues of right to counsel and due process protection at pretrial identification. However, recent decisions indicate that the protection offered by the court against a mistaken identification is minimal. Excluding unreliable identifications, requiring corroborating evidence, and issuing cautionary instructions to the jury are three partial solutions which fail to provide an adequate answer. Allowing the jury to hear expert testimony on the factors affecting the reliability of eyewitness identification evidence appears to be a more satisfactory solution in many respects. But its merits have yet to be consistently recognized by our legal system.

The role that a psychologist might play in this situation is part of a larger issue concerning the relationship between the law and social science. At the beginning of the century, Munsterberg (1908) was arguing for more interaction between the two fields, perhaps at times in a way that was insulting to the legal profession: "It seems indeed astonishing that the work of justice is ever carried out in the courts without ever consulting the psychologist and asking him for all the aid which the modern study of suggestion can offer" (p. 194). In fact, at that time the legal profession apparently was somewhat insulted. At least this can be inferred from reading a wonderfully satirical article by Wigmore (1909) about a trial that took place on April 1, 1909. The plaintiffs were members of the bar of the Supreme Court. The defendant was Munsterberg, who had just published his soon-to-be-famous *On the Witness Stand* (1908). The plaintiffs argued that Munsterberg had made untrue and damaging assertions about them. Specifically, the plaintiffs argued that Munsterberg asserted that:

(1) Psychology had developed very precise methods of determining the accuracy of testimony and of diagnosing guilt. These methods were endorsed by psychologists as applicable to American judicial practice.
(2) These methods were superior to those in use in American courts, and by not using these methods lawyers were being grossly negligent.

The plaintiffs argued that Munsterberg's claims were untrue, that their good name had been injured, and they asked for a sum of one dollar in compensation for damage. Their case consisted of providing evidence that (1) the methods of psychology were not very precise; (2) the methods were not generally endorsed as applicable to the American judicial system; (3) the methods had not been shown to be superior to those in use (in fact they were not even available in English-language journals); and (4) the members of the legal profession had not been grossly negligent in rejecting these methods.

The defense attorney argued that his client had not intended any disrespect to the plaintiffs but wanted to stir them to a sense of their responsibilities. After the closing arguments, the judge instructed the jury to retire and consult on their verdict. The jurors whispered for only an instant, and then announced that they were agreed on a verdict without the need for further deliberation. The foreman then read the verdict: "We find for the plaintiffs, with damages of $1."

Before the jurors left the courtroom to go home, the judge took a few moments to express his personal view. He said essentially this: In no other country in the civilized world had the legal profession taken so little interest in finding out what psychology and other sciences had to offer that might contribute to the nation's judicial system.

The trial, of course, never happened. It gradually becomes evident that the article is satirical when the reader learns that the trial took place on April Fool's Day, that the suit had been entered in the Supreme Court of Wundt County (Wilhelm Wundt is widely acknowledged as the father of experimental psychology), and that a Mr. X. Perry Ment assisted with the defense. Nonetheless, the article contained many truthful elements of the legal profession's reaction to Munsterberg's book.

It has been seventy years since this "trial" took place. Now, the methods of psychology are substantially more precise, and it is reasonable to apply them to the American judicial system. Research efforts are widely published, and almost invariably in English-language journals. The legal profession seems to be paying them a good deal of attention, so times have changed. Munsterberg would have smiled.

11

An Actual Case of Murder: People v. Garcia

O N OCTOBER 12, 1977, at approximately 8:30 p.m., two men entered a liquor store in Watsonville, California (fig. 11.1). The first robber stood directly across from a young male clerk, pointed a gun at him, and demanded all of his money. The second robber stood four or five feet away with a gun pointed at an older male clerk who was standing beside the younger clerk. The first robber told the clerk, "Don't move, give me the money. Put it in a bag. Don't panic. Give me the wallets too. Give it to me anyway." When the young clerk turned to replace his wallet in his rear pocket, a shot was fired. The young clerk dove to the floor and as he looked up, the first robber was almost out the door. The second robber was still in the doorway with a smile on his face. The older clerk had been shot dead.

In early 1978 two men were tried for this murder, and I was called by the defense to testify on the psychological findings relating to the fallibilities of eyewitness identification.

Background

Within five minutes from the time that two strange men entered George's Liquor Store, a seventy-two-year-old clerk named Norman Glover was dead. An autopsy suggested that he had died from what appeared to be a .38 caliber soft-lead bullet. The angle indicated that he must have been bending over when the bullet entered his body. Bone fragments revealed that the bullet ricocheted downwards, rupturing the stomach and severing the aorta.

Figure 11.1. The liquor store in Watsonville, California, where a robbery and murder took place in October of 1977. (Photograph by Douglas Cole.)

Joseph Melville, a young clerk, witnessed the entire incident. As soon as the robbers left, he hit the alarm and a merchant patrolman, Roy Campbell, responded almost immediately. Campbell reported that Melville, who was in a state of shock, could say only "Two men, one with a mustache, two men, one with a mustache." Campbell then called the police and an ambulance and left the scene. Joseph Melville was taken to the Watsonville Police Department for an interview. Portions of a transcription of his initial statement to the police give some idea of what happened (Watsonville, California, October 13, 1977):

Q: Okay, Joe. I want you to go back to a few minutes before this thing happened tonight and tell me exactly what you can remember.

A. Before the . . .

Q. Before it ever happened. Before they came in the store.

A. I was in the middle stocking boxes at the store . . . I quit doing that at 8:20 and I took . . . I was going to take a ten minute break in the front to help Norman out with the customers and it must have been about 8:25 and I was ready to go back and stock and these two guys came in with guns.

Q. They just walked right in the store . . . ?

A. Walked right in the store with guns and pointed it at us and said, "Give us the money," and then I took the money out of the register . . .

Q. Who opened the register?

A. I did. I put the money . . . I was going to give the money and he said put it in a bag. So I stuck it in a bag and I dropped some on the floor . . . because I was going really fast and I remember him saying, "Don't panic." That caught me kind of funny. "Don't panic." Then I put it in a bag; he asked me for my wallet. I put my wallet on the counter. Gave him a five and told him that's all I had, all I had. Next minute I was putting my wallet back in my pocket. I was trying to put it back in my pocket. I heard a gun shot; I hit the floor; I saw Norman down there; I looked up and they were gone . . .

After some discussion of the guns that were used, and the number of shots that were fired, the interview turned to focus upon the description of the man whom Melville got the best look at:

Q. He was a male Mexican adult?

A. Right.

Q. How old would you say he is?

A. About thirty-five.

Q. At the very oldest how old was he?

A. 37 was the oldest I would say.

Q. And the very youngest?

A. 32.

Q. So, somewhere between 32 and 37 years.

A. Right.

Q. How tall would you say he is?

A. I say 5-7/5-8. I stood up and he came like this and I am about 6-1 so I would say 5-8.

Q. Were you standing on the same level he is?

A. No I was taller than he. The floor beneath us? yeah, yeah, right.

Q. So you are guessing about 5-8?

A. Yeah.

Q. Weight wise?

A. Kind of heavy. 175/180. About that size.

Q. Real stocky build?

A. Yeah.

Q. Okay, color of hair?
A. Black.
Q. Black or dark brown?
A. Dark, it was black.
Q. Was it straight, curly?
A. It was kind of a . . . bushy. Like mine but spread out like that. You know.
Q. How long?
A. My length, maybe a little shorter.

  . . .

Q. Okay, when you say bushy you mean . . .
A. It's hard to describe.
Q. Was it messed up or unkept?
A. It was unkept.
Q. Did you notice anything about his face?
A. Moustache.
Q. Okay, what type of moustache?
A. Like that, you know, like yours.
Q. A little like mine. Did it come below the corners of his mouth?
A. I think it did, a little bit below there.
Q. A black moustache?
A. Right.
Q. Okay, what else can you remember about his face?
A. Kind of round. Really round face. Really round face.
Q. Okay, how about this guy's teeth, now?
A. Nothing I can tell about his teeth.
Q. Did you notice any scars on his face?
A. No.
Q. Eyes? Anything unusual about the eyes? What struck you most about him?
A. The gun in his hand. He just had the gun in his hand. When he came in I thought he was joking.
Q. Okay, what was he wearing as far as a shirt or jacket?
A. He wasn't wearing a jacket.

There followed a series of questions about the clothes that the robber was wearing. And then:

Q. Okay, and what type of weapon was he carrying?
A. It was a revolver pistol. I believe it was a .38.
Q. When you say "revolver" it was like this one here?

A. Right.

Q. You believe it was a .38?

A. Yeah. When I was in the cadets here I shot .38's and it sure looked like it. Either that or .357, but I know . . .

Q. .38 caliber, right?

A. But I know darn well it wasn't a .22.

Q. Blue steel?

A. Yes. I wish I could remember what the handle looked like.

Q. How long would you say the barrel is?

A. How long is that one there?

Q. That's a two inch.

A. I'd say 4". That's my first guess.

   . . .

Q. Okay, we are going to refer to him as #1. A male Mexican adult, 32-37, about 5-8, 175/180 pounds, stocky build, black collar-length hair, unkept. Was it parted in any particular way?

A. No, I don't think it was. I don't remember but I don't think it was.

Q. A black moustache just below the corners of the mouth, round face, a short-sleeve colored shirt?

A. Right.

Q. And you believe it was a .38 caliber, blue steel, 4-inch revolver.

The interview also covered a description of the second robber, a discussion of how the money was taken, what words were exchanged, and how the police were notified.

There are some interesting things to notice about this interview. First, it might have been best for the police officer conducting the interview to begin by letting Melville tell the story in his own words. This could be followed with a controlled narrative, similar to the form used here. This would be the optimal procedure in terms of accuracy and completeness.

The controlled narrative used in this case was fair in places, but could have been improved in others. "How old would you say he is?" is about as neutral as you can be. But a few questions later the officer asked: "Real stocky build?" suggesting a terminology that the witness himself never used. Later in the interview when the officer was summarizing Melville's description, he again used the expression "stocky build," essentially suggesting that it had originated with Melville.

It is also evident from this interview that the witness is guessing in places. He guessed about the length of the barrel of the gun, and he guessed about the height of the robber. There is a reasonable chance that these guesses will become, over time, firm memories on the part of the witness. Finally, there is some evidence here for the phenomenon of weapon focus; at the very least there is ample evidence that Melville paid a good deal of attention to the gun in the hand of the robber. He was asked "What struck you most about him?" His answer: "The gun in his hand."

Together Melville and the police constructed a composite drawing of the robber who stood over the counter (fig. 11.2). On October 15, 1977, Melville went to a lineup in the jail in Santa Cruz and picked no one. On October 26 he went to the Monterey jail in Salinas for a lineup and picked no one. That same day,

Figure 11.2. Composite drawing of a suspect of the Watsonville liquor store robbery and murder. (By Tom Macris, police artist, San Jose Police Department, October 13, 1977.)

back at the Watsonville Police Department, Melville was shown a large set of black-and-white photographs, and he reported that one of them looked very similar to the robber who did all the talking. The person in that photograph was José Garcia. Actually, there had been two photos of Garcia in the set. Melville passed over the first and picked out the second. Later that week the officers showed Melville the same photographs again, and Melville picked the same one of Garcia. On October 31 Melville was shown six color photographs. He thumbed through them and came to Garcia's. He placed it aside and continued looking at the remaining photos, then picked up Garcia's picture and stated, "This is the guy. I wouldn't forget the face."

On November 3 Melville was taken to a lineup in Oakland where he picked a man out of the lineup because his voice sounded like the robber. This man was an Oakland police officer. Later in the week officers met with Melville again, at which time he asked to see the six color photographs once more. He wanted to see which was a stronger inclination—the man he picked out of the lineup because of his voice or the man he picked from the photographs because of his looks. He decided the photograph was correct.

José Garcia was arrested for robbery, murder, and use of a firearm in the commission of a felony. His booking sheet on November 11, 1977, shows that he was born in 1948, was 5'10" tall, and weighed 242 pounds. Garcia, who has a heavy Spanish accent, was known to be a member of the Nuestra Familia, a Mexican-American prison gang in California; he has a tattoo of Fresno Neustra Familia in large letters on his back. Tattoos line both arms; on the left arm there are thick dark blue lines and flowers, a large pirate face with long Fu Manchu mustache; on the right arm from the elbow to the armpit is a woman in a bathing suit, Because of a sawblade accident, Garcia's second, third, and fourth fingers on the left hand are permanently bent downward at the second knuckle area. The word "Fresno" with a cross below it is tattooed just above his thumb joint.

A preliminary examination was held for Garcia on November 29. Melville was the key witness (from transcript, Santa Cruz, California):

Q. And then what happened after they entered the store?
A. They demanded—one guy went to the cigar cabinet in the

corner here, and the other one was right in front of me . . .

Q. What happened next?

A. Number one demanded the money.

Q. How far were you from him at that time?

A. Approximately two feet.

Q. What part of his body were you able to see?

A. Waist up.

Q. With what hand?

A. I can't say for sure, but I think it was his right hand, also. The gun hand. He grabbed it with the same hand he had the gun in, but I am not sure because I never did see his left hand.

Q. Why didn't you see his left hand?

A. I never noticed it at all. It might have been in his pocket or something. I am not sure.

Melville went on to recount the shooting, his hitting the alarm button, the arrival of the police, his interview at the police station, the making of the composite, the police attempt to hypnotize him in order to improve his recollection, his appearances at various lineups, and so on. And finally:

Q. Is the individual, either one of the two persons who entered the store on the night of October 12, 1977, at approximately 8:30 p.m., here present in the court?

A. Yes, the defendant.

Q. Would you point the person out for purposes of the record.

A. (Indicating)

THE COURT: What is he wearing? Where is he seated?

THE WITNESS: Orange jumpsuit on the left side.

THE COURT: Orange jumpsuit and left side?

THE WITNESS: Of the counter.

THE COURT: Let the record show the witness has pointed to and identified the defendant Garcia.

Before the preliminary hearing, Garcia's defense attorneys were asking: "If it was really Garcia, why didn't Melville mention the deformed left hand? Why didn't he mention the heavy Spanish accent?" Melville's preliminary hearing testimony attempted to deal with the first apparent contradiction—he claimed he never saw the suspect's left hand. He had the suspect holding a gun in his right hand and grabbing the bag of money at the same time. The second apparent contradiction was never addressed at all.

Q. Do you recall what that individual said?
A. "Don't move. Hand it over."
   . . .
Q. Were you able to see the individual's hand at that time?
A. Just the gun hand.
Q. What did you see in his hands, if anything?
A. The revolver.
   . . .
Q. After he said, "Don't move. Hand it over," what did you do next?
A. I reached into the register, took the money out, and was going to hand it to him. He told me to put it in a bag.
   . . .
Q. And after you removed the money, what happened then?
A. He asked for the wallet.
Q. What did you do with the money after you removed it from the cash register?
A. I handed it to him, and he told me to put it in a bag.
Q. Which hand did you use to hand it to him?
A. My hand, right hand.
Q. What was your other hand doing at that time?
A. Well, I put the money—I had the bag in my right hand, put it in with my left hand and handed it to him like that.
Q. Then what happened?
A. Then he took it and asked for the wallet.
Q. Did he speak to you at that time?
A. He said, "Come on, come on. Don't panic, don't panic."
   . . .
Q. And after placing the money in the bag, what did you do with it?
A. I handed it to him.
Q. And did he touch it?
A. Yes. He grabbed it.

Joseph Melville was not the only witness to identify Garcia. On December 5, 1977, Roy Campbell came forward to give a statement to the police. By accident Campbell was speaking to a district attorney in Watsonville regarding another case and said that he saw two people in the liquor store probably two to three minutes prior to the call for the armed robbery (which he heard on the short-wave radio in his car). He did not come forward earlier, he said, because he believed that the people he saw did not fit the description given out by the police as two Mexicans, both slender, one tall, one short. Campbell was driving by the store at ten to twenty miles an hour and saw two Mexicans inside. The bodies were at a forty-five-degree angle as he drove by. He was able to pick Garcia out of six color photographs. However, Campbell admitted seeing Garcia's photograph in the paper when he was being transported to the preliminary examination.

The Trial

Garcia was tried for the crime. His defense attorney, Gerald Christensen of Santa Cruz, California, and Chief Investigator Douglas Cole decided there was a need for a psychologist to testify on the subject of eyewitness accounts, particularly since this was to be the sole evidence produced in the case. A minimally edited transcript of that testimony appears in the appendix of this book.

The testimony began with a discussion of my qualifications. It was necessary to show the court and the jury that the psychologist (or any expert, for that matter) was qualified to testify on the subject at hand. The substance of the testimony began with a brief discussion of the nature of human memory: Memory does not work like a videotape recorder; people do not sit and passively take in information, recording it the way a videotape recorder would record it. Rather, they take in information in bits and pieces, from different sources, at different times, and integrate this information together. In a sense, people actually construct memories.

I went on to explain that psychologists make a distinction between three major phases in the memory process: the acquisition phase, the retention phase, and the retrieval phase. During the acquisition phase, one actually witnesses some event, takes in information about it. This is followed by the retention phase, the period of time in which information resides in memory before it is needed. Finally, there is the retrieval phase, the time during which people are asked questions about their recollection and they respond. At this time the contents of the memory are revealed. Many factors come into play that affect the accuracy and completeness of an eyewitness's report at each of these three stages.

There followed a discussion of those psychological factors affecting eyewitness testimony that were relevant to the case of *People v. Garcia*. Experimental research on each factor was described. The first factor was the retention interval, the period of time between the incident and the witness's recollection of that incident. Melville's identification occurred a couple of weeks after the crime, but Campbell's was over seven weeks later. The second factor was stress. It is reasonable to presume that a witness to a robbery and murder would be suffering extreme stress. In fact, when Campbell arrived on the scene after the murder, he described Melville as being in a state of shock. Third is the factor of weapon focus. Both robbers in this incident carried guns, and it is clear that these weapons captured a good deal of Melville's attention.

Next came a discussion of the cross-racial identification phenomenon. Melville and Campbell were both white; the robbers were Mexican. The testimony then went on to cover the factor of postevent information. This was relevant because the newspaper photograph of Garcia that Campbell saw before he identified him could have supplemented his memory in the same way that it does in laboratory experiments. Unconscious transference was also a relevant phenomenon. When a witness looks at a photograph and is uncertain, and later looks at a new photograph of the same person and is suddenly more certain, it is possible that some sort of unconscious transference is taking place: the familiarity experienced with the second photograph might be mistakenly related by the witness back to the incident, rather than back to the prior viewing of photographs where it might belong. Melville expressed some doubts at his first identification but became more positive when he looked at other photographs later on.

Finally, testimony was introduced about people's tendency to overestimate the duration of a complex event. Melville said the robbery took about five minutes. Campbell said his view was about thirty seconds.

The trial ended, and the jurors began their deliberations. They were unable to reach a verdict on Garcia. The chief investigator interviewed some of the jurors after the trial and in a letter to me on May 1, 1978, wrote: "The most important thing was that, whether they liked you or didn't like you, they spent a great deal of time discussing your testimony."

Garcia was retried later in May of 1978. The testimony was nearly identical, and again the jurors were unable to reach a verdict. From interviews with them it was determined that the final count was nine for acquittal and three for conviction. In a letter of June 23, 1978, the chief investigator wrote: "There seems to have been a consensus within the jury that your testimony was not only valuable but also a useful tool."

Appendix

This is a slightly edited version of the testimony I gave in the case of *People v. Garcia*, March 23, 1978, Santa Cruz, California. The background of the crime and circumstances leading to the arrest of Garcia are described in chapter 11. The prosecution's entire case against Garcia rested on the identification of the defendant by two witnesses, Melville, the clerk, and Campbell, the security guard. Thus, after the prosecution (led by Mr. Harry) had rested its case, the defense (led by Mr. Christensen) began calling its witnesses — character witnesses, alibi witnesses, and expert witnesses.

The testimony began in the same way that all testimony does, with the solemn oath that the testimony is the truth, the whole truth, and nothing but the truth. Next, my qualifications were presented to the court. These included my education, teaching experience, publications (books and articles), professional lectures, government grants supporting my laboratory research, and prior testimony offered in criminal cases.

There followed a series of questions by the district attorney about the methods that I use in collecting data. He objected to the introduction of the expert testimony on several grounds, arguing in part that (1) I could only reach very general conclusions about human perception and memory, and not about the two eyewitnesses, Melville and Campbell; (2) the purpose of the testimony was to unfairly impeach the eyewitnesses; (3) the experimental situations are very different from the specific robbery-murder crime. The judge ruled that the testimony would be admitted, and the defense attorney resumed his direct examination. Through a long series of questions he attempted to bring before the jury the factors in the criminal incident that are known from the psychological literature to produce problems for an accurate eyewitness account.

217

Here is a portion of that testimony that deals with the issue of admissibility, and the relevant psychological factors:

MR. HARRY: Your Honor, my objection is based upon the proffered testimony of Dr. Loftus that, first of all, she is an expert in conducting experiments and giving addresses and writing of articles regarding the results of those tests, but she is not an expert in determining the ability to perceive, recollect, and identify based upon Mr. Melville and Mr. Campbell. She can only talk about her general testing that she has conducted, and I think that from the questions on voir dire, it's very clear that they have not been conducted on actual eyewitness victims of robberies and murder, and that she has really no expertise that she can bring to this court except for one purpose and this is the purpose which I feel the defense is offering the evidence. And that is to somehow collaterally impeach Mr. Melville and Mr. Campbell as to their ability to perceive, recollect, and describe what happened. And I would cite *People v. Johnson*, 38 Cal. 3d 1.

MR. CHRISTENSEN: It's not Cal. 3d 1.

MR. HARRY: Cal. Appeals 3d 1. My eyesight isn't too good. And on page six at the bottom, it reads: "Evidence Code Section 780 enumerates the varieties of impeachment evidence that the jury may consider, including subdivision (c), the witness' capacity to perceive, recollect and communicate. Contrary to defendant's arguments, it does not follow that a party has a right to impeach a witness by calling another witness to testify as to the former's capacity."

THE COURT: This testimony is not being offered for that purpose, Mr. Harry. It's been specifically rejected for that purpose, as you have heard the Court reject it previously.

MR. HARRY: I am reinforcing my point on that, your Honor. Evidence Code Section—

THE COURT: I don't understand why you are reinforcing a point that has already been made clear.

MR. HARRY: All right. I will withdraw the point, then.

THE COURT: All right. Go ahead.

MR. HARRY: Evidence Code Section 801, subdivision (a) limits expert testimony to subjects beyond the range of common experience, thus modifies the decisional role vested in the trial court with the discretion of admitting expert testimony. The purpose of this, your Honor, appears to be—and that's why the question was asked what did she do? She said she read Mr. Melville's report and she read Mr. Campbell's report and she read over the police report dealing with those individuals. She didn't mention the preliminary hearing transcripts. She may have seen those, also. I don't know. But if she did, the only reason she could be reading those and the only reason she would be offering any evidence regarding those is to impeach those witnesses.

THE COURT: I disagree with you. I want you to hear this, too, Dr. Loftus, so you understand what the ground rules are. I have previously indicated that, as far as I'm concerned, relevant evidence for the jury to consider, if it comes from somebody who has expertise in knowing what the factors are, are the factors that go into identification. Now, you mentioned acquisition, retention, retrieval. Previously, you testified at the hearing we had regarding what the important factors are and the way in which there are certain misconceptions about how important these factors are. Do you follow me?

THE WITNESS: Yes.

THE COURT: Now, those things, as far as I'm concerned, are relevant for the jury to consider here. The only purpose in terms of what we are talking about here, of Dr. Loftus having read the reports, the preliminary hearing transcript, and so on, is to allow her to know what the facts are in this case. I am not going to allow Mr. Christensen to ask her questions that would indicate in any way an opinion on her part about whether this is a good identification or a bad identification by either Mr. Melville or Mr. Campbell. But she is entitled to talk about the factors that would be involved if somebody was robbed at gunpoint in a store of the kind that we are dealing with under the circumstances that we are dealing with. Do you understand what I'm saying?

MR. CHRISTENSEN: I certainly understand what you are saying.

THE WITNESS: Me, too.

MR. HARRY: Your Honor, for clarification, the factors involved are factors that would come into play from her experiments and not from the facts as existing in this—

THE COURT: Let me deal with that for a moment. Now, Dr. Loftus, you have, as I understand it, conducted, among the many experiments you have conducted, experiments which, in your opinion, would entitle you to discuss the kind of factors I'm talking about. Is that correct?

THE WITNESS: Yes.

THE COURT: Now, are there also books, articles, things of this kind that are written in the area?

THE WITNESS: Hundreds of articles written in the area.

THE COURT: And I take it you probably have read most of those?

THE WITNESS: Yes, I have.

THE COURT: Do you also talk with and consult with other people who have the kind of credentials you do in the field of psychology?

THE WITNESS: We have annual meetings, most of the societies I belong to, and there we meet and discuss our research, new findings, and new theories every year.

THE COURT: Now, with regard to the experiments that you have been involved with, have you specifically worked on experiments which were intended to attain the kind of information we are talking about here? What are the important factors—

THE WITNESS: Yes.

THE COURT: —when somebody is robbed and they are later asked to recall what happened?

THE WITNESS: Yes.

THE COURT: That is, some studies have been specifically directed toward that?

THE WITNESS: Yes, they have.

THE COURT: And have any of these studies actually involved human beings being observed as well as just movies?

THE WITNESS: Yes.

THE COURT: Okay. Mr. Harry, as far as I'm concerned, Dr. Loftus is qualified to testify. I do not, once again, believe that anybody should be able to express an opinion, no matter what their experience, on whether somebody has properly identified somebody or not, because I don't think it's humanly possible. Only the person who saw the event knows. But she is certainly entitled to talk about what, from her expertise, are the important psychological and other factors that go into identification.

MR. CHRISTENSEN: Your Honor, purposefully, I did not use the hypothetical—I did not set the stage to duplicate this case. And I purposefully asked her, and which she has done before, whether or not she had reviewed these materials. I thought that was the most fair way of getting into the factors that may be involved in this particular case, without having her express an opinion, because if we get into a particular thing, "What if two people walk into a particular liquor store on such and such a night and point guns at someone?" I thought that's what you wanted me to stay away from. So what I have asked her to do is review the material and I will ask her a leading question on certain factors that may be involved in this particular case and ask her what those factors are, what they mean, and not ask her any questions about what Mr. Melville's opinion could have been in that particular situation and Mr. Campbell's. I will not ask that.

MR. HARRY: That's what I expected he would do. I would object to the question including the portion which may be involved in this case. I don't think she can give that kind of an answer, unless it's much more specific than that.

MR. CHRISTENSEN: I think she most certainly may say it may be involved.

She's done studies. She's done all these studies and I will not ask her: "Based upon that, what is your opinion of the identification of Mr. Melville?" I will not ask that. I know the court does not want me to ask that and I will not. But that is the only legitimate way of getting into the area, other than asking a hypothetical question, and I think it makes a lot more sense and it's a lot more fair to let the jury determine what the facts are, ultimately, and plug it into argument.

THE COURT: All right. As far as I'm concerned, you are entitled, at this point, to ask her what psychological factors would be involved in acquisition, retention, and retrieval in a situation where somebody is robbed.

MR. CHRISTENSEN: See, it goes further than that, and I wanted to bring up some factors that are involved in, in fact, how much time goes by, for example. Rather than specifically referring it to this particular case, and it is a fact that she can testify to, I again would just ask her whether she reviewed the materials, whether there are certain facts that may be involved in this case. I won't go any further than that, and then certain factors, and then leave it up to the jury and I can also argue it.

THE COURT: As far as I'm concerned, you are entitled to do that.

MR. CHRISTENSEN: Thank you.

THE COURT: Bring the jury in, would you please?

THE BAILIFF: Yes, your Honor. (The jury enters the courtroom at 2:00 p.m.)

THE COURT: Go ahead, Mr. Christensen.

MR. CHRISTENSEN: Thank you, your Honor.

DIRECT EXAMINATION resumed by MR. CHRISTENSEN:

Q. Dr. Loftus, before Mr. Harry engaged in voir dire with you, I had asked you whether or not you had a familiarity with this case, and I believe you stated you did. Is that correct?

A. Yes.

Q. You also, in describing the function of memory earlier, referred, at least very briefly, to certain factors that may affect eyewitness identification, did you not?

A. That's correct.

Q. And I would like to ask you whether or not there are certain factors that may affect eyewitness identification in the case of *People v. Garcia and Losoya*. Do you understand what I'm saying?

A. Yes.

Q. All right. First, the retention interval. You mentioned that earlier in your discussion with Mr. Harry, also. Can you explain for me what that is?

A. Yes. The retention interval is simply the period of time between a crime or some other incident and a witness's recollection of that incident.

Q. Are there any studies in that particular area?

A. There are many studies which looked at the effects of varying the length of the retention interval.

Q. And have psychologists reached any conclusions in that area?

A. Yes, they have.

Q. Can you tell me what those are?

A. Well, if I could use the paper?

THE COURT: Please do. There are a number of sheets there.

THE WITNESS: Well, I will keep this one for the time being. If you look at — this is the conclusion that psychologists have reached about the relationship between memory and the retention interval. The function between these two is a negatively decelerating function. That means it drops off quite rapidly at first and then the decay is much more gradual. And this was first discovered by Ebbinghaus in 1885. It's called the forgetting curve and it's been replicated in laboratories across the country with different kinds of material and different kinds of witnesses. And what this basically says is that we remember much less after a long retention interval than after a shorter one.

Q. So what it generally says is as time goes by you forget. Is that right?

A. Well, in simple terms, yes.

Q. But you also forget in a particular manner. You forget more at a particular stage and less at another stage?

A. That's correct.

Q. Okay. Thank you. What about the factors of stress? Do you know what I mean by that?

A. Yes.

Q. What does that mean?

A. Well, stress is typically used to—there are different definitions of stress that are used by psychologists, but it commonly means the feeling of being aroused, afraid, upset. That's a popular use of the term "stress." There are much more technical definitions.

Q. Does it have a meaning in relation to eyewitness identification?

A. Well, yes, it does, because there is a relationship between stress and memory or eyewitness ability.

Q. Can you describe what that relationship is?

A. Yes. I will use the diagram.

Q. Would you use a new sheet of paper?

A. Again, while the relationship between memory and stress is some-what more complex, this is memory or any sort of cognitive performance, and this is stress or fear or arousal, the relationship is an inverted U-shape function and this is called the Yerkes-Dodson law, named after the two psychologists who discovered it in 1908. What this is saying is that under very high stress or fear or arousal and also under very, very low stress, such as when you are just waking up in the morning, we are less good rememberers and perceivers than we are under ordinary optimal moderate levels of stress.

Q. Which means when you are nice and wide awake, you are remembering the best. Is that correct?

A. That's true. And up here you can imagine if you have just gotten into an auto accident or something very stressful and upsetting that happened to you, you wouldn't want to sit down and start to try to work a crossword puzzle or do something that required some concentration.

Q. What you mean in relation to memory is, this is like the better memory as we go up the line, right?

A. That's true.

Q. And with high stress or very low stress, memory is going to be at the lower level or not as good. Is that what you are saying?

A. That's correct.

Q. Okay. Is the presence of a weapon a factor that is involved in how good or bad an eyewitness identification is?

A. Yes, it is. It's a factor and, in fact, the factor has been called "weapon focus," because what happens when a weapon is present is it tends to capture some of the witness's attention and some of the witness's processing time and capacity, leaving less time available for other details and other aspects of the incident, and this has the effect of reducing the ability to describe other details, although, often, people have a very good ability to describe the weapon. That's what is meant by weapon focus.

Q. Have there been studies on this to know why that is the case that people can identify the weapon?

A. Well, there is one study that was performed at Oklahoma State University within the last couple of years, showing that weapon focus did occur—that in a condition where there is a weapon present, people are good at remembering the weapon, but less good at remembering the person who was holding the weapon than in the corresponding controlled condition. However, we don't have a very detailed understanding of why this occurs. Just that it does occur and it probably has something to do with how much time the witness is spending on the weapon versus the other details.

Q. That's a "probably." Can you say that with any amount of certainty?

A. No. I think, actually, it would be possible to do it if you had an experiment in which you could measure eye movement patterns, but it hasn't been done with that sophisticated equipment.

Q. What do you mean by "measure eye movement patterns"? What does that have to do?

A. That the experiment I just described in which it was shown that a condition in which a weapon was present caused people to focus on the weapon and look at other details less often. We only know that because we look at their final reports. We ask them questions at the very end and they can remember the weapon very well, but they don't remember the faces well. To really know that that is because they were focusing on the weapon, it would be nice to have a study in which you recorded eye movements—there is equipment which you can use which allows you to see where people are looking, but this is very fancy and expensive equipment and it's not available for most of the scientific studies where it would be nice to have it.

Q. So the concept has been called "weapon focus." Is that correct?

A. Yes.

Q. But that doesn't necessarily mean people are focusing in on the weapon?

A. We assume they are, because they remember the weapon later and there is a detriment in their ability to remember other details.

Q. In regard to stress and weapon focus, those factors, have you heard the statement involved in—a statement by an eyewitness in a stressful situation: "I will never forget that face"?

MR. HARRY: Object to this, your Honor. Calls for something that the witness has no expertise on. She hasn't conducted such an experiment with people involved in a holdup.

THE COURT: Well, Mr. Harry, I think she has indicated earlier that she has conducted experiments intended to obtain the kind of information that you can obtain about what might be involved in the identification process as a result of such an experience. Now, are you saying that the only way you can obtain information about what happens when something occurs is to have that exact same thing occur? I mean, is that the basis?

MR. HARRY: That's not what I'm saying.

THE COURT: Okay. Mr. Christensen, can you rephrase that question somehow?

MR. CHRISTENSEN: Q. Well, let's see. Has it been shown in the studies that you have read about or conducted yourself, and your readings in the area, that a statement under a stressful condition, "I will never forget that face," has it been shown whether or not that would be a valid or invalid statement?

MR. HARRY: Your Honor, I would object. She has not said that she has conducted any experiments where people say—

MR. CHRISTENSEN: She is an expert from reading—

THE COURT: Why don't you ask Dr. Loftus whether, in her experience with all of these experiments she has conducted, some people tend to overrate their identification. Isn't that the point?

MR. CHRISTENSEN: Yes. In particular, in regards to stress, yes.

THE COURT: All right.

MR. CHRISTENSEN: Q. The question has already been stated. Can you give me an answer?

A. Yes. People do overrate their identification, partly because they don't understand the operation of stress and how it affects memory.

Q. Thank you. Are you familiar with the concept called "cross-racial identification"?

A. Yes, I am.

Q. And what is meant by that?

A. A cross-racial identification is one in which a member of one race attempts to identify a member of a different race.

Q. Has that concept been studied by psychologists?

A. Yes, it has.

Q. And what results?

A. The repeated finding in studies of cross-radical identification is that we are less good, less accurate at identifying a member of another race than we are at identifying members of our own race.

Q. Have studies been done, particularly, with Mexican-Americans?

A. No. The experiments — quite a few experiments that have been done in cross-racial identification have involved whites, blacks, Japanese-Americans, and Chinese-Americans. And the conclusion that is reached in the studies is based upon subject populations involving those races. Mexican-Americans have not been studied as a group.

Q. Based upon your background, experience, education, do you have an opinion as to whether or not the concepts would apply to a Caucasian and Mexican-American?

A. In my opinion, the cross-racial problem that exists with these other groups would extend into a cross-racial identification with whites and Mexican-Americans, yes.

Q. Thank you. Has there been any determination of why it's more difficult to identify a person of a different race?

A. Well, there have been many hypotheses that have been proposed. One of the leading ones is it has something to do with how much experience or training you have had with members of a different race versus members of your own race, but even that hypothesis has not held up. That is, there have been studies that have shown that even individuals who have extensive experience and training with faces of a different race still have the cross-racial problem. So there really exists no good explanation for this finding, although the finding holds up repeatedly.

Q. It's there, but you don't know why?

A. That's correct.

Q. Have you heard about a concept called "postevent information"?

A. Yes.

Q. Big word.

A. Yes.

Q. What does that mean?

A. Postevent information simply refers to information that is presented in some way to a witness after a to-be-remembered event is completely over.

Q. And has that been studied by psychologists, the effects that may have on a subsequent identification?

A. Yes, it has.

Q. In fact, you have indicated a study you have recently done yourself. Is that correct?

A. That's correct.

Q. Is there a particular result that you have reached?

A. In the experiments which studied postevent information, they have found that people will take this information that comes in during the retention interval, as that information about the barn came in during the retention interval in one of my experiments. They will take this information and integrate it into their memories, either supplementing their memory or altering or adding to their memories, and it now becomes, in a sense, a part of their recollection. Now, what percentage of the people do this depends completely on other factors: how good a look the witness got at what is going to be remembered; how convincing the postevent information is. But it can come in in a number of different ways. You saw an experiment, or I described an experiment, in which it came in during questioning. It can also come in in the course of overhearing a conversation or engaging in a conversation or reading a newspaper article. And information supplied in this way can become a part of a witness's memory and a witness can be very confident about—very confident that the witness actually saw what the witness has only heard about.

Q. Or seen somewhere else other than at the time it happened?

A. Well, that's true, too.

Q. Does this get back to the fact that the brain is, again, not a video—memory is not videotaped?

A. Well, the studies involving this factor—nice examples of how you can take information from different sources and even from different modalities. In one case you are actually seeing the events, but you are hearing or reading a piece of postevent information and you take this information or we all take this information, integrate it together to produce something that is different from what we actually, ourselves, experience.

Q. Again, that has been studied over a period of time?

A. Yes.

Q. "Unconscious transference," does that mean anything to you?

A. Yes. That's a term which means the mistaken recollection or the confusion of a person seen in one situation with a person that has been seen in a different situation or in a different context. And that definition is somewhat confusing and I can best explain what it means by using an example from Patrick Wall's book—the book is called *Eyewitness Identification in Criminal Cases*. Mr. Wall brings up an example of a train clerk who was robbed. I believe it was at gunpoint. The train clerk subsequently went to a lineup and picked a sailor out of the lineup. The sailor did not commit the robbery, had a very good alibi, but had purchased tickets from this train clerk on three prior occasions. So you can see what is happening in this situation. The train clerk, the witness, goes to the lineup. In fact, there is a face in the lineup that looks familiar and that familiarity is mistakenly related back to the crime, rather than back to the purchasing of tickets where it properly belongs. That's a classic example of unconscious transference.

Q. Other than Mr. Wall's example, has that concept been studied?

A. Yes, it has.

Q. And what result reached?

A. Well, the major thing we know from the experiments on unconscious transference is that it is a real phenomenon and you can produce it in a controlled laboratory situation. That people will look at faces that they have seen at different times in different contexts and mistakenly relate those faces back to an incorrect situation.

Q. Thank you. I have one final question, and I'm not sure it's a concept or a factor that may involve or affect eyewitness identification, but what about time perception? Do people correctly perceive the amount of time an event takes, particularly a stressful event?

A. No. As a matter of fact, people almost invariably overestimate the amount of time that something took. When the event is over and they are now thinking back and trying to provide an accurate estimate of how long it took, classically, they estimate a duration that is too long.

Q. They wouldn't be lying at that point. I mean, they are not intentionally telling an untruth?

A. No, it's an attempt to give an accurate estimate, but it typically is wrong. "Typically" is even too weak a word to use in this case. Most everybody overestimates the amount of time that something took.

Q. And I take it that's been studied?

A. Yes, it has.

Q. And the result reached is, as you have stated, almost always?

A. Yes.

Q. Do you know why? Do psychologists know why?

A. Well, psychologists have tried to find out why by asking questions such as: does it matter whether the interval was filled with activities or whether there were relatively fewer activities in the interval? And they will, to an experiment in which they manipulate that factor and, in fact, the answer to that question is, yes, it does matter. Filled intervals are perceived to be longer. So it may be that it has something to do with the fact that many things are happening in the interval and, in a stressful interval, relatively, even more things are happening within the interval. So you do find that even with stressful situations or even with people who are ordinarily stressful, they tend to even more than average overestimate the amount of time that something took.

MR. CHRISTENSEN: Thank you, Dr. I have nothing further.

. . .

CROSS-EXAMINATION by MR. HARRY:

Q. Dr. Loftus, is this your Yerkes-Dodson law? Does it matter what the stress factor is down here whether that curve works in the same way each time?

A. Well, the Yerkes-Dodson law really talks about the overall shape of the curve, but you do have an inverted U-shape curve. But exactly how high and exactly how wide and so on is going to depend on a number of different things.

Q. So at the low point we could say that someone getting up in the morning with a good night's sleep would be in a situation of low stress?

A. Well, usually, the low stress really means very—even with a good night's sleep, immediately, as one is awakening.

Q. So immediately after being awakened, the curve rises rather quickly?

A. Well, not necessarily, but during one's ordinary everyday activities where things are happening around you and it's perhaps the middle of the day, it's thought to be this moderate stress level where optimum performance is possible.

Q. So we are supposed to strive for the top of the curve; is that right?

A. Well, I don't know whether you want to strive for the curve. It depends on whether you want to perform well or not.

Q. But if we want to have a good memory, we should strive for the top of the curve, not the low end or the high end, is that what you are saying?

A. That's correct.

Q. Does the measurement in the test depend upon the significance of the event causing the stress?

A. I'm not sure I understand the question.

Q. Okay. Well, let's use your weapon focus example. If someone is using a weapon and the person observing the weapon has a rather high stress from that, it may not bother some people and it may cause a very high stress factor for some other people. Is that correct?

A. Well—

Q. According to your tests.

A. Well, I think it's possible that someone could feel very comfortable around weapons and not become stressed by them and such a person might even, in the presence of a weapon, still be at a moderate stress level.

Q. Okay. That's what I was trying to understand from your example. So if the event is significant and the person has the capacity or ability to observe, then according to your analogy here with the Yerkes-Dodson law, if it produces high stress, how would the significance of that be affected, if it's a very significant event to the perceiver or an insignificant event?

A. Well, if an event—if an overall event is significant to someone, the person's probably going to be able to remember that that event happened, but if the person was extremely stressed, would not be able to remember the details of that event particularly well. Now, if, by "significance," you mean some particular detail which captures the attention of the person such as a weapon would, and a good deal of processing capacity and attention were focused on that weapon, you might find that details about that weapon were remembered reasonably well, despite distractions. However, if you looked under high stress at a weapon and then had to describe it, you probably would not do as well as if you looked for the same amount of time under moderate stress.

Q. So the significance depends upon the person perceiving it. Isn't that right?

A. Well, significance would depend on the witness, yes.

Q. And doesn't it also depend on whether it is a central or a peripheral event?

A. Yes.

Q. So if you are testing, asking questions about what someone saw in one of your movies, if it's a central event, you would expect that the persons answering the questions would be more accurate in the details of that particular event, right, on the significant portion of the event?

A. It's true that central events are recalled better than peripheral events. That's true.

Q. So when the stress factor is high, we sometimes find various significant events occurring to cause that high stress, do we not?

A. That's true.

Q. And if something is central during that significant event and also is highly central and significant to the perceiver, the likelihood of their memory is better. Is that not right?

A. That's true.

Q. As to those central factors?

A. It would be as to the central rather than the peripheral factors.

Q. And the peripheral factors are likely to drop off down on your memory curve back in 1880 whatever, the forgetting curve. Is that right?

A. Well, everything is subject to the negatively decelerating forgetting curve, both central and peripheral events.

Q. But it is accurate to say, is it not, that the more significant the event, the less likely it is to drop off the end of the curve, even though the curve may be extended for quite some length of time?

A. If, by "significant," you mean an object which is central to the event that has been witnessed, yes, it probably has a slower decay rate than an object which is peripheral.

Q. Now, if a person observing an event and under your testing pattern they do not receive false information like the barn that wasn't there, and they are later then tested as to what they saw, the significance of the event not being known to them until a later date, but upon being known as to the significance of it, would it be more or less likely for that person to have a better memory after determining that the event was significant?

MR. CHRISTENSEN: I object. I think it's ambiguous. At least to me.

THE COURT: Did you understand the question?

THE WITNESS: No. Could you repeat the question?

MR. HARRY: Q. Let me try it this way: if someone observes something in your testing laboratory and it doesn't really mean much to them at the time and later they learn somehow during this test that the event that they observed has some significance, when they then are tested as to their memory, are they more or less likely to remember that significant event?

A. More or less likely than what?

Q. Than if they didn't know its significance.

MR. CHRISTENSEN: That assumes facts not in evidence as to how they found out anything was significant. Who told them it was significant? Did they tell them it was significant because they told them what it was?

MR. HARRY: Your Honor—

MR. CHRISTENSEN: May we also approach the bench? I think it's important. (A discussion was held at the bench, not reported.)

THE COURT: Okay. Go ahead, Mr. Harry.

MR. HARRY: Q. Dr. Loftus, do people have the ability to remember events, even though they were not significant when they first observed them?

A. Certainly, things that are not particularly significant happen to us all the time and we can remember some things about those events.

Q. Would it be fair to say that high stress interferes with the ability to remember the details?

A. Yes.

Q. But it would also be fair to say that if it is an important event, then the focus is on a particular significant event and that the memory is improved?

A. Something that is particularly significant or important which causes one to focus on it would tend to improve or enhance the memory for that aspect, yes.

Q. Is the experience of the observer for observing a particular kind of object or location important in determining what they remember after the testing?

A. Well, definitely. When we have prior knowledge about some particular object or kind of objects, we can perceive and remember them more easily. Scientists who study certain kinds of leaves can look briefly at a special kind of leaf and perceive and remember what kind it is.

Q. And in your testing that you give, have you ever given a test where you have shown the same subject the same material at a later date and retested them regarding what they saw?

A. Well, often, I think in most of my experiments we have shown them the incident only once.

Q. That's the movie incident?

A. The film, yes. Because we are trying, to some extent, to simulate the conditions of a naturally occurring event, which usually only happens once.

Q. And in your testing, did you ever find an individual who had been a participant in a similar situation that is shown in the movie or the film?

A. In other words, might we have a crime that is actually in our experiment?

Q. Yes.

A. I don't know that.

Q. You weren't testing for that result?

A. No.

Q. And is it fair to say that even though you have tested and experimented with the weapon focus aspect of your work, that there are people who, even though the weapon is there and the stress situation is high, they do remember things. Is that right?

A. Well, that would certainly be true, yes.

Q. But they remember the more central portions and they forget the details?

A. Well, one can only say that people in general tend to remember central objects, central events better than they do peripheral ones.

MR. HARRY: Nothing further. Thank you, Dr. Loftus.

THE COURT: Mr. Christensen?

MR. CHRISTENSEN: I have no further questions.

THE COURT: I have a couple of questions, but first some of the jurors have questions and I will read the questions and I think the easiest way to handle it is to read them. I'm familiar with some of the handwriting by now, so these are two questions from the same person and I think I will read them to you together, because they may be related. The first part of the two questions is, "Do the subjects ever see an actual event instead of sitting in a room reviewing a film?"

THE WITNESS: Yes. In some of the experiments that we have done, they do look at actual live events and in many of the experiments that have been performed by my colleagues around the country, with which I am familiar and have studied their methods, they use live events. They are purse snatchings or staged assaults, either on college campuses or on the streets somewhere, and so it's relatively common to use a live event, but not as common as films, because the psychologists want to have some control of the materials so you know every time you are presenting it to a new group of people you are presenting exactly the same thing, whereas a live event might change a little bit each time it's presented.

THE COURT: The other two portions of these questions: "Were they ever tested after one or two months?" And the second one is: "Can a time span be put on the retention curve?"

THE WITNESS: Retention interval studies have ranged from moments after an incident to months and months afterwards. One study that is on the top of my mind used a four-month retention interval finding relatively poor performance after four months. Putting a time span on that forgetting curve is not really possible to do. It depends completely on the kind of material that you are looking at, how many times you see it, how good a look you get, and so on. All we know is the general shape of the curve, but we can't put a time frame on it. We can't say it will plateau always after two weeks or something like that.

EXAMINATION BY THE COURT:

Q. All right. You are a psychologist and I assume you have had some experience with hypnosis.

A. I have had minimal experience with hypnosis. I have an acquaintanceship.

Q. I'm going to ask you a question and leave it up to you as to whether you are able to answer it or not. If a witness was under hypnosis, would this unconscious transference that you have talked about still apply?

A. Well, let me give you the basis for my knowledge about hypnosis so you understand how minimal it is. I spent a year on fellowship at Harvard, 1975-76. While I was there, I had extensive conversations and even conducted a study with a professor there who is an expert in hypnosis and we together attempted to perform an experiment on hypnosis and memory. Through my conversations with him and a couple of articles that I have read, I know that there is a great controversy about hypnosis, about what hypnosis can do or what it is, and it is my opinion that material produced — hypnosis causes a person to be relaxed, occasionally, more cooperative. There is nothing particularly magic about it. In this cooperative, relaxed state, a person can produce ideas and thoughts that are sometimes true and sometimes not true.

Q. I think you probably would rather not answer that question. I mean in the sense that it deals with this unconscious transference, would there be any way of knowing whether somebody, under hypnosis, whether this unconscious transference condition would apply or not?

A. No. All we really know now is that it is a real phenomenon. We can produce it in the laboratory, but we don't know what conditions make it more or less likely to happen.

Q. The next question here: are the results of the doctor's tests, experiments, and resulting papers considered theories or accepted as facts?

A. Well, it depends on which thing you are referring to. I would say nearly everything I have said here today is an established fact. I mean the Yerkes-Dodson law is a law that was discovered long before I was born. The Ebbinghaus forgetting curve is a well-established theoretical notion in psychology. My experiments have been published in the best journals that exist.

Q. They represent the concensus of the people in your field, anyway; is that correct?

A. I would say so, yes.

Q. I have one question about the stress business. That Yerkes-Dodson curve, as I understand it, deals with the actual time when the person is observing what the person was observing, what they are later called upon to recall. Is that correct?

A. At the time of the initial observation, yes.

Q. Okay. Now, does somebody being under stress at the time they are asked to recall something have any effect on their ability to recall?

A. Well, I believe that work has been done on stress at the time of re-trieval, but I don't know enough about that to be able to talk about it here today.

Q. So this definitely deals —

A. With the time of acquisition, yes.

THE COURT: Anything further, Mr. Harry?

MR. HARRY: Yes, your Honor. I'd like to ask one other question.

FURTHER CROSS-EXAMINATION:

MR. HARRY: Q. Dr. Loftus, you indicated to Mr. Christensen earlier that memory, when he asked you about the accepted definition of "memory," and you said, well, it is not a videotape, but you did not say what it really is.

A. Well, experimental psychologists, talking about the facts — when we say it is not a videotape, we mean it does not come in and passively reside in memory untouched, unscathed by future events. What seems to happen is we pick up fragments and features from our environment. These go into memory, they interact with our prior knowledge and expectations, what is already there, and when the event is completely over, yet new information comes in and be-comes added to it and this — we think of memory as being an inte-grative process, a constructive process rather than a passive record-ing process.

Q. Doesn't it depend on whether the person is able — strike that. You and your colleagues have determined it is not a videotape because of your testing. Isn't that right?

A. In part, yes.

Q. So, then, from that, have you come to a conclusion that there is absolutely no person who would have what is called a photographic memory?

A. Well, "photographic memory" is a popular term. The closes thing that we actually have to it is something called eidetic imagery, which is a capability that is found, occasionally, in children and rarely in adults where someone can actually look at a scene and then look away and have a very complete and clear mental image of it for a relatively long — a couple of seconds, maybe a minute — period of time, but it's very rare.

Q. But if they did have that, would that not be identical to the video-tape?

A. Well, in the few — the rare, rare occasions with adults that possess eidetic imagery, I am not sure how long — I mean, they can cer-tainly maintain an image for a couple of seconds, maybe even a couple of minutes, but I don't know just how long they can main-tain it. It's such a rare phenomenon. At least in adults. Very rare.

Q. If you drew a curve, the normal population bell-shaped curve, you would result with very, very few people out here who could remember everything and very, very few people over here on the bottom or the other end of the curve that couldn't remember anything. Isn't that right?

A. Well, there are certain brain damaged conditions which cause total deficits in memory.

Q. And most people fall somewhere between these two extremes, do they not, and they can remember events and they can change what they saw and they can retrieve it from their memory and tell you about it. Isn't that right?

A. That's something that most of us can do reasonably well—

Q. And you are—

MR. CHRISTENSEN: May she finish?

THE COURT: Go ahead.

THE WITNESS: In most of the situations we encounter, very, very precise memory isn't required of us, so we don't know our fallibilities and we don't know our strengths very well, because they are not tested to their fullest.

MR. HARRY: Q. And what you are involved in doing is testing people's memory and taking that material and drawing up the statistics and writing books about it. Is that not accurate?

A. That's part of what I do, yes.

MR. HARRY: Thank you.

MR. CHRISTENSEN: No further questions.

THE COURT: Thank you very much.

THE WITNESS: Thank you.

In his closing argument, the defense attorney made many references to the expert testimony, pointing out to the jury the numerous factors that could have affected the accuracy of the eyewitness accounts. In the end, the jury was unable to reach a verdict about the guilt of José Garcia. A specific reaction to the testimony on the part of individual jurors is difficult to obtain, but when several jurors were informally interviewed after the trial was over, they indicated that they had spent quite some time discussing the testimony. After the deliberations, some of them felt the identification was still likely to have been accurate despite the presence of several debilitating factors. For others, a reasonable doubt was raised, substantial enough for "not guilty" to be the only verdict they could render.

References

Abernathy, E. 1940. The effect of changed environmental conditions upon the results of college examinations. *Journal of Psychology* 10: 293-301.

Allport, G. W., and L. J. Postman. 1947. *The psychology of rumor.* New York: Henry Holt and Company. Also in *Readings in social psychology,* ed. E. E. Maccoby, T. M. Newcomb, and E. L. Hartley. New York: Holt, Rinehart and Winston, 1958.

Anderson, J. R., and G. H. Bower. 1973. *Human associative memory.* Washington, D.C.: V. H. Winston and Sons.

Baddeley, A. D. 1972. Selective attention and performance in dangerous environments. *British Journal of Psychology* 63: 537-546.

Baltes, P. B., and K. W. Schaie. 1976. On the plasticity of intelligence in adulthood and old age. *American Psychologist* 31: 720-725.

Bartlett, F. C. 1932. *Remembering: a study in experimental and social psychology.* London: Cambridge University Press; New York: Macmillan.

Berkun, M. M., H. M. Bialek, R. P. Kern, and K. Yagi. 1962. Experimental studies of psychological stress in man. *Psychological Monographs* 76, no. 15.

Bird, C. 1927. The influence of the press upon the accuracy of report. *Journal of Abnormal and Social Psychology* 22: 123-129.

Blakemore, C. 1977. The unsolved marvel of memory. *The New York Times Magazine,* Feb. 6. (Rpt. in *Readings in psychology 78/79.* Guildford, Conn.: Annual Editions, Dushkin Publishing Group, 1978.)

Block, Eugene B. 1976. *Hypnosis: a new tool in crime detection.* New York: David McKay.

Borchard, E. M. 1932. *Convicting the innocent: errors of criminal justice*. New Haven: Yale University Press.

Bornstein, M. H. 1974. Perceptual generalization: a note on the peak shift. *Psychological Bulletin* 81: 802-808.

――――. 1976. Name codes and color memory. *American Journal of Psychology* 89: 269-279.

Bower, G. H., and M. B. Karlin. 1974. Depth of processing pictures of faces and recognition memory. *Journal of Experimental Psychology* 103: 751-757.

Bregman, A. S. 1966. Is recognition memory all or none? *Journal of Verbal Learning and Verbal Behavior* 5: 1-6.

Bricker, P. D., and A. Chapanis. 1953. Do incorrectly perceived tachistoscopic stimuli convey some information? *Psychological Review* 60: 181-188.

Brigham, J. C., and P. Barkowitz. 1978. Do "they all look alike?" The effect of race, sex, experience, and attitudes on the ability to recognize faces. *Journal of Applied Psychology* 8: 306-318.

Brown, E., K. Deffenbacher, and W. Sturgill. 1977. Memory for faces and the circumstances of encounter. *Journal of Applied Psychology* 62: 311-318.

Brown, M. R. 1926. *Legal psychology*. Indianapolis: Bobbs-Merrill.

Bruner, J. S., and L. Postman. 1949. On the perception of incongruity: a paradigm. *Journal of Personality* 18: 206-223.

Buckhout, R. 1974. Eyewitness testimony. *Scientific American* 231: 23-31.

――――. 1975. Nearly 2000 witnesses can be wrong. *Social Action and the Law* 2: 7.

――――. 1977. Eyewitness identification and psychology in the courtroom. *Criminal Defense* 4: 5-10.

Buckhout, R., D. Figueroa, and E. Hoff. 1975. Eyewitness identification: effects of suggestion and bias in identification from photographs. *Bulletin of the Psychonomic Society* 6: 71-74.

Bugelski, B. R., and D. A. Alampay. 1961. The role of frequency in developing perceptual sets. *Canadian Journal of Psychology* 15: 205-211.

Burtt, H. E. 1948. *Applied psychology*. New York: Prentice-Hall.

Cady, H. M. 1924. On the psychology of testimony. *American Journal of Psychology* 35: 110-112.

Carmichael, L. C., H. P. Hogan, and A. A. Walter. 1932. An experimental study of the effect of language on the reproduction of visually perceived form. *Journal of Experimental Psychology* 15: 73-86.

Cattell, J. M. 1895. Measurements of the accuracy of recollection. *Science*, n.s. 2: 761-766.

Charrow, V. R., and R. P. Charrow. 1978. The comprehension of standard jury instructions: a psycholinguistic approach. Unpublished (American Institutes for Research).

Clifford, B. R., and J. Scott. 1978. Individual and situational factors in eyewitness testimony. *Journal of Applied Psychology* 63: 352-359.

Cole, W. G., and E. F. Loftus. In press. Incorporating new information into memory. *American Journal of Psychology*.

Crowder, R. F. 1976. *Principles of learning and memory*. Hillsdale, N.J.: Erlbaum Press.

Dale, P. S., E. F. Loftus, and L. Rathbun. 1978. The influence of the question on the eyewitness testimony of preschool children. *Journal of Psycholinguistic Research* 7: 269-277.

Davis, R. D., and D. Sinha. 1950. The effect of one experience upon the recall of another. *Quarterly Journal of Experimental Psychology* 2: 43-52.

Devlin, Honorable Lord Patrick (chair). 1976. *Report to the secretary of state for the home department of the departmental committee on evidence of identification in criminal cases*. London: Her Majesty's Stationery Office.

Doob, A. N., and H. M. Kirshenbaum. 1973. Bias in police lineups — partial remembering. *Journal of Police Science and Administration* 1: 287-293.

Dooling, D. J., and R. E. Christiaansen. 1977. Episodic and semantic aspects of memory for prose. *Journal of Experimental Psychology: Human Learning and Memory* 3: 428-436.

Dritsas, W. J., and V. L. Hamilton. 1977. Evidence about evidence: effects of presuppositions, item salience, stress, and perceiver set on accident recall. Unpublished (University of Michigan).

Eagly, A. H. 1978. Sex differences in influenceability. *Psychological Bulletin* 85: 86-116.

Easterbrook, J. A. 1959. The effect of emotion on the utilization and organization of behavior. *Psychological Review* 66: 183-201.

Ebbinghaus, H. E. 1885. *Memory: a contribution to experimental psychology*. New York: Dover, 1964.

Ellis, H., J. Shepherd, and A. Bruce. 1973. The effect of age and sex upon adolescents' recognition of faces. *The Journal of Genetic Psychology* 123: 173-174.

Erickson, B., E. A. Lind, B. C. Johnson, and W. M. O'Barr. 1978. Speech style and impression formation in a court setting: the effects of "power" and "powerless" speech. *Journal of Experimental Social Psychology* 14: 266-279.

Evans, F. J., and J. F. Kihlstrom. 1975. Contextual and temporal disorganization during posthypnotic amnesia. Paper presented at the American Psychological Association, Chicago.

Eysenck, H. J. 1967. *The biological basis of personality*. Springfield, Ill.: Thomas.

Federal Rules of Evidence for United States Courts and Magistrates. 1975. St. Paul, Minn.: West Publishing Company.

Feingold, G. A. 1914. The influence of environment on identification of persons and things. *Journal of Criminal Law and Criminology* 5: 39-51.

Feuerlicht, R. S. 1977. *Justice crucified: the story of Sacco and Vanzetti*. New York: McGraw-Hill.

Fischhoff, B. 1975. Hindsight ≠ foresight: the effect of outcome knowledge on judgment under uncertainty. *Journal of Experimental Psychology: Human Perception and Performance* 1: 288-299.

———. 1977. Perceived informativeness of facts. *Journal of Experimental Psychology: Human Perception and Performance* 3: 349-358.

Fisher, G. 1968. Ambiguity of form: old and new. *Perception and Psychophysics* 4: 189-192.

Frankfurter, F. 1927. *The case of Sacco and Vanzetti*. New York: Little, Brown. (Rpt. Universal Library edition, 1962.)

Garcia, L. T., and W. Griffitt. 1978. Impact of testimonial evidence as a function of witness characteristics. *Bulletin of the Psychonomic Society* 11: 37-40.

Gardner, D. S. 1933. The perception and memory of witnesses. *Cornell Law Quarterly* 8: 391-409.

Gerbasi, K. C., M. Zuckerman, and H. T. Reis. 1977. Justice needs a new blindfold: a review of mock jury research. *Psychological Bulletin* 84: 323-345.

Gilbert v. California. 1967. 388 US 263; 87 S Ct 1951; 18 L Ed 2d 1178.

Goldstein, A. G., and J. Chance. 1964. Recognition of children's faces. *Child Development* 35: 129-136.

———. 1965. Recognition of children's faces II. *Perceptual and Motor Skills* 20: 548-549.

Hall, D. R., and T. M. Ostrom. 1975. Accuracy of eyewitness identification after biased or unbiased instructions. Unpublished (Ohio State University).

Hall, J. A., R. Rosenthal, D. Archer, M. R. Dimatteo, and P. L. Rogers. 1978. Decoding wordless messages. *Human Nature* 1: 68-75.

Harris, R. J. 1973. Answering questions containing marked and unmarked adjectives and adverbs. *Journal of Experimental Psychology* 97: 399-401.

Hart, J. T. 1967. Memory and the memory-monitoring process. *Journal of Verbal Learning and Verbal Behavior* 6: 685-691.

Hastie, R., R. Landsman, and E. F. Loftus. 1978. Eyewitness testimony: the dangers of guessing. *Jurimetrics Journal* 19: 1-8.

Hastorf, A. H., and H. Cantrill. 1954. They saw a game: a case study. *Journal of Abnormal and Social Psychology* 97: 399-401.

Hilgard, E. R., R. C. Atkinson, and R. L. Atkinson. 1975. *Introduction to psychology*, 6th ed. New York: Harcourt, Brace, Jovanovich.

Hooker, B. 1914. Hugo Munsterberg's "Psychology and social sanity." *The Bookman* 39: 454-457.

Johnson, C., and B. Scott. 1976. Eyewitness testimony and suspect identification as a function of arousal, sex of witness, and scheduling of interrogation. Paper presented at the American Psychological Association, Washington, D.C.

Jones, A. 1977. The Narciso-Perez case: nurse hunting in Michigan. *Nation* 224:584-588.

Kagan, J., R. E. Klein, M. M. Haith, and F. J. Morrison. 1973. Memory and meaning in two cultures. *Child Development* 44: 221-223.

Kay, H. 1955. Learning and retaining verbal material. *British Journal of Psychology* 46: 81-100.

Kintsch, W. 1974. *The representation of meaning in memory*. Hillsdale, N.J.: Erlbaum Press.

Kirby v. Illinois. 1972. 406 US 682; 92 S Ct 1877; 32 L Ed 411.

Kosslyn, S. M. 1975. Information representation in visual images. *Cognitive Psychology* 7: 341-370.

Lakoff, R. 1975. *Language and woman's place*. New York: Harper and Row.

Laughery, K. R., J. E. Alexander, and A. B. Lane. 1971. Recognition of human faces: effects of target exposure time, target position, pose position, and type of photograph. *Journal of Applied Psychology* 55: 477-483.

Lavrakas, P. J., and L. Bickman. 1975. What makes a good witness? Paper presented at the American Psychological Association, Chicago.

Leippe, M. R., G. L. Wells, and T. M. Ostrom. 1978. Crime seriousness as a determinant of accuracy in eyewitness identification. *Journal of Applied Psychology* 63: 345-351.

Lesgold, A. M., and A. R. Petrush. 1977. Do leading questions alter memories? Unpublished (University of Pittsburgh).

Levine, F. J., and J. L. Tapp. 1973. The psychology of criminal identification: the gap from Wade to Kirby. *University of Pennsylvania Law Review* 121: 1079-1131.

Lipmann, P. 1911. Pedagogical psychology of report. *Journal of Educa-*

tional Psychology 2: 253-261.

Lipton, J. P. 1977. On the psychology of eyewitness testimony. *Journal of Applied Psychology* 62: 90-93.

Loftus, E. F. 1974. Reconstructing memory: the incredible eyewitness. *Psychology Today* 8: 116-119.

————. 1975. Leading questions and the eyewitness report. *Cognitive Psychology* 7: 560-572.

————. 1976. Unconscious transference in eyewitness identification. *Law and Psychology Review* 2: 93-98.

————. 1977. Shifting human color memory. *Memory and Cognition* 5: 696-699.

————. 1978. Reconstructive memory processes in eyewitness testimony. In *Perspectives in law and psychology*, ed. B. D. Sales. New York: Plenum.

Loftus, E. F., D. Altman, and R. Geballe. 1975. Effects of questioning upon a witness' later recollections. *Journal of Police Science and Administration* 3: 162-165.

Loftus, E. F., D. G. Miller, and H. J. Burns. 1978. Semantic integration of verbal information into a visual memory. *Journal of Experimental Psychology: Human Learning and Memory* 4: 19-31.

Loftus, E. F., and J. C. Palmer. 1974. Reconstruction of automobile destruction: an example of the interaction between language and memory. *Journal of Verbal Learning and Verbal Behavior* 13: 585-589.

Loftus, E. F., and G. Zanni. 1975. Eyewitness testimony: the influence of the wording of a question. *Bulletin of the Psychonomic Society* 5: 86-88.

Loftus, G. R., and E. F. Loftus. 1976. *Human memory: the processing of information*. Hillsdale, N. J.: Erlbaum Press.

Luce, T. S. 1974. Blacks, whites and yellows: they all look alike to me. *Psychology Today* 8: 106-108.

Maccoby, E. E., and C. N. Jacklin. 1974. *The psychology of sex differences*. Stanford: Stanford University Press.

Malpass, R. S., and J. Kravitz. 1969. Recognition for faces of own and other race. *Journal of Personality and Social Psychology* 13: 330-334.

Manson v. Brathwaite. 1977. 429 US 1058; 97 S Ct 2243; 50 L Ed 2d 774.

Marquis, K. H., J. Marshall, and S. Oskamp. 1972. Testimony validity as a function of question form, atmosphere, and item difficulty. *Journal of Applied Social Psychology* 2: 167-186.

Marshall, J. 1966. *Law and psychology in conflict*. New York: Bobbs-Merrill. (Rpt. New York: Anchor Books, Doubleday, 1969.)

Marshall, J., K. H. Marquis, and S. Oskamp. 1971. Effects of kind of question and atmosphere of interrogation on accuracy and completeness of testimony. *Harvard Law Review* 84: 1620-1643.

McCarty, D. G. 1929. *Psychology for the lawyer*. New York: Prentice-Hall.

McKelvie, S. 1976. The effects of verbal labeling on recognition memory for schematic faces. *Quarterly Journal of Experimental Psychology* 28: 459-474.

Michigan State Bar Special Committee on Standard Criminal Jury Instructions. 1977. *Michigan criminal jury instructions* 1. Ann Arbor: Institute of Continuing Legal Education.

Moskowitz, M. J. 1977. Hugo Munsterberg: a study in the history of applied psychology. *American Psychologist* 32: 824-842.

Mueller, J. H., K. L. Bailis, and A. G. Goldstein, 1978. Depth of processing and anxiety in facial recognition. Paper presented at Midwestern Psychological Association, Chicago.

Mueller, J. H., M. Carlomusto, and A. G. Goldstein. 1978. Orienting task and study time in facial recognition. *Bulletin of the Psychonomic Society* 11: 313-316.

Munsterberg, H. 1908. *On the witness stand*. New York: Doubleday, Page.

———. 1914. *Psychology and social sanity*. New York: Doubleday, Page.

Murdock, B. B., Jr. 1974. *Human memory: theory and data*. Hillsdale, N. J.: Erlbaum Press.

My. 1978. The door in the wall. Part 2: Theodore X. Barber. *Human Behavior* 7: 43-46.

Neil v. Biggers. 1972. 409 US 188; 93 S Ct 575; 34 L Ed 2d 401.

Norman, D. A., and D. E. Rumelhart. 1975. *Explorations in cognition*. San Francisco: Freeman.

O'Barr, W. M., and J. M. Conley. 1976. When a juror watches a lawyer. *Barrister* 3: 8-11, 33.

Paivio, A. 1971. *Imagery and verbal processes*. New York: Holt, Rinehart and Winston.

Patterson, K. E., and A. D. Baddeley. 1977. When face recognition fails. *Journal of Experimental Psychology: Human Learning and Memory* 3: 406-407.

Pearlman, S. 1977. The Sawyer brothers. *Good Housekeeping*, August, pp. 82-88.

Penfield, W. 1969. Consciousness, memory, and man's conditioned reflexes. In *On the biology of learning*, ed. K. Pribram. New York: Harcourt, Brace and World.

Penfield, W., and L. Roberts. 1959. *Speech and brain mechanisms*. Princeton: Princeton University Press, 1959.

Penry, J. 1971. *Looking at faces and remembering them: a guide to facial identification*. London: Elek Books.

People v. Anderson. 1973. 389 Mich 1530221; 205 NW 2d 461.

People v. Johnson. 1974. 38 CA 3d 1; 112 Cal Rptr 834 (3rd dist.).

Peterson, M. A. 1976. Witnesses: memory of social events. Ph.D. diss., University of California, Los Angeles.

Piaget, J. 1962. *Play, dreams and imitation in childhood*. New York: W. W. Norton.

Porter, K. A. 1977. The never-ending wrong. *Atlantic Monthly*, June, pp. 38-64.

Powers, P. A., J. L. Andriks, and E. F. Loftus. 1979. The eyewitness accounts of females and males. *Journal of Applied Psychology* 64: 339-347.

Putnam, B. In press. Hypnosis and distortions in eyewitness memory. *International Journal of Clinical and Experimental Hypnosis*.

Pylyshyn, A. W. 1973. What the mind's eye tells the mind's brain: a critique of mental imagery. *Psychological Bulletin* 80: 1-24.

Regina v. Audy. 1977. *Canadian Criminal Cases* (2d), 228-237.

Rouke, F. L. 1957. Psychological research on problems of testimony. *Journal of Social Issues* 13: 50-59.

Rumelhart, D. E., and A. Ortony. 1976. The representation of knowledge in memory. In *Schooling and the acquisition of knowledge*, ed. R. C. Anderson, R. J. Spiro, and W. E. Montague. Hillsdale, N. J.: Erlbaum Press.

Sales, B. D., A. Elwork, and J. J. Alfini. 1978. Improving comprehension for jury instructions. In *Perspectives in law and psychology*, ed. B. D. Sales. New York: Plenum.

Salzberg, H. C. 1977. The hypnotic interview in crime detection. *The American Journal of Clinical Hypnosis* 19: 255-258.

Sarason, I. G., J. H. Johnson, and J. M. Siegel. 1978. Assessing the impact of life change: the development of the Life Experiences Survey. *Journal of Consulting and Clinical Psychology* 46: 932-946.

Sarason, I. G., and R. Stoops. 1978. Test anxiety and the passage of time. *Journal of Consulting and Clinical Psychology* 46: 102-108.

Schaie, K. W., and K. Gribbin. 1975. Adult development and aging. *Annual Review of Psychology* 26: 65-96.

Scott, W. C., and V. Foutch. 1974. The effects of presentation order and ethnicity on facial recognition. Paper presented at the Oklahoma Academy of Science, Duran.

Shepard, R. N. 1967. Recognition memory for words, sentences and pictures. *Journal of Verbal Learning and Verbal Behavior* 6: 156-163.

Shepard, R. N., D. W. Kilpatrick, and J. P. Cunningham. 1975. The internal representation of numbers. *Cognitive Psychology* 7: 82-138.

Siegel, J. M., and E. F. Loftus. 1978. Impact of anxiety and life stress upon eyewitness testimony. *Bulletin of the Psychonomic Society* 12: 479-480.

Siipola, E. M. 1935. A group study of some effects of preparatory set. *Psychological Monographs* 46: 27-38.

Simmons v. United States. 1968. 390 US 377; 88 S Ct 967; 19 L Ed 2d 1247.

Smith, A. D., and E. Winograd. 1977. Age differences in remembering faces. Paper presented at the Southeastern Psychological Association, Hollywood, Fla.

Snee, T. J., and D. E. Lush. 1941. Interaction of the narrative and interrogatory methods of obtaining testimony. *The Journal of Psychology* 11: 229-336.

Sobel, N. R. 1972. *Eyewitness identification: legal and practical problems.* New York: Clark Boardman. (1976 supplement.)

Sommer, R. 1959. The new look on the witness stand. *Canadian Psychologist* 8: 94-99.

Stafford, C. F. 1962. The child as a witness. *Washington Law Review* 37: 303-324.

Stein, E., ed. 1978. *New frontiers in litigation: twenty-ninth annual Advocacy Institute course handbook.* Ann Arbor: Institute of Continuing Legal Education.

Stern, W. 1910. Abstracts of lectures on the psychology of testimony and on the study of individuality. *American Journal of Psychology* 21: 270-282.

Stovall v. Denno. 1967. 388 US 293, 302; 87 S Ct 1967, 1972; 18 L Ed 2d 1199, 1206.

Stump, A. 1975. That's him — the guy who hit me. *TV Guide,* October 4-10.

Sulin, R. A., and D. J. Dooling. 1974. Intrusion of a thematic guide in retention of prose. *Journal of Experimental Psychology* 103: 255-262.

Swets, J. A., W. P. Tanner, and T. G. Birdsall. 1961. Decision processes in perception. *Psychological Review* 68: 301-340.

Thomas, D. R., and A. L. DeCapito. 1966. Role of stimulus labeling in stimulus generalization. *Journal of Experimental Psychology* 71: 913-915.

Thomas, D. R., A. D. Caronite, G. L. LaMonica, and K. L. Hoving. 1968. Mediated generalization via stimulus labeling: a replication and extension. *Journal of Experimental Psychology* 78: 531-533.

Thorson, G., and L. Hochhaus. 1977. The trained observer: effects of prior information on eyewitness reports. *Bulletin of the Psychonomic Society* 10: 454-456.

Tickner, A. H., and E. C. Poulton. 1975. Watching for people and actions. *Ergonomics* 18: 35-51.

Trankell, A. 1972. *Reliability of evidence*. Stockholm: Bechmans.

Tversky, A., and D. Kahneman. 1977. Causal schemata in judgments under uncertainty. In *Progress in social psychology*, ed. M. Fishbein. Hillsdale, N. J.: Erlbaum Press.

United States v. Amaral. 1973. 488 F 2d 1148 (9th Cir.).

United States v. Brown. 1974. 501 F 2d 146 (9th Cir.).

United States v. Nobles. 1975. 422 US 225.

United States v. Telfaire. 1972. 469 F 2d 552; 152 US app DC 146.

United States v. Wade. 1967. 388 US 218; 87 S Ct 1926; 18 L Ed 2d 1149.

Varendonck, J. 1911. Les témoignages d'enfants dans un procès retentissant. *Archives de Psychologie* 11: 129-171.

Vidmar, N. 1978. Effects of adversary versus non-adversary investigative procedures on testimonial evidence. Paper presented at the Law and Society Association, Minneapolis.

Wall, P. M. 1965. *Eyewitness identification of criminal cases*. Springfield, Ill.: Charles C. Thomas.

Wells, G. L. 1978. Applied eyewitness-testimony research: system variables and estimator variables. *Journal of Personality and Social Psychology* 12: 1546-1557.

Wells, G. L., M. R. Leippe, M. H. Baumgartner, D. D. Simpson, J. Lingle, N. Geva, R. E. Petty, R. L. Bassett, and T. M. Ostrom. 1977. Guidelines for empirically assessing the fairness of a lineup. Unpublished (Ohio State University).

Wells, G. L., C. L. Lindsay, and T. J. Ferguson. 1979. Accuracy, confidence, and juror perceptions in eyewitness identification. *Journal of Applied Psychology*.

Whipple, G. M. 1909. The observer as reporter: a survey of the "psychology of testimony." *Psychological Bulletin* 6: 153-170.

Whipple, G. M. 1911. The psychology of testimony. *Psychological Bulletin* 8: 307-309.

———. 1912. Psychology of testimony and report. *Psychological Bulletin* 9: 264-269.

———. 1913. Review of "Les témoignages d'enfants dans un procès retentissant," by J. Varendonck. *Journal of Criminal Law and Criminology* 4: 150-154.

———. 1918. The obtaining of information: psychology of observation and report. *Psychological Bulletin* 15: 217-248.

Wigmore, J. H. 1909. Professor Munsterberg and the psychology of evidence. *Illinois Law Review* 3: 399-445.

Witryol, S., and W. Kaess. 1957. Sex differences in social memory tasks. *Journal of Abnormal and Social Psychology* 54: 343-346.

Woocher, F. D. 1977. Did your eyes deceive you? Expert psychological testimony on the unreliability of eyewitness identification. *Stanford Law Review* 29: 969-1030.

Woodhead, M. M., A. D. Baddeley, and D. C. V. Simmonds. In press. On training people to recognize faces. *Ergonomics*.

Yerkes, R. M., and J. D. Dodson. 1908. The relation of strength of stimulus to rapidity of habit-formation. *Journal of Comparative and Neurological Psychology* 18: 459-482.

Zanni, G. R., and J. T. Offermann. 1978. Eyewitness testimony: an exploration of question wording upon recall as a function of neuroticism. *Perceptual and Motor Skills* 46: 163-166.

Zuckerman, M., and B. Lubin. 1965. *Manual for the multiple affect adjective checklist*. San Diego: Educational and Industrial Testing Service.

Index